The Energy Crisis and U.S. Foreign Policy

edited by
Joseph S. Szyliowicz
Bard E. O'Neill
foreword by
John A. Love

The Praeger Special Studies program—utilizing the most modern and efficient book production techniques and a selective worldwide distribution network—makes available to the academic, government, and business communities significant, timely research in U.S. and international economic, social, and political development.

The Energy Crisis and U.S. Foreign Policy

PRAEGER SPECIAL STUDIES IN INTERNATIONAL POLITICS AND GOVERNMENT

Praeger Publishers   New York   Washington   London

Library of Congress Cataloging in Publication Data

Main entry under title:

The Energy crisis and U.S. foreign policy.

(Praeger special studies in international politics and
government)
Bibliography: p.
Includes index.
1. Energy policy—United States—Addresses, essays,
lectures. 2. Petroleum industry and trade—United
States—Addresses, essays, lectures. 3. United States—
Foreign relations—Addresses, essays, lectures.
I. Szyliowicz, Joseph S., ed. II. O'Neill, Bard, ed.
HD9502.U52E484   327.73   74-3140
ISBN 0-275-09040-X
ISBN 0-275-88840-1 pbk.

PRAEGER PUBLISHERS
111 Fourth Avenue, New York, N.Y. 10003, U.S.A.
5, Cromwell Place, London SW7 2JL, England

Published in the United States of America in 1975
by Praeger Publishers, Inc.

75-10998

Printed in the United States of America

To Irene and Nancy, and our children, Michael and Dara
and Suzanne, Andrew, and Sarah

FOREWORD
John A. Love

The reaction to the energy crisis by the great majority of U.S. citizens was one of shock and disbelief. On the basis of our entire national experience, we believed that resources were endless and only needed proper organization and capital investment to bring them to general and plentiful use.

Leaving behind the "scapegoat" or "evil plot" explanation, we still have serious problems. The ups and downs of energy statistics, and obvious discrepancies and distortions in spot surplus or shortages, serve to strengthen our suspicions and cynicism.

But the problem of matching the supply and cost of energy with future demand in a viable economy and with a good standard of living, not only in the United States but throughout the world, may well be both one of the most difficult problems we have ever faced and an early warning of other profound adjustments facing the explosively increasing population of this planet.

A vague unease in current comment and writings that all is not well, that perhaps the old rules no longer apply, confirms the need to look, to analyze, and to study. Although, at the time this is written, domestic supplies seem to have leveled out at a lesser but adequate amount, it is certain that we have not yet solved the problem even for the near or middle term. It is unarguable that even the current levels of supply and price will have continuing, and ever more serious, effects on our international relations, the world's economy, and our hopes for the future.

For this and other reasons, I was pleased to learn of the proposed publication of this book. Certainly every effort must be made to know the facts, and to attempt to identify the options for future action.

The articles presented in this book offer a valuable and needed contribution to the kind of understanding that is a vital ingredient and starting place for any acceptable solutions to the multitude of problems that lie ahead. By systematically analyzing the impact of the energy crisis, the contributors to this volume have been able to isolate areas of special concern such as Europe and the Middle East and have suggested some of the specific reasons for the difficulties we face in the wake of the embargo. More important, their examination of the present context and substance of American foreign policy also alerts us to issues that must be confronted if we are to conduct a free and unfettered foreign policy.

Well before the embargo dramatized the reality of the energy crisis to both decision-makers and the American people, we had, on several occasions, discussed the possibility that the Arab states might unite to use oil as a political weapon. As students of the Middle East our attention was drawn to that possibility through the increasing attention given to this matter in official Arab statements, radio broadcasts, and the press. We became more and more concerned with the consequences of such an action, not only in terms of the political configurations in the Middle East but also with the effect that it would have on the policy of the great powers, particularly on that of the United States, towards the region.

Accordingly, in the spring of 1973 we proposed, at a meeting of the executive committee of the Colorado Association for International Education, that the organization sponsor a faculty seminar on the Energy Crisis and American Policy in the Middle East. The other members accepted our proposal and we began to plan for a seminar to be held in November 1973. In October 1973, what had been an academic issue suddenly occupied headlines throughout the world and made our conference both topical and timely.

Hosted by the Air Force Academy on behalf of the CAIE, that seminar enabled us to bring together several scholars who eventually became contributors to this book and to discuss with them our concern with the role of energy in contemporary international affairs. The quality of the discussions, the success of the conference, and the warm reception accorded to the published proceedings, encouraged us to continue our work on this topic.

One other important conclusion that we reached as a result of the conference was that our focus had been too narrow and that to understand the impact of the energy crisis one had to broaden the focus to include all of America's global relations. It was therefore apparent that a wide range of expertise would be required to deal effectively with this topic and we were fortunate to obtain the cooperation of a number of prominent scholars.

We were not satisfied, however, with compiling the usual edited volume and we therefore undertook to integrate and supplement the contributions with our own research. Besides examining all available materials, we took advantage of opportunities to visit the Middle East and Western Europe in order to do further research and are indebted to those scholars and government officials who kindly gave of their time.

We were also fortunate to be living in Colorado. Colorado is justly famous for its climate and scenery but it is also the home of two men who have had direct high-level administrative responsibilities for energy policy. General George A. Lincoln, former head of the Office of Emergency Preparedness, encouraged us in our efforts and proved to be a stimulating colleague and cooperative contributor. John A. Love, the former governor of Colorado who served as the nation's energy chief also deserves our gratitude. He was most gracious when we discussed our project with him and he kindly agreed to write a foreword.

We are also indebted in various ways to many individuals. Our colleagues, Professors Josef Korbel, John de Gara, and Bernhard Abrahamsson of the Graduate School of International Studies, together with Mr. Bashir Al-Samarrai made many constructive suggestions which greatly strengthened our concluding chapter. We are especially grateful to Stephen J. Rossetti, a very gifted and dedicated young scholar, for his substantive criticisms and editorial assistance. Dorothea Blair of GSIS patiently took care of our administrative requirements and clerical assistance; Caryn Friedman and Shirley Taylor were both patient and personable while typing the manuscript and Carol Roark revealed her artistic talents in various ways including preparation of the charts in Chapter 1.

We also wish to thank our wives in more than routine manner. Although they had ample cause to complain because we were forced, owing to our different locations, to spend many long hours away from our families, they were most helpful and supportive.

Finally, we must note that views expressed herein are those of the authors alone and, in the case of Major O'Neill, do not necessarily reflect the views of the United States Air Force or the Department of Defense.

CONTENTS

LIST OF TABLES AND FIGURES

LIST OF ABBREVIATIONS

b/d   Barrels per day

Btu   British thermal units

CESC   Conference on European Security and Cooperation

CPSU   Communist Party of the Soviet Union

FEO   Federal Energy Office

FPC   Federal Power Commission

FPDMS   Foreign-policy decision-making system

IMF   International Monetary Fund

MBFR   Mutual and Balanced Force Reductions

OAPEC   Organization of Arab Petroleum Exporting Countries

OECD   Organization for Economic Cooperation and Development

OPEC   Organization of the Petroleum Exporting Countries

SC.242   Security Council Resolution 242

The Energy Crisis and
U. S. Foreign Policy

1

THE ANALYTICAL
FRAMEWORK
Bard E. O'Neill

In October 1973 the Organization of Arab Petroleum Exporting Countries (OAPEC) sent shock waves through the world when it announced that it had decided to decrease the production of crude oil and to embargo the United States and Holland. This historic decision represented a major turning point in Middle Eastern politics, in the relationships between the Arab states and the rest of the world, and, in a wider sense, between raw material-producing and -consuming nations.

Until now the increasing use of energy had been viewed as desirable and advantageous by all nations. Oil had rapidly displaced competing forms of energy until it accounted for 46 percent of all energy produced in the United States in 1973. True, there had been some signs before October 1973 that the vision of the industrialized nations of an ever-expanding use of oil might not be fulfilled—talk of an energy shortage can be traced back to the early 1950s—and in the early 1970s several Arab states, such as Libya, had spoken of the need to conserve their resources and to obtain the highest possible revenues for their nonreplenishable resource. Nevertheless, few persons in academia, government, or even in the oil industry itself were prepared for the development of an oil shortage in the United States in 1972 or the subsequent decision by OAPEC to use oil as a political weapon to further Arab aims in the Arab-Israeli conflict.

The impact of these developments was immediate and far-reaching. Oil had become a vital part of every developed country's economy; and the United States, Western Europe, and Japan were suddenly confronted with the prospect of recession and even depression, of millions of unemployed, and, at best, a tremendous increase in the costs of their products. The developing nations too were deeply affected, for their aspirations to rapid economic development were suddenly crushed as the price that they had to pay for oil increased sharply, thus draining precious, scarce resources from investment projects. In short, what had once been taken largely for granted—the supply of oil at reasonable prices, suddenly became a vital issue for political decision-makers throughout the world. And because of its international dimensions, it was clearly an issue that would deeply affect the political and economic interrelationships of states, their foreign policies, and even the structure of the international system itself.

Evidence of this fact was not long in coming. Both developed and developing nations focused their attention on conservation measures to minimize the impact of the energy crisis, gave priority to consideration of the development of domestic oil and other energy resources, and began a search for long-term petroleum supplies at reasonable prices. The profound effect of the scramble for oil on the foreign policies of many countries was obvious as most of the European states, Japan, and the majority of developing countries moved to endorse the Arab version of Security Council Resolution 242 (November 1967), which called for a total Israeli withdrawal from lands occupied in 1967. As far as the United States was concerned, this was an unacceptable course of action.

Because of its moral obligations to Israel and its perceptions of the costs that would be incurred in terms of the credibility of its international commitments, the United States could not afford to turn its back on Israel. Yet, since the American government was acutely aware of the future importance of the Middle East in terms of U.S. energy supplies, it could scarcely ignore the Arab point of view. Thus, while emissaries from many nations were arriving in Arab capitals seeking agreements on oil supplies, Secretary of State Kissinger began his own trek in search of a peace settlement that would both guarantee Israeli security and reopen the Arab spigot. His success in achieving military disengagements between Israel and Syria, and Israel and Egypt, paved the way for President Nixon's visit to the Middle East in the early summer of 1974. Although U.S. diplomacy proved remarkably successful and obtained the lifting of the embargo, it would be premature to assume that the underlying issues could be resolved quickly or easily. Both the Arab-Israeli and energy issues are extraordinarily complicated matters that require a delicate blend of statesmanship and understanding if they are to be successfully dealt with.

It is the purpose of this book to systematically examine the multifaceted relationship between the energy crisis and American foreign policy, both at present and in the future. Although in retrospect the embargo lasted for but a few months and, at most, merely inconvenienced the American public, its impact on policy was profound and its ramifications wide-ranging. U.S. relations with the USSR, Western Europe, Japan, and the middle East were affected, as was the distribution of economic and political power within the international system. How America's complicated international relationships were altered by the energy crisis that the oil embargo dramatized is the central concern of this book.

From an academic viewpoint, therefore, the energy crisis provides us with an excellent opportunity to analyze the substance and character of the U.S. response to a major development within the international system over which it had little or no control. In an age of increased interdependence and accelerating international crises, the United States will inevitably continue to be confronted with unexpected challenges that will touch on such sensitive questions as its security, power, and economic well-being. The energy crisis therefore may well represent a threshold in international and national politics; and a careful study of its origins, development, and foreign-policy implications and of the U.S. response may well provide valuable insights for decision-makers who may have to cope with similar situations in the future and for citizens whose life styles may be dramatically altered by the policies that are formulated.

Moreover, although many decisions have already been made as a result of the energy crisis, many issues are yet to be resolved; questions involving energy will be with us for years. The continuing importance of energy is further emphasized by the fact that the United States will be substantially dependent on external sources of oil through the 1980s, and thus its relations with both friends and adversaries will be subject to further reappraisal. It is therefore imperative that we not only reflect on the changes that have already occurred but also consider the difficult questions that lie ahead and will confront decision-makers with agonizing choices.

Any effort to analyze the origins, effects, and consequences of the energy crisis for U.S. foreign policy requires the knowledge and insights of scholars in various fields. It demands familiarity with the domestic energy situation, the international aspects of the oil industry, regional political dynamics in the Middle East, and U.S. foreign policy toward major international actors. Accordingly, we have brought together a number of prominent scholars with specialized competence to provide an understanding of different aspects of the topic. Their contributions, combined with our own research, make it possible for us to address the problem in its totality.

FRAMEWORK FOR ANALYSIS

We are not satisfied, however, with merely discussing this vital topic in a purely descriptive way. As scholars of international relations, we are committed to the systematic accumulation of knowledge and particularly to the development of foreign-policy analysis in a scientific manner. Thus, while we acknowledge that good descriptive work is indispensable, we endorse the view that "the ideal goal of those performing case studies is the development of concepts and propositions that are useful across a number of cases" (Coplin 1971, p. 150). Accordingly, we have chosen to elaborate and apply a conceptual framework that not only describes reality but also identified dependent and independent variables, suggests relationships, clarifies linkages, and provides for the ordering and classification of data. It should be emphasized that this effort does not represent a scholastic exercise but stems from our profound belief that in this way we can not only further the development of our own field but also aid the reader by synthesizing and integrating the findings in such a way that explanation and understanding of this complex problem are facilitated. Hence, in the remainder of this chapter we shall outline a framework for analyzing the relationship between the energy crisis and American foreign policy. In the final chapter we shall apply that framework to this issue-area in a substantive manner, drawing upon the findings of our contributors and our own research.

The field of foreign policy is littered with analytical approaches. Some focus upon the international system, others upon individual actors, still others on domestic conditions and political processes. Only recently have attempts been made to develop integrative frameworks that permit consideration of all the critical variables that different scholars have identified. Such an approach possesses obvious theoretical drawbacks. Aside from the problems that result from shifting levels, about which much has been written (Singer 1969, pp. 28-29; Teune and Prezeworsky 1970, pp. 47-74), it represents what is, at best, "concatenated theory" (Mayer 1972, pp. 62-64) or "loose factor theory" (Meehan 1965, p. 133). That is, while these schemes suggest a number of variables that account for foreign policy and a number of relationships among these variables, they do not permit precise measurement of the variables. (See also McCloskey 1956; Kaplan 1964, Ch. 8.) Nevertheless, in our view such an approach is essential if we are to explicate as clearly and fully as possible the many relevant dimensions of the nexus between the energy crisis and U.S. foreign policy.

None of the available frameworks, however, met all of the criteria that we established for this study: the framework should permit the effective ordering of the substantive data contained in the various chapters; it should permit us to identify the significant dimensions of this multifaceted problem; and it should facilitate the integration and analysis of the data and permit their presentation in a manner that is meaningful to a varied audience. Accordingly, we felt compelled to devise our own framework, and we decided to base it on the well-known systems approach.

In this schema outputs, the foreign policy of the United States (our dependent variable), are produced by the foreign-policy decision-making system (FPDMS), which consists of both individual and institutional actors that are affected by inputs: demands by particular interest groups or the general public, as well as supports, particularly the resources and capabilities of the state.

FIGURE 1 The International Environment

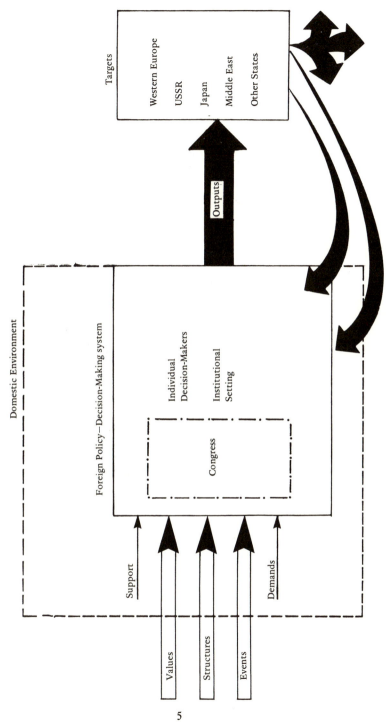

Clearly, foreign-policy decisions are also affected by the international environment: its structure, its values, and specific events that may occur therein. Figure 1 illustrates these components and their interrelationships. We shall discuss the conceptualizations of each part of the system in detail below.

FOREIGN POLICY OUTPUTS

We begin with the main focus of our book, the foreign policy (output) of the United States. Though scholars have debated over the precise definition of "foreign policy," most authorities now agree that it consists of the actions of states toward their external environment and the factors that account for those actions (Sondermann 1961; Lerche and Said 1970, pp. 30-31). Such a gross definition, however, merely represents the first step toward analysis and explanation, for unless the outputs of a system can be conceptualized in a meaningful manner, it is impossible to develop and test any theory that seeks to relate policy to its determinants. Unfortunately, progress in this regard has been slow and marked by confusion and lack of consensus at the most elementary level, that of classification. As a recent analysis of the field noted: "A problem of particular importance . . . is the absence of a widely accepted typology of foreign policy behavior" (McGowan and Shapiro 1973, p. 222). The importance of this point cannot be minimized, because without consensus upon the conceptualization and operationalization of policy outputs, it is impossible to carry out comparative and cumulative research (McGowan and Shapiro 1973, conclusion; Kegley 1973, p. 7).

The degree of idiosyncracy that reigns in this area can easily be illustrated by the writings of well-known scholars. Lerche and Said (1970, pp. 35-38), for example, stress the difference between status quo and revisionist policies; Holsti (1972, pp. 101-70), orientations, national roles, objectives, and patterns of influence; and Wolfers (1961, pp. 146-51), goals of self-extension, self-preservation and self-abnegation. In fact, not only do different scholars stress different dimensions of foreign policy, but they conceptualize the same dimensions in conflicting ways. For example, the dimension "policy toward change" is conceptualized by some scholars in terms of status quo and revisionist policies; by others in terms of avoidance and conquest, submission and withdrawal, compromise and awards; and by still others in terms of defensive and community building (Kegley 1973, pp. 10-13).

Given this state of affairs, we have decided to categorize foreign policy in terms of interests, goals, objectives, and methods—concepts familiar to decision-makers and intelligible to the informed public. Unhappily, a careful reading of the literature that employs these concepts reveals disagreement among scholars on the meaning of these terms as well as substantial terminological confusion. The latter takes one of three forms: a scholar may present general definitions without any clarifying examples, or may use the same term in two different senses, or may identify differences between two concepts and then ignore the distinctions. To cite but a few illustrations: Lerche and Said (1970, pp. 25-30) define their concepts but fail to give any examples; Richard Rosecrance (1973, pp. 17, 67) uses goals in two different ways—national expansion, national consolidation, and national preservation on the one hand, and territory, prestige, power, glory, security, and ideological gain on the other. Coplin et al. (1974) define national interests, goals, and objectives, and then proceed to use these terms to refer to different phenomena (compare pp. 69-70, 86-90). Finally, Deutsch (1968, pp. 14-15, 80) stresses the goal-seeking behavior of states but then uses the term interchangeably with "vital interests" and gives different kinds of examples. Because of our concern with conceptual clarity, we shall define as precisely as possible the concepts that we use and give examples of each.

Our first concept, the national interest, represents the general and continuing purposes that governments see themselves as serving on behalf of the nation. Essentially this refers to the enhancement of the nation's security, well-being, prestige, ideology, and power. Which of these interests or purposes will receive the most attention will, of course, vary from state to state and from time to time within a given state. As most students of foreign policy are well aware, however, the generality of this concept substantially undercuts its explanatory power. Thus, we shall concentrate our attention on the goals, objectives, and methods that are chosen by policy-makers because these concepts enable us to discuss and analyze foreign policy in a more specific and concrete manner.

Goals may be defined as the general, long-term, and best conceivable outcomes that policy-makers seek to establish during a time span that can be reasonably anticipated. In other words, goals refer to what is most desirable in the foreseeable future vis-a-vis some other nation or group of nations. An example would be the Nixon administration's goal of "establishing civilized discourse" with the People's Republic of China.

Objectives

Objectives, on the other hand, are the more precisely defined short-range preferred outcomes that are attainable at any particular time, given the existing configuration of the domestic and international environments. As such they represent specific steps that are designed to achieve a particular goal. In the case of the goal of establishing "civilized discourse" with China, for example,

U.S. policy-makers have identified several objectives that, if achieved, would contribute to its fulfillment. They include the establishment of full diplomatic relations, increased economic contacts, the institutionalization of consultations, and the avoidance of military confrontations.

Closely related to and often profoundly affecting the definition of objectives is one of the major inputs to the FPDMS—the capabilities available to the state. As every student of international politics knows, capabilities play an important role in foreign policy-making. The amount and types of resources— economic, diplomatic, military, demographic—can scarcely be ignored when objectives are chosen and assigned priorities. Capabilities will limit the definition and achievement of goals and objectives; states with greater capabilities have more options available to them in establishing ojbectives and policies designed to achieve those objectives. This does not mean, however, that actual influence (the ability of a state to change the behavior of another actor in a desired direction) over the behavior of others will always be commensurate with capabilities; the United States, for example, despite its impressive capabilities in terms of the accepted indices of national power, exerted little influence in international affairs in the interwar period.

Many factors play a role in determining whether a state will seek to translate its capabilities into influence. First, the resources to be employed must be mobilized and usable. Second, the willingness to expend resources must be present and credible to others. Third, in particular interstate relationships the degree of need or dependency of one party will be important in establishing how much influence can actually be exerted. Finally, in situations where dependency is not a factor, one party may still have significant influence, depending on the extent to which the other party is well disposed toward it. In short, if we are to analyze the impact of U.S. foreign policy, however roughly, we must specify in what way, for what objectives, and in relation to whom the United States exerted its influence and with what results. Moreover, it is necessary to examine the methods or techniques used in a particular case.

Various types of actions are available to decision-makers seeking to exert influence in relation to another actor in the international arena. One scholar has classified them as follows: persuasion (initiating or discussing a proposal); offering rewards; granting rewards; threatening punishment; infliction of non-violent punishment; and the application of force (Holsti 1972, pp. 167-68). The important question, of course, is which method(s) are employed in specific situations in the hope of achieving which national objective(s).

This depends to a large extent on the pattern and character of the relationships between particular states. Where there is a consensus on objectives and friendly relations, the emphasis will be on persuasion and offering and granting rewards. Conversely, in situations involving states that disagree on important foreign-policy objectives, one can expect an emphasis on threats and

FIGURE 2 Outputs: U.S. Foreign Policy Vis-a-Vis China

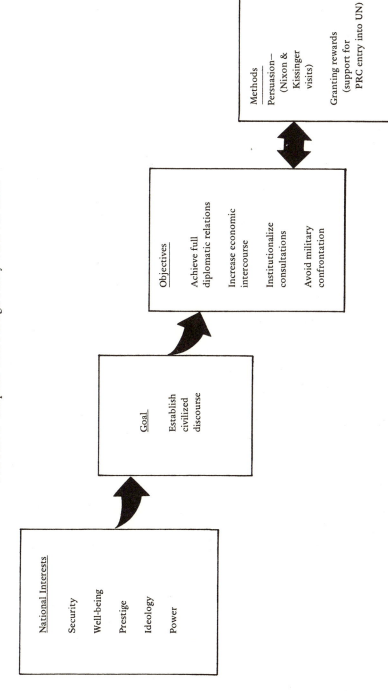

National Interests

Security

Well-being

Prestige

Ideology

Power

Goal

Establish
civilized
discourse

Objectives

Achieve full
diplomatic relations

Increase economic
intercourse

Institutionalize
consultations

Avoid military
confrontation

Methods

Persuasion—
(Nixon &
Kissinger
visits)

Granting rewards
(support for
PRC entry into UN)

punishments. Examples of each can easily be found in U.S. policy toward the Middle East. On the one hand the United States reached an understanding with Iran that the flow of oil must be maintained and has sold that country sophisticated military hardware. On the other, the United States mobilized forces during the Jordanian civil war of September 1970 and sent a warning to Syria to cease its support for the armored invasion of Jordan.

In short, we have chosen to categorize foreign policy outputs in terms of national interests, goals, objectives, and methods, with an emphasis on the latter three concepts. In our conclusion we shall be particularly concerned with how they were affected by the energy crisis. Figure 2 presents a graphic description of the relationship among these concepts, using U.S. policy vis-a-vis China as an illustration.

FOREIGN-POLICY DECISON-MAKING SYSTEM

In this book we are of course interested in assessing not only whether American foreign-policy goals, objectives, and methods vis-a-vis Western Europe, Japan, the USSR and the Middle East have changed as a result of the energy crisis but also the factors (our independent variables) that account for change. Hence we must examine the major components of our FPDMS as well as the exogenous factors that influence and are influenced by it.

When analyzing the FPDMS there are three aspects that must be considered. First we must identify the key individuals, assess their impact on policy, and examine personality and background characteristics that influence their decisions (Greenstein 1969). In the making of U:S. foreign policy, for example, it is clear that one must look at the role of the president and his principal advisers. Second, one must analyze the organizational setting in which foreign policy is made. Both the formal structures and the informal relationships within and among the State and Defense departments and the CIA may be relevant to achieving an understanding of how and why a particular policy decision was reached. Third, one must consider the role of the legislature. Congress obviously plays an important role, but it often does so indirectly and intermittently. For this reason we have included Congress within the FPDMS and shall discuss its role within the context of domestic inputs which often are mediated through the legislature.

The Role of Psychological Variables

There is widespread agreement among scholars that to understand why choices are made, one must examine the decision-makers' perceptions or images of reality. Different scholars have used different labels for this variable, including "psycho milieu," "phenomenological approach," and "operational code" (Sprout and Sprout 1965, pp. 28-30; Singer 1969, pp. 26-29; Apter and Andrain 1972, pp. 9-11; George and George 1964, passim). These perceptions and images result from differential interactions of attitudes, values, beliefs, ideologies and analogies; and it is not surprising that they often diverge from reality and vary among individual policy-makers.

Holsti (1972, pp. 362 ff.) makes useful distinctions among these concepts in the following manner. *Attitudes* are general evaluative propositions about some object, fact, or condition, more or less friendly, hostile, desirable, or dangerous. They often influence the reactions of policy-makers to the signals, actions, and demands of other states, the perceptions of the other governments, and the definition of their own objectives toward others. *Values* are general conceptions of the good toward which actions are directed (such as individual liberty, equality) and by which they are often judged. Although they may not always explain or prescribe responses in specific cases, they often establish attitudes toward a situation and provide justifications and suggestions for policies designed to deal with it. *Beliefs* are defined as propositions that decision-makers hold to be true. They are particularly important in the study of foreign policy because they often are the basis for policy choices (for instance, Woodrow Wilson's belief that secret diplomacy and autocracy were roots of war). *Analogies* are images of reality that are based on or compared with a previous set of circumstances. Policy-makers, either explicitly or implicitly, often rely on such comparisons when characterizing situations and deducing appropriate actions to cope with them. One sell-known example is Anthony Eden's belief that the 1956 Middle East crisis represented another Munich and that Nasser was comparable with Hitler.

Perceptions and images are also influenced by doctrinal and ideological factors. *Doctrines* are explicit sets of beliefs that purport to explain reality and/ or prescribe goals for political action, whereas *ideologies* are composed of comprehensive sets of doctrines. Both doctrines and ideologies may be important determinants of policy because they provide an intellectual framework for interpreting messages from the environment; help set the long-range goals of a state; rationalize policy; and prescribe ethical criteria for judging one's own and others' actions.

Only in recent years have scholars emphasized the importance of such variables. Traditionally most analysts have viewed the making of foreign policy through a problem-solving paradigm that emphasizes maximal information-gathering, a conscious definition of goals, and a search for the most effective means of achieving the goals. It has become increasingly apparent, however, that this model suffers from severe deficiencies; in particular it deemphasizes the role of bureaucratic and psychological variables in decision-making.

Despite its limitations, however, the rational problem-solving model can be used to indicate the role of both psychological and organizational factors in the making of foreign policy. Accordingly, following the example of W. Coplin (1971, pp. 33-54), we shall discuss the relationship between psychological and bureaucratic variables and the tasks involved in this model—definition of the situation, selection of goals, search for alternatives, and selection of an alternative—in order to illustrate their significance in policy-making.

In the first task, defining a situation, perceptions are of obvious importance. A decision-maker's perceptions may be relatively open, adjusting easily to new information, or closed. Since the international milieu is often complex and uncertain, policy-makers tend to develop relatively closed images of international conditions. This happens partly because, once they officially define a situation, they create an investment they are unwilling to lose. To continuously reevaluate existing images would engender a sense of insecurity because it could lead to a loss of support for the decision-makers and their policies. Moreover, it could result in an individual policy-maker's losing his political efficacy and status in the eyes of his colleagues. One analyst has gone so far as to argue that this factor accounts for such "fiascos" as the Bay of Pigs, Vietnam, and Pearl Harbor (Janis 1972). Hence, when a change of image does occur, it is often the result of dramatic events.

In terms of the second task, goal selection, the primary psychological consideration is an individual's perceived need to stay in power and to increase the influence of his office (Wriggins 1969). Whether or not an actor's domestic position influences this task will depend in part on his assessment of his political position at the time.

Psychological factors will also affect the third task, the search for alternatives. Because of the complexity of issues, the stress of policy-making, and the limited attention span of most individuals, the consideration of various alternatives tends to be narrowed. Moreover, there is a tendency to rely on past formulas that have proved successful and, in Herbert Simon's phrase, to "satisfice" (1957, passim). That is, policy-makers do not search for the most desirable option but are satisfied with a course of action that is minimally acceptable.

The fourth task, choosing among alternatives, also is affected by such considerations and is further complicated by the fact that it is difficult to determine the consequences and value of actions. Since the possibility of loss can be great, decision-makers tend to opt for choices involving low negative consequences and a high probability of success.

The specific role of psychological factors within each of these tasks is, obviously, not constant and will vary from case to case, depending on such variables as the strength of an actor's personality and the restraints upon a particular leader.

In general, however, two important conclusions can be drawn concerning the role of perceptions, images, and other psychological variables in the making of foreign policy. First, the net effect tends to be toward what Lindblom (1959) called "incrementalism." As suggested above, foreign-policy actors tend to possess relatively closed images of the international environment, to rely on analogies with past situations, and, being concerned with maintaining their position, to prefer options with low risks. Hence most policy, whether domestic or foreign, tends to be characterized by incremental change—that is, by continuity with the past and minor changes over the status quo.

Second, psychological variables may be especially important explanatory factors when dealing with leaders who single-handedly formulate policy. However, these variables are especially difficult to identify and measure in cases where policy is the result of compromise and bargaining among many individual actors (Holsti 1972, pp. 368-72).

Thus, we shall analyze the role of major actors in the making of foreign policy during the energy crisis to determine whether one or two decision-makers played dominant roles. If such is the case, we shall utilize whatever psychological data is available to help explain the policy outcomes.

The Role of Bureaucratic Variables

Our second and no less significants tructural dimension is the bureaucratic setting within which decision-makers operate. Foreign policy is not made in a vacuum; in the words of one scholar:

> . . . how top-level policy makers see a problem, and the alternatives they contemplate, are an amalgam of how bureaucrats have characterized the situation and what positions they have come up with, taking into consideration organizational rivalries and bureaucratic traditions (Holsti 1972, p. 388).

Essentially administrators carry out a variety of functions, all of which influence the definition of any problem and of the available options. Problems are studied by various experts, extensive data-gathering is carried out, and formal recommendations are made that reflect the organizational traditions and biases of the different government agencies involved, so that policy often results more

from the interplay of contending bureaucratic advocates than from any conception of an overall purpose (Kissinger 1969, p. 40).

As we shall see, one of the basic reasons why U.S. energy policy developed
in the manner that it did was the number of administrative units involved. Energy fell within the purview of such departments as State, Defense, Interior,
Commerce, and Treasury, as well as such agencies as the Federal Power Commission and the Atomic Energy Commission. Any integrated policy on energy,
therefore, had to accommodate the various interests represented through these
units.

One way to clarify the impact of organizational factors on the FPDMS is
by relating them to the four tasks of rational decision-making. First comes the
definition of the situation, where these variables often are particularly important because the bureaucracy has to refine and condense large amounts of data
into a form useful to the decision-maker. In doing so the psychological variables discussed earlier may come into play, for administrators may skew information in order to serve their own implicit or explicit purposes.

The bureaucracy is also deeply involved during the goal-selection stage,
for particular agencies tend to interpret general goals in light of their own, often
undefined, interests (Downs 1967, p. 180). Furthermore, the indeterminacy
inherent in attempting to judge the success or failure of any foreign-policy initiative, owing partly to the conflicting criteria of various organizations involved,
stifles individual initiative in expanding the alternatives to be considered.

In the search for alternatives, the functional division of labor makes it
hard to deal with new conditions, particularly since agencies have a strong
tendency to defend old roles and search for new ones. The clash of views within
the bureaucracy often leads to a search for compromise solutions, which, in
turn, tends to rule out radical policy departures at the outset.

Finally, when it comes to a choice of alternatives, there is little inclination to break with the past or to follow a course of action pregnant with high
risk. One reason for this is that the longevity of bureaucrats leads them to
identify with and defend past policies because radical change would threaten
their position and imply criticism of their past performance. Even in cases
where bureaucrats resign themselves to new policy initiatives, they can have a
conservative impact because they can slowly alter them through their implementing actions. The decision-maker who wishes to escape this dilemma may
try several approaches—reshape the bureaucracy, set up an alternative bureaucracy, or use a crisis situation to effect a radical change in procedure.

Thus, like the psychological variable discussed earlier, organization tends
to make foreign policy decision-making a rather conservative process, leading
to a situation in which ". . . foreign policy decision makers tend to avoid new
interpretations of the environment, to select and act upon certain goals, to limit the search for alternatives to a small number of moderate ones, and finally to
take risis which involve low costs if they prove unsuccessful" (Coplin 1971, p. 56).

It is, however, necessary to note that this conclusion does not apply in all cases and that the impact of the organization variables also depends on the strength of the major decision-makers and on the kind of issue involved. In a crisis situation, for example, the effect of bureaucracy may be minimized because under the press of time there can be little, if any, attention given to preparation of position papers or detailed consultations (Holsti 1972, pp. 391-92). Whether this was the case in the energy crisis is one of the many issues connected with the bureaucratic setting that we shall discuss in detail in our conclusion.

DOMESTIC AND INTERNATIONAL INPUTS

The third dimension of our framework, inputs, can be divided into two categories: those derived from the domestic environment, and the structure and values of the international system and the events occurring therein. The national inputs consist of demands and support. Under demands we are concerned principally with public opinion and the activities of interest groups.

Public Opinion

Public opinion is, of course, an important ingredient in the formulation of foreign policy in democratic societies such as the United States. But in order to assess its impact on any problem such as the energy crisis, one must disaggregate the citizenry into various groups, each of which plays a different role in shaping the inputs on foreign policy. First comes the small but influential group, perhaps 1-15 percent—usually with higher education, urban location, professional occupation, and higher income—that is well-informed, articulate, and concerned. Next comes a large group, the "attentive public," which consists of those citizens (30-50 percent) who have established attitudes toward other countries, some knowledge about specific issues, and a willingness to express opinions. Their views are often inculcated by parents, teachers, peer groups, parties, interest group, the media, and/or the government (Dawson and Prewitt 1969). Finally, we must consider the majority of the people. Survey research suggests that most persons are apathetic and uninformed on matters of foreign policy; few Americans, for example, could locate Libya on a map, let alone a small sheikhdom like Abu Dhabi. They also tend to remain passive actors unless they become interested in an issue and mobilized for political action.

Nevertheless, even though most persons may not be very concerned with

foreign policy issues in general, they do have general attitudes and predisposi-
tions, a phenomenon that is often referred to as a mood. While moods may not
identify concrete objectives, they do seem to set limits around policy alternatives. Japan, for example, would find it hard to embark on a nuclear weapons
program because of the widespread revulsion among her people toward nuclear
forces. The vast majority of citizens therefore play a role in policy, although
primarily to the extent of setting bounds on alternatives (Key 1972, p. 552).

Whether or not a large segment of the population expresses opinions also
appears to be related to the degree of urgency or threat in a situation. However, it seems accurate to suggest that during crises (characterized by sudden,
unanticipated actions, high perceptions of threats, and feelings that something
should be done immediately) public opinion is still not an important factor:
decisions are usually made by a few policy-makers because they have little time
for consultation (Almond 1960, pp. 69-86; Holsti 1972, pp. 81-86).

Interest Groups

In addition to public opinion in general, one must also consider the role
of organized interest groups in terms of the demands that are placed on the
FPDMS. For, in sharp contrast with the rather limited impact of public opinion
on foreign policy-making, some interest groups, especially economic and ethnic
ones, can have, and have had, a substantial impact on policies that are related
to their areas of concern. The Zionist lobby's success in matters related to
Israel is an obvious and well-known example (Cohen 1965, pp. 101-06). Less
well-known but equally significant have been the activities of the oil lobby concerning both domestic and international petroleum policy.

Interest groups have been studied intensively, and scholars have identified
several factors that contribute to a group's effectiveness. The structure of a
group is very important; most effective groups have been noticeably well-
organized. But, although a permanent and sophisticated organization may be
necessary for effective articulation, it is by no means sufficient. Equally important is the identification and successful exploitation of channels of access to
policy-makers. This may take a variety of forms. Most desirable is the use of
personal connections based on local, school, family, or social ties to establish
face-to-face communication with policy-makers. Another channel is elite representation, which can take the form of having either a group member or a
sympathetic independent actor involved in the policy-making structure. Access
may also be gained through skillful use of the formal and institutional channels
that exist in modern democratic polities, such as political parties, legislatures,
bureaucracies, cabinets, and the media. In decentralized political systems such as

the United States, effective groups usually try to articulate their demands through all these channels and to do so at all levels of government. Finally, interest groups may resort to extralegal measures, such as physical demonstrations and/or violence, as a means of registering their demands. Although this usually occurs when other channels are perceived as blocked or ineffective, extralegal measures can be used to complement the others (Almond and Powell 1966, pp. 80-86; Merkl 1970, pp. 320-22). A classic example of an interest group's using all these channels, except violence, at all levels of government was the Zionist lobby in the late 1940s, when it obtained U.S. support for and recognition of Israel. The direct and indirect channels used by this lobby to influence the FPDMS are indicated in Figure 3.

The second factor that may have a bearing on the success of an interest group is the style of articulation. This can be manifest or latent, specific or diffuse, general or particular, instrumental or affective. Manifest articulation is the explicit formulation of a demand, whereas latent articulation refers to behavioral or mood cues (such as vague grumbling). Obviously, when demands are latent, it is harder for policy-makers to accurately assess and respond to them. Once a demand has been articulated, it may be expressed in specific or diffuse terms. Specific demands, such as a request to end the oil depletion allowance, suggest appropriate corrective measures; diffuse statements, such as "the oil companies are dishonest," tend to indicate dissatisfaction but not the desired policy response. Demands may also be defined with varying degrees of generality. General demands are phrased in class or associational group terms, a recent example being the demand of truck drivers that the speed limit be raised. Particular demands, on the other hand, are stated in individual or family terms (such as offering a bribe for a favor). Finally, articulation may be instrumental or affective. The former takes the form of a bargain with policy-makers (offering electoral support in return for a favorable policy response to the group's demands). Affective articulation, by contrast, takes the form of simple expressions of anger, disappointment, hope, or gratitude (Almond and Powerll 1966, pp. 86-88).

Politically astute interest groups in the United States will emphasize manifest, specific, general, and instrumental styles of articulation, because these styles make it easier for policy-makers to ascertain the exact nature of group demands, to aggregate those demands with requests from other groups, and to arrive at acceptable compromises. Conversely, policy-makers have difficulty in reacting to ambiguous demands that are made in emotional tones, since it is very difficult to assess the costs, risks, and benefits of alternative responses in such cases.

Two final conditions that, although not essential, certainly contribute to successful interest articulation deserve mention: the absence of formidable counterlobbies and lack of public interest. Where well-organized and active

FIGURE 3 Channels Used by Zionist Lobby to Influence Foreign Policy
Decision-Making System (FPDMS)

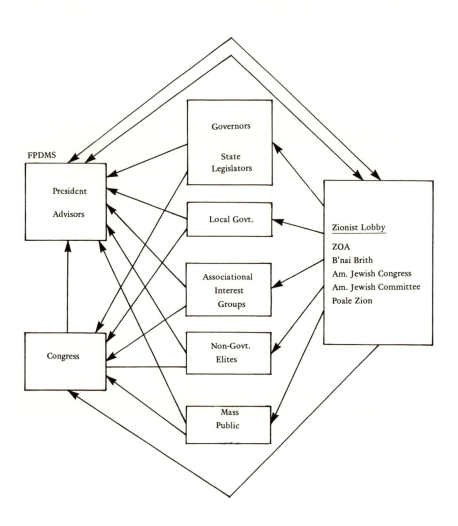

opposition groups exist, they may influence decision-makers to deny another group complete fulfillment of its demands or they may cancel out their opponents' efforts completely. As far as public interest is concerned, it is easier for interest groups to establish the fact that their views are representative of the only segment of the population concerned with an issue when the attentive public is small (Cohen 1965, p. 107).

In summary, we would expect that interest groups that are successful in influencing the FPDMS would be well-organized; would use many channels of access; would voice their demands in manifest, specific, general, and instrumental terms; and would have little or no effective opposition to or public interest shown in the issue at hand. The oil companies and the Zionist lobby meet these criteria and, as we shall see, together with other interest groups of various kinds, have utilized various techniques and channels to achieve varying degrees of success in their attempts to influence U.S. domestic and international policy on energy matters.

Both public opinion and interest groups tend to work through other institutions, notably Congress. Its constitutional powers are well-known and include the ratification of treaties, confirmation of executive appointments, control over appropriations and the national defense budget, the right to declare war, and through its general legislative authority, the establishment of the administrative structure for the foreign-policy decision-making system. In addition to its Constitutional powers Congress also possesses various extra-Constitutional and informal techniques that can be used to influence foreign affairs. These include legislative investigations, the passage of Congressional resolutions, and the activities of individual Congressmen (Crabb 1965, Ch. 5). The extent and manner in which these powers are utilized depend on numerous factors, as does the impact that they actually produce on foreign policy. In our conclusion we shall seek to assess the role that Congress has played in the energy-foreign-policy field.

Legitimacy

The third input to the FPDMS support essentially consists of two dimensions. The first of these is the capabilities of the state, which are derived from the exploitation of its resources, both human and material. We have already discussed the relationship between capability and foreign policy outputs. Whether or not these capabilities become available and can be utilized to serve foreign-policy ends, however, is in large part a function of the second dimension of support, the degree of legitimacy that citizens accord the political system. In the United States, legitimacy is usually taken for granted but, because of Watergate and related matters, this concept suddenly acquired new relevance and must therefore be discussed briefly so that we may later assess whether and how it affected the formulation and implementation of foreign policy during the energy crisis.

Legitimacy, according to Charles Andrain (1970, pp. 137 ff.), deals with whether or not the citizens acknowledge the moral right of political leaders to make binding decisions over them. Actually, there are five levels that may receive or be denied the moral support of the people: the political society, the laws, political institutions, specific political leaders, and particular policies (Easton 1965, pp. 171-219; Lipset 1960, pp. 72-83; Friedrich 1968, pp. 232-46). Although the analyst may wish to focus on these separately, he must bear their interrelationships in mind. That is, if citizens do not agree that they should live together in the same society, it is doubtful that they will accept the laws designed to govern their behavior and the institutions that make those laws. Likewise, if the laws and institutions are not granted legitimacy, the leaders and their policies will not be accepted (as is the case with the Kurds in Iraq). If one reverses the order, on the other hand, the process need not be cumulative. That is, the population may reject policies but not leaders, leaders but not institutions, institutions but not laws, and all of the others but not the political society.

Legitimacy may also be analyzed in terms of the forms that it may take. Scholars have identified five types—traditional, personal, ideological, procedural, and instrumental. The first is characteristic of states where legitimacy is derived from such sources as immemorial norms, ascriptive status, and ancestral wishes. Personal legitimacy, by contrast, stresses the attractiveness, magnetic personality, and extraordinary qualities of "great men." Charisma, one form of personal legitimacy, is used to describe those leaders whom the people accept as having a "gift of grace" and supernatural abilities (such as Nasser). Ideological legitimacy is operative in those cases where large segments of the citizenry accept the political society, laws, institutions, leaders, and policies because they reflect a higher set of principles that are considered to be a "true" explanation of past, present, and future phenomena (such as Marxism in the USSR).

While traditional, personal, and ideological types of legitimacy may exist among certain segments of the population (there is always a mixture), in modern democracies more emphasis is placed on procedural and instrumental sources as a moral basis for accepting political objects. Where procedural legitimacy prevails, leaders and policies receive moral support because they are placed in power; and they make decisions in accordance with laws that both the leaders and the masses accept. In such cases, citizens consent to impersonal legal principles rather than obeying a person. Instrumental legitimacy exists in cases where leaders are able to provide concrete benefits and services to society or when they possess acknowledged expertise—leaders and their policies are supported because of widespread recognition that knowledgeable individuals made the policy.

When relating support, conceptualized as legitimacy, to foreign-policy decision-making, we are interested in two somewhat contradictory effects. First, legitimacy, by creating stability and moral support, makes it easier for leaders to obtain backing for policy initiatives and expands their power to make decisions under difficult conditions. The latter is particularly important where the institutions and leaders are considered legitimate, for it provides the diffuse support necessary for the radical changes that are sometimes required during crises. A case in point was the U.S. worldwide alert during the October 1973 Middle East war, when it appeared that the USSR might send troops to Egypt. Because of the strong procedural legitimacy and the instrumental legitimacy derived from Secretary of State Kissinger's acknowledged expertise, this action could be implemented successfully despite doubts expressed by certain opinion leaders and segments of the attentive public about the domestic political motivations for this action.

In contradistinction to the above, legitimacy restricts decisional options because the principles of legitimacy place certain obligations and limitations on leaders. In the case of the United States, for example, procedural legitimacy is based on specific formalized rules that are designed to constrain the use of power and to restrain arbitrary decisions (such as President Truman's failure to seize the Youngstown Steel Company in the 1950s). Likewise, instrumental legitimacy restricts rulers, because it forces them to deliver on their promises in terms of concrete benefits and services.

THE INTERNATIONAL ENVIRONMENT: STRUCTURE, VALUES, AND EVENTS

Finally, we turn to the international environment and consider the inputs that derive from outside the domestic political system. These may be analyzed under three distinct headings. First is the structure of the international system, which may be defined in terms of its configuration of power and influence or its persistent forms of stratification. It is here that we address some familiar aspects of international politics, such as the degree of polarity within the system, the distribution of power, and the structure of regional and functional subsystems. Given our focus on the energy crisis, we are particularly interested in whether changes in the international structure of power and influence are discernible or likely, and what the impact of such changes may be on American policy. It is worth noting in this context that we do not identify the contemporary structure of power in the international system with the balance of military forces; we see it, instead, as rather diffuse and varying according to issue area. That is, we accept the notion that there are different structures of power and influence in various issue and geographic areas. Thus, while the international structure of power may still be considered bipolar, at least to an extent, because of the obvious dominance of the Soviet-American diplomatic and conflict subsystem, there are deviations from the dominant pattern in specific areas, such as foreign trade, where the ability to provide or withhold raw materials—as was the case with oil—may give minor states great potential for power and influence.

Second are the systemic values, the values that transcend local and national concerns—such as social, economic, and political development, self-determination, territorial integrity, and the peaceful resolution of conflict. Although the significance for policy-makers of the structure of power in the international system has long been recognized, the impact of systemic values is not as clear. While it is no doubt true that system-wide values, such as economic development, have a subtle influence on foreign policy (Holsti 1972, pp. 373-74), we hold the view that they are, at best, secondary considerations and have minor influence on policy-making. For one thing, as Werner Levi (1969, passim) has pointed out, normative systems are composed of a multitude of values that not only change but also tend to be compartmentalized, with different values justifying different behavior. Moreover, the nature of normative systems is conducive to different interpretation, to the choice of expediently useful norms from the total constellation, and to the suppression of inconvenienc norms that are not intensely held. Finally, there is a methodological problem that stems from the fact that values are often inferred from the very behavioral patterns for which they are supposed to account, at least in part (Apter and Andrain 1972, pp. 155-59).

Finally, we must consider the fact that foreign policy is often a response to immediate events and conditions abroad, many of which are unanticipated, and that feedback mechanisms relate the outputs of the FPDMS to all of its components. These aspects, of course, seem especially significant in the case of the energy crisis.

ORGANIZATION OF THE STUDY

The data and insights that are essential for the application of this conceptual framework will be provided in the following chapters, which have been organized around three major dimensions: the background and significance of the problem, the situation in the Middle East and the content and goals of U.S. foreign policy and security policy in the area, and U.S. policy vis-a-vis other major international actors. In this manner the reader will be able to obtain an understanding of particular critical energy problem areas.

Specifically, Chapter 2 considers the background to the U.S. energy revolution; Chapter 3 examines the domestic factors that caused an energy shortage; Chapter 4 looks at the change in character of the international petroleum enterprise and its implications; Chapter 5 reviews political dynamics in the Middle East and their relationship to energy considerations; Chapter 6 focuses on U.S. policy in the Middle East; Chapter 7 considers the role of the Persian Gulf in U.S. security policy; Chapter 8 assesses the energy predicament of America's allies and how this situation affects U.S. policy; and Chapter 9 analyzes the impact that energy considerations may have on America's adversary relationship with the USSR. In our concluding chapter, 10, we shall synthesize, interpret, and supplement with our own research the findings of our contributors. We shall do so within the framework elaborated above, focusing specifically upon the impact on U.S. foreign policy of the Arab oil embargo of October 1973.

2

BACKGROUND TO THE
U.S. ENERGY REVOLUTION
George A. Lincoln

In the summer of 1972, Undersecretary of State John Irwin sought a personal conference with each Cabinet officer and other agency heads responsible for energy matters. He indicated grave concern that the increasing dependency on foreign energy supplies, principally oil, would inevitably result in losing our freedom of action in foreign policy. His concern was underlined with a presentation of some of the considerations in this chapter concerning the energy situation in the United States, its background and development, and some of the options the future holds.

Irwin's efforts in mid-1972 to alert the top level of the government may have represented the first time that energy received top institutional attention from U.S. foreign-policy machinery. Nothing spectacular came of his efforts at the time, though some shared his concern (Akins 1973, pp. 462-64). Policy, or lack thereof, implicitly continued to assume an expanding dependence on foreign oil, principally Middle Eastern, until at least the 1980s. It was not until September 1973, when the President, in commenting on the country's energy problems, said that the United States cannot be at the mercy of the Middle Eastern oil producers, that formal recognition that the security of our energy was in jeopardy finally reached the top level of foreign policy.

Within a few weeks, following the outbreak of Arab-Israel hostilities, the Arab states had curtailed oil production and halted shipment of oil to the United States (also to the Netherlands and Denmark). Short-term crisis measures were necessary, but so also were a policy review and revision for the longer term.

The President, in a speech on November 7, 1973, advocated a "Project

24

Independence" in energy; this was a far cry indeed from the previous relative complacency of the leadership. Within a few weeks the chairman of the Atomic Energy Commission gave the President a $10 billion, five-year plan for an energy research and development budget that outlined measures for moving to self-sufficiency by 1980-85. The President, in an energy message to Congress on January 23 and in his State of the Union address of January 30, 1974, outlined a program for energy self-sufficiency, noting that, as 1970 had been the year of the environment, 1974 should be the year of energy (Nixon 1974, pp. 123-25).

At the invitation of the President, a top-level conference of the principal energy-deficient consuming states convened in Washington on February 11, 1974. The conference discussed not only the current crisis generated by the Arab boycott but also the sobering longer-term implications of prices and international behavior in energy matters, and such remedial measures as sharing knowledge in the area of energy conservation and research and development. Energy had leaped to the top level, internationally, as a critical issue and problem.

The plan and program presented in the President's energy message of January 1974 had the objective of placing the United States in a position of being essentially independent of foreign energy producers by 1980. The message described Project Independence as entailing three essential concurrent tasks: rapidly increasing domestic energy supplies, reducing demand by conserving energy, and developing new technologies through a massive new research and development program. The proposal was sufficiently drastic to generate skepticism concerning achievement on the proposed schedule. But the important point was, and is, that the nation was at last both alerted to the hazard facing the security of its energy and was beginning to do something about it—a transition in policy and public awareness of a rapidity rarely before accomplished except on outbreak of war. The Arab oil boycott of the United States was substantially ended in mid-March 1974. But, it was hoped, the nation would not slip back into the energy complacency that existed prior to that boycott.

The general public attitude and de facto policy of the United States prior to that boycott is well described in the following quotation from the AEC report mentioned above:

So long as supplies of oil imports seemed to be insured there was little cause for concern about domestic self-sufficiency. United States companies owned controlling interests in the firms producing and delivering foreign oil, and there seemed to be no practical limit on foreign production capacity, that much of the refining was done abroad and products were imported was no cause for concern so long as continuous flow of fuel was reasonably ensured. Failure to use cheap foreign fuel

would have caused an unnecessary rise in cost of energy at home and
slow progress toward meeting environmental goals. The result has
been an increasing dependence on foreign imports. (AEC 1973, p. 40)

True, there were warning voices, and one national security energy program—
the mandatory oil import program. This program alone was, however, an inadequate instrument, operating by limiting imports and thereby providing some
incentive to domestic refining and some price protection to domestic crude oil.
In hindsight, the country needed a long-range integrated program encompassing
all significant aspects of energy and encouraging domestic production and use
of fuels, such as coal, from domestic sources while stressing energy conservation.

In any case, it can be argued that the American way of dealing with a
large unexpected problem is, first, to be skeptical of its existence, then to
search for scapegoats, and finally to settle down to dealing with the problem.
One of the ironic aspects of the energy crisis, both short- and long-term, is that
the more successful the measures to deal with it, the more likely there will be a
haunting skepticism concerning its necessity and/or reality.

Even for those who charged conspiracy rather than focusing on the reality
of energy crisis and crunch, the problem was hydra-headed. First, there is the
immediate problem, related to the Arab-Israeli issue, of restrictions and threatened restrictions on U.S. oil imports, a significant possibility foreseen by Secretary Irwin and others concerned with energy security. This leverage on U.S.
policy could have been a hammerlock if the trend of increasing U.S. dependency had continued unchecked for several more years before the boycott occurred. Indeed, some argued that the United States experienced a great good
fortune in being awakened to its peril before it was too late to recover energy
freedom.

Second, there is the problem created by interpolation of energy issues
into the complicated system of U.S. alliances and other relations. Economic
threats tend to generate "go it alone" policies much more than military concerns, which tend to generate cohesion.

Third, there is the problem created by the sudden, vast escalation in the
price of international oil, with consequent leverage on the complex of both
international and domestic economic matters. The effect of the price increase
on those developing countries needing capital for development, and foreign
exchange for such essentials as fertilizer to support the essential food supply, is
potentially devastating. Related to the explosive change in price is a rapid shift
in control of export oil from private companies to the producing countries.
This new control system is bound to be administered with political as well as
economic objectives.

Finally, there is, for the United States, the vast problem of adjusting domestic energy policies to accord with the newly sensed foreign energy realities.

We require a background, an overview, of central energy facts and considerations in order to comprehend the foreign-policy aspects of these related problems. That requirement is what this chapter is about.

BASIC CONCEPTS

Energy

Energy, according to Webster, is the capacity for doing work. This means that energy manifests itself in such ways as heat, light, and power that drives machinery and vehicles. Also, a small amount of energy fuels is essential to vitally important nonenergy industrial uses, such as manufacture of petrochemicals.

Energy is generally measured in the United States in BTU (British thermal units), which is the amount of heat required to raise the temperature of one pound of pure water one degree Fahrenheit. A thousand cubic feet of normal natural gas contains about 1 million BTU, and a barrel of normal crude oil contains about 5.8 million. A short ton of bituminous coal contains about 24-28 million BTU, and a short ton of lignite about 17-20 million. The United States in 1973 consumed 75.6 quadrillion BTU of energy, equivalent to about 36.6 million b/d (barrels per day) of crude oil. About 17 million b/d of crude oil (6.1 million b/d imported) was consumed. The remainder of energy consumption was provided from other sources. Obviously, an action making a change equivalent to as much as 1 million b/d of oil could be considered significant; a change of the order of 100,000 b/d is hardly significant.

A kilowatt hour contains 3,142 BTU. A watt is the power conveyed by an electric current of one ampere flowing under a tension of one volt, and a kilowatt is equal to 1.34 horsepower. Electricity, however, is not a basic energy source, as are coal and oil, but is intermediate energy, which (except for hydropower) has to be produced by using some basic fuel (such as coal) and then transmitted to an energy-using source (such as a light bulb or an electric motor providing power).

Energy Conservation

Energy conservation is a concept having both a production dimension and a consumption dimension. The conservation concept has long been associated with maximizing the efficiency of extraction of fuels (particularly oil and gas) from the ground. For example, oil recovery efficiency from U.S. producing wells in 1970 averaged only 31 percent (NPC 1972, p. 66) of these known reserves. With higher prices or improved technology, or both, a much greater efficiency should be forthcoming. A rise to 50 percent efficiency, adding as much as 80 billion barrels to U.S. proved reserves by 1985, has been suggested as possible (*Oil Daily,* Apr. 24, 1974).

Now, however, the term "energy conservation" is more generally applied to various actions for reducing consumption of energy while achieving substantially the same ends. The opportunities are as great for energy conservation as for "energy efficiency." For example, the furnaces of electric power plants have an average efficiency of less than 40 percent, now decreasing because of environmental requirements; and around 10 percent of generated electricity lost in line transmission to the user. Another obvious example is the fuel consumption of automobile motors. The preliminary report of the Energy Policy Projects of the Ford Foundation (1974, p. 4) notes that in 1958 the average American car got over 14 miles per gallon; by 1973, the rate had dropped to less than 12. The principal reasons were increased weight, additional equipment, and the extra fuel used by emission controls.

Conservation is an energy policy offsetting otherwise needed production and also supporting the security of our energy, our foreign policy posture, and economies for the consumer, as well as environmental aspirations. Most other energy programs, however, are in some degree of conflict with those environmental aspirations, since the production and consumption of energy usually necessitates some pollution, or environmental change, or threat thereof.

Production Lead Times

Production lead times between initiating a project and getting the energy product to the consumer are generally long. The lead times between research and development and the consumer are much longer. While policies on energy can be changed in a day—the initiation of the boycott by the Arabs in October 1973—the adjustments of production and of consumption, except for voluntary conservation and rationing, have entirely different order of timing magnitude. For example, nuclear power plants are requiring over eight years from initiation of planning to production, although the Japanese build them in five; an oil refinery requires three to five years; and development of a new oil field requires several years. Any new process or product is likely to take as much as 10 years from research concept to mass distribution. On the consumption side, some measures can happen in a short time, such as turning down the thermostats. But others, such as shifts from individual cars to use of mass transit, or from large cars to small cars, require significant time.

The long lead time aspect is stressed to show the importance of forecasts (discussed below). There are serious time lags in recovering a secure energy situation impaired by faulty estimates in forecasts of production and/or consumption. The same time lags exist when a threatened or actual change of policy, such as the Arab actions of 1973, alerts the country to the need for energy security.

Energy Security

Energy security is a central aspect of the difficult complex of national security, which is a main purpose of foreign policy. Energy security is a problem area of our economy that, like our social system and way of life, depends on adequate energy at an acceptable cost. That cost must be appraised both from the standpoint of the individual consumer and from the balance-of-payments and other international standpoints. Energy security, also and not least, is the assurance against coercion by the foreign possessors of those energy resources that make possible our way of life (Lincoln 1973a).

As a problem area in our economy, energy security is in sharp contrast with nuclear security. As in the case of nuclear security, however, our country has now passed over a divide to a situation where absolute energy security has been lost. The free action of our foreign policy, as well as of our economy, is now subject to significant influence by foreign energy producers. True, we have some chance of recovering that freedom by wise and vigorous energy measures— but not soon.

USES AND SOURCES

The United States has about 6 percent of the world's people and consumes over 30 percent of the energy used in the world. Since there is some correlation between gross national product and consumption of energy, those statistics are not as surprising as they might first seem. In fact, the United States used 44 percent of world energy in 1950, leading to the sobering thought that if major portions of the rest of the world achieve their objectives of greatly increased per capita gross national product, the consequent worldwise energy consumption will bring the fossil fuel age more quickly to an end.

The U.S. five-year annual rate of growth (in percent) has been:

1957	1962	1967	1972
2.73	2.60	4.20	4.35

Source: "The United States Energy Through the Year 2000," Department of Interior (1972).

The Department of Interior reports that U.S. energy consumption grew 5 percent in 1972 and 4.8 percent in 1973. Consumption of petroleum increased 5.1 percent despite the Arab boycott of October 1973. World energy consumption has been growing at a rate of 6 percent a year, and world petroleum consumption increased over 9 percent in 1973.

The overall U.S. trend to an annual increase in energy consumption in the 1960s and early 1970s is disturbing from the foreign-policy standpoint, since the United States is now an energy deficient country. The U.S. presentation to the International Energy Conference of February 1974 forecast an annual increase of 3.6 percent before the turn-around of U.S. energy policy toward a drastic conservation program. But the turn-around has to start from annual increases of well over 4 percent during the previous few years and move toward suggested goals of as low as 2 percent or even less.

The use of energy in 1973 can be categorized by sectors of the economy (the percentages are approximate):

Industry	40 percent
Transportation	25 percent
Residential	20 percent
Commercial	15 percent

Another way of looking at energy is to note that "business," according to the Department of Commerce, consumes about 70 percent of energy. Hence we must look to business to play a large part in checking the high rate of expansion of energy consumption.

The transportation sector most directly affects, and is most directly affected by, our domestic petroleum deficiency. That sector draws its energy almost entirely from petroleum, using about half of total petroleum consumption (about a quarter of total energy consumption).

Our energy comes from oil, gas, coal, hydropower, and, currently, a small amount from nuclear power. The consumption of energy by basic energy sources in 1973 was as follows:

Oil	45.9 percent
Natural gas	31.2 percent
Coal	17.9 percent
Hydropower	3.9 percent
Nuclear power	1.1 percent

Source: Bureau of Mines, as reported in *Coal News,* March 15, 1974.

The production of electricity—intermediate energy—consumed about 25 percent of primary energy (coal, oil, gas, and uranium) by 1973. This consumption is estimated to rise to 38 percent by 1990. Electricity is distributed principally among the industrial, residential, and commercial sectors. Its consumption grew at an annual rate of 7.4 percent between 1960 and 1970 and is projected to expand much more rapidly than the consumption of the primary fuels (Ford Foundation 1974, p. 5).

In 1973 slightly over half of the electricity was generated from coal, which the United States has in abundance. The remainder was generated from oil, gas, hydropower, and a small but expanding proportion from nuclear fuel. Obviously, from the standpoint of energy security (including our balance of payments), the United States should maximize its production of electricity from coal and should press expansion of the nuclear power program. Until the shock of the Arab embargo, however, the electric power industry was shifting from coal to oil to meet environmental standards. The nuclear power program, producing 5 percent of our electricity at the end of 1973, is scheduled to be producing 23 percent by 1980 (AEC 1973, p. 107). It should be noted that because of long lead times, all nuclear power plants that will be producing in 1980 were under construction by 1974.

Since indigenous fuels are foreign-policy/national-security-supporting fuels, these policy areas are best served by making our electricity from coal and nuclear power.

Along with the fall in use of coal, there has been a leveling off of production of natural gas and a compensating rise in the use of oil. Since U.S. petroleum production leveled off in the early 1970s, our energy consumption increases had to be provided principally by foreign oil imports. These imports increased by only 6 percent a year in the 1960s but increased by 18 percent a year during the first four years of the 1970s, so that in 1973, U.S. production met only 65 percent of our demand for oil.

The United States relied primarily on Canada and Venezuela until early in the 1970s. From that time, additional oil imports had to come primarily from the Middle East, on which the remainder of the oil-deficient non-Communist world was already primarily dependent. The exact U.S. dependency on Arab oil in early 1974, assuming unchecked demand, was a matter of some statistical controversy; but a generally used estimate was 2.4 million b/d, or about 14 percent of our petroleum consumption. If consumption expanded at

the 1973 rate (5.1 percent) with provision almost entirely from the Middle
East, including Iran, the dependency by 1980 would be sobering indeed. The
dependency of other energy-deficient countries had been building for a long
while. From 1960 to 1972, oil consumption grew at an annual rate of 11.0 percent in Western Europe and 17.4 percent in Japan. When the United States also
became seriously dependent, the market power of the cartelized oil-exporting
states have them a strong position to raise prices and realize monopoly profits—
which they did.

Forecasts for the future have generally shown the natural gas proportion
of consumption falling because of the leveling off of U.S. production, coal declining further because of ecological restraints, hydropower remaining about
constant, and nuclear power climbing, at first slowly. The forecasts have shown
a significant increase in the proportion of consumption provided from oil. This
increase would be occasioned principally by the anticipated shortfalls in supply
of natural gas compared with demand and also by the environmental controls
on use of coal.

All of these forecasts are now in question because of the revolutionary
change in both price and U.S. energy policy triggered by the Arab oil boycott
of 1973-74.

During the period considered in this discussion (until about 1985), the
expansion of nonfossil fuel sources is unlikely to provide a significant portion
of energy needs except for nuclear power, which, according to a Federal Energy Office estimate, will not provide more than about 5 percent of energy by
1985. There is a long-term need to shift to the breeder reactor, which produces
more nuclear fuel than it consumes, since the known sources of uranium are
finite. During the period under discussion, nuclear power will be from light-
water or high-temperature gas reactor plants; the breeder reactor will come into
production later. Of the nonfossil sources, hydropower is generally estimated
to maintain about its current status of supplying no more than 4 percent of
energy. Expansion of hydroelectric power has serious environmental aspects.
Who, for instance, wants to dam the Grand Canyon? Geothermal and solar
power arouse the most interest and also, particularly solar power, considerable
controversy.

As to geothermal power, the National Petroleum Council estimates geothermal power as reaching no more than 1 percent of the electric energy requirement by 1985 (NPC 1972, p. 53). The AEC's *The Nation's Energy Future*
is only slightly more optimistic. The Joint Committee on Atomic Energy notes
that geothermal power capabilities are fairly predictable and provides an estimate of about 3 percent of energy consumption by the year 2000, commenting
that a massive effort would be required in California and a few other states.

Solar energy has attracted, and is attracting, a great deal of attention.
There is no doubt that the sun projects enough energy to the earth for all conceivable needs. Research on this energy source is not new. In 25 years solar

research centers expanded from three (M.I.T., Algeria, and Tashkent) to 38 (Hottell and Howard 1971, p. 334). The search for effective utilization of solar energy has been particularly attractive to poorer and developing countries, according to Hottell and Howard. If solar energy is ever harnessed, that achievement will drastically change the world's energy balance of power. The prospects are, however, speculative; and any significant contribution will come in the more distant future. Those prospects are best for space heating and cooling in sunny climes. The AEC's *Nation's Energy Future* suggests that someday solar power might provide up to 30 percent of residential heating and cooling, or about 6 percent of U.S. energy requirements. The report of the Joint Committee on Atomic Energy suggests the provision by solar energy of about 2 percent of our requirements by the year 2000. Two of the negative aspects have been the adverse environmental impact of covering large areas with solar energy apparatus if production of electric power is undertaken and the high projected costs of any solar energy installation even after technological problems are solved. With rising conventional energy costs, the latter point may, however, cease to be pertinent.

To meet energy needs during the period under consideration, we must depend on oil, gas, coal, small amounts of hydropower, and conventional nuclear power. On the demand side, we have to depend on an energy conservation/efficiency program that dampens the previously projected increases in consumption.

THE UNITED STATES AND WORLD ENERGY DEPENDENCY

The focus of world attention in international energy trade has been on oil. There is, however, a considerable trade in electricity, coal, and natural gas, as well as significant prospects for nuclear power plants. The last are a particularly sensitive commodity because of the concern that nuclear fuel might be diverted to weapons. Nuclear power plants (and there is a design for floating plants) might, however, become a commodity in significant international demand both because of the high price and possible scarcity of other energy sources, and because of the eventual waning of the world's fossil fuel supply. For example, despite his country's oil-surplus status, the Shah of Iran has suggested that oil and gas should be conserved for such long-term use as petrochemicals, and that the world should turn quickly to less exhaustible energy sources, such as nuclear power.

The United States exports coal, principally to Europe, Japan, and Canada, and imports a significant amount of natural gas—over 4 percent of U.S. consumption—overland from Canada. The Canadians, however, sensitive about preserving energy resources for the next generation, have limited both gas and oil exports.

Starting in the early 1970s, there has been intensive consideration by industry and government of imported liquid natural gas (LNG). The first trickle
of imports was from Algeria to New England. The LNG projects are costly in
capital, ambitious, and land the gas in the United States at several times the
U.S. regulated wellhead price. There are proposals for LNG from Siberia, which
has vast gas reserves, for our west coast and east coast. The dependency resulting from a significant LNG import program would seriously impair energy security and would be directly against the policy of Project Independence. The
fact remains, however, that by 1973 the production of U.S. natural gas had
nearly leveled off while demand steadily increased for this desirable fuel. A way
must be found to close the gas gap—by conservation (60 percent of gas is
burned, some think wastefully, under industrial boilers), by switching to other
fuels (also in short supply), by increased production (for which offshore discoveries and Rocky Mountain gas with nuclear or other stimulation have the
best prospects), by coal gasification, by imports, or other means. Gas require
ments pose substantially the same problems as oil, except that gas lacks some
of the energy-insecurity temptation of oil because it has been more difficult to
import from overseas.

Interpenetration of Energy Policies

Energy is an all-pervasive factor in both domestic and foreign policy; but,
more often than not, in the past it was not recognized as significant. Instead,
attention usually has been directed to two favorite whipping boys—the tax depletion allowance and the mandatory oil import control program initiated in
1959. The latter was put into effect on the basis of legislation requiring the
President "to act" if an investigation showed that imports of a commodity
threatened the national security of the United States. The oil import program
controlled less than 7 percent of U.S. energy in the last year (1972) of its
existence—not a very large part of the energy elephant. Certainly, in light of
the Arab embargo, there can be no argument that oil imports eventually
threatened the national security of the United States.

The money value of the depletion allowance was minor compared with
total taxation or the gross national product. It did benefit foreign operations of
U.S. companies as well as domestic operations—the argument being that such
development helped U.S. interests. Certainly both programs contributed to
encouraging development of domestic production. The unpopularity of the
programs, which conflicted with other national objectives, such as acceptance
of taxation systems as fair and hopes for lower energy costs to the consumer,
may, however, have distracted attention from the threats of the future, thereby

illustrating the conflicts inherent in designing and administering an energy program.

The hard fact is that the traditional U.S. energy program was overrun by the rapid evolution of the domestic and international energy situation. This is not necessarily meant to be a critical statement; the needed changes were so drastic that a time-consuming program of education and realization was necessary in our political, social, and economic systems. A shock such as the Arab embargo may have been necessary to gain quick consideration of those changes.

Three specific examples of interpenetration of energy with other policies usually considered as nonenergy are given to illustrate the point.

The belated adoption of environmental programs by the United States in the Clean Air Act of 1970 had major energy implications, yet none were appraised at the time. For example, the Cabinet Task Force report on the Oil Import Program of 1970 did not consider environmental factors in estimating future consumption and supply. Yet, with the production and consumption of energy generating a significant part of our pollution and of environmental impacts, this program was bound to have a significant effect: coal, long the stepchild of policy despite its domestic abundance, would be further disadvantaged; consumption of oil and of gas, if available, would be increased; expansion of energy facilities, such as the Alaska pipeline, would be delayed by administrative requirements, including environmental impact statements. Inevitably, there would be an impetus toward increased foreign dependency.

As another example, gas, the most desirable fuel for many purposes, was obviously peaking out in production by the early 1970s, yet the price of interstate transported gas had long been controlled for the desirable objective of lower costs to the consumer. Though commonly accepted economic theory recognizes that there is an elasticity of supply and that increased prices generate more supply, and though U.S. companies have negotiated with foreign countries, particularly the USSR, to import natural gas in liquid form at several times the wellhead price of domestic gas, the Congress, as of this writing, had not acted on the President's recommendation that the price of new gas at the wellhead be freed from controls.

As a third example, chosen in the international policy field, the United States has had a policy of a special relationship with Israel. The Arabs and Israel have been involved in a deadly quarrel. The Arab states threatened an oil cutoff in 1967 and demonstrated their ability by 1971 to collaborate in economic measures to raise oil prices and expand control of their one important resource. Yet the United States continued energy policies, or lack thereof, that moved toward a significant dependence on Arab oil. Clearly, in hindsight, this was an imprudent choice by default of conflicting policies gravely threatening the security of the United States. Any effective option was a hard and costly choice indeed—until the Arab embargo and simultaneous price rise made the policy options that moved toward much greater domestic self-sufficiency seem comparatively less costly. Recognizably, there are understandable time lags in appreciation of situations, even of perils. The U.S. problems of 1973-74, triggered by only a limited dependence on Arab oil, lead reasonably to a comment on the perils of energy forecasting.

The Perils and Policy Implications of Energy Forecasting

The policy-maker, whether he be an energy business executive deciding on where and how to invest capital or the President proposing national energy policy, is significantly captive to forecasts of what the energy world will be five, ten, and more years ahead. Forecasts, sometimes called "intelligence estimates," are an essential element of policy-making, giving a base line for policy action. The policy-maker may have the objective of trying to turn the forecasts into realities, or he may seek to create a reality much different from the forecasts. The President's call in November 1973 for a program of self-sufficiency, for example, was a call to invalidate drastically the generally accepted forecasts that, by 1980, the United States would have a foreign petroleum dependency of about 50 percent, about 25 percent of U.S. energy consumption, rising still higher by 1985.

Part of the hazard of energy forecasting lies in assumptions as to the mix of energy fuels used, even if overall energy consumption forecasts prove sound. In the 1950s, for example, there was a general belief that U.S. coal would give way fairly rapidly to nuclear fuel for electric power plants. This did not happen, but U.S. coal was a laggard industry until sudden popularity came with the Arab embargo of 1973. As another example, an article entitled "The Coming Energy Glut" (*Economist,* January 9, 1974) points out that after World War II there was a general assumption that European coal mines would prosper for a long while. Within 20 years, however, Europe was importing coal from the United States and had switched to oil as a principal fuel, thereby leading to a critical dependence of Western Europe on the Middle East.

Forecasts require that more-or-less scientific and reasoned assumptions be made on political, social, economic, technological, environmental, and other changes. These assumptions can be highly controversial, and the possible options on even one assumption permit a wide range of policy choice. When the United States was an energy-surplus country able to use energy lavishly—and we did—forecasting did not seem a critically important art.

The February 1970 report by the Cabinet Task Force to the President on oil import control provides a case study on the perils of forecasting and their effects on policy. The membership was Cabinet-level and the task force staff was large and of outstanding quality. The study analyzed massive data from the oil industry, governmental agencies, and other informed sources. While there was disagreement over the future method of import control, there was no recorded feeling that oil imports did not threaten the security of the United States (the legal basis for the control program) or disagreement over the forecasts of production and consumption. Industry and government were in substantial agreement on those forecasts and, presumably, planned their domestic and foreign affairs accordingly. How did these forecasts look compared to the realities four years later, when the Arab embargo had been imposed? (Akins 1973, pp. 462-63). Considering the lead times involved, four years is hardly enough to build a new refinery or develop an already discovered oil field.

The report gravely underestimated oil consumption, overestimated U.S. oil production, overestimated the supply available from the Western Hemisphere, and hence gravely underestimated both the timing and extent of dependence on the Eastern Hemisphere—principally the Middle East. Specifically, U.S. consumption for 1974, without the Arab boycott and other constraints, equaled the report's estimate for 1980. Imports for 1973 were 20 percent above those estimated for 1980 in the report. Whereas the early 1970 report estimated only a 27 percent foreign dependency by 1980, in 1973 that dependency had already reached 35 percent and was then estimated to reach 50 percent by 1980 and 57 percent by 1985.

There was an even more drastic shift in prices between forecasts and quickly changing reality. In early 1970 the generally accepted assumption was that imported crude oil would continue to be priced to land on the U.S. east coast at around $2 a barrel. With effective cartelization by the principal oil-producing and -exporting countries, the price rose significantly by the fall of 1973, and then exploded to approximately $10 a barrel shortly after the boycott. Whether such high prices, reflected in increases in U.S. domestic crude oil prices, proved temporary or permanent, there was a fundamental change in world and domestic economics of petroleum.

The funamental change in price, together with the unforecasted quick leap in petroleum demand, rendered obsolete all previous predictions of consumption and production of energy. The projections of the oil companies were equally erroneous.

The chief executive officer of Exxon, the world's largest oil company, stated in a speech in early 1974: "Aside from the Arab embargo, the domestic energy shortage is a result of 1973 demand exceeding long-range prediction." Since the misestimates applied generally, Exxon was short on foreign as well as U.S. refining capacity (*Oil and Gas Journal,* Feb. 4, 1974, p. 50).

The reasons for the miscalculations were several and sometimes controversial. There was the high increase in overall energy consumption. Use of energy forms other than oil turned out to be less than expected. Natural gas production leveled off, with the unmet gas demand shifting principally to oil. Whereas Exxon, for example, estimated an annual 4 percent increase in coal consumption, coal increased by only 1 percent a year. Environmental programs were pressing usage away from coal to oil. Those same programs generated an absolute increase in energy consumption with such requirements as emission controls and unleaded gasoline. The accumulation of the faulty estimates in different sectors of the energy system added up to a quickly developing requirement for oil to full the supply gaps, just as U.S. oil production (Alaska having been delayed by environmental difficulties) peaked.

Hence foreign oil had to fill the oil supply gap, but the Cabinet report also miscalculated the foreign supply situation. It estimated that most of our foreign oil could be obtained from the Western Hemisphere and that, even by 1980, U.S. imports from the Eastern Hemisphere should not be consequential. The report recognized that such dependence was an element of insecurity and that measures should be taken to avoid it, but foreign Western Hemisphere availabilities were critically overestimated: by 1972 Venezuela was limiting production to conserve declining reserves (a policy that, incidentally, paid off well when the price of oil tripled or more in late 1973) and Canada, with limited production compared with its estimated national needs, set a ceiling on exports in 1973. Further, while Indonesia and Nigeria are signficant producers of the particularly desirable low-sulphur oil wanted worldwide, the great mass of foreign productive capacity is in the Middle East, including North Africa.

Recognizing that the principal Eastern Hemisphere sources are less secure than those in the West, the Cabinet Task Force report proposed that if Eastern Hemisphere imports increased to 5 percent, remedial action should be taken, and that 10 percent should be an absolute maximum. In fact, according to testimony of a Federal Energy Office official, the dependence on Arab oil alone in 1974 was estimated to be about 14 percent of U.S. consumption (*Oil and Gas Journal,* Jan 28, 1974, p. 79).

Toward Energy Security

The United States was an energy-surplus country until about 1969. Our foreign energy policies were principally those dealing with the large investments and operations overseas of U.S.-based companies and a program limiting oil imports for national security purposes. The latter had the objective of encouraging a healthy domestic industry by protecting against "cheap" foreign oil. The former—the affairs of overseas U.S. investment—provided welcome earnings to help the balance of payments, but most of those overseas operations had to do with the supply of oil to energy-deficient countries rather than to the United

States. We could afford to look at policy in compartments, an approach that extended to handling domestic policy by compartments of oil, coal, gas, hydropower, nuclear power, and environmental policy.

The situation is now completely changed by the United States becoming an energy-deficient country and by "cheap" foreign energy, principally oil, becoming a thing of the past.

As to first great change, the forecasters, and hence the policy-makers, now have to consider the entire "energy pie" made up of all energy fuels. Oil is the swing fuel, both because of its versatility in meeting the variety of demands and because more oil can be provided quickly from abroad (under normal circumstances) to fill any energy gap, whereas domestic expansion of fuel supply has a long time lag. Put another way, the energy requirements not met during the 1975-85 decade by domestic coal, oil, gas, hydropower, and a limited but expanding nuclear power must be met principally by imported oil. Since there are de facto ceilings on foreign sources other than the Middle East, these short-falls below optimum production of other fuels, if supplied at all, are going to have to come substantially from the Middle East. Admittedly the foregoing statements are unduly simplistic, since there is a demand side to the equation—energy conservation can help significantly, as can a maximum emphasis on substituting coal for imported oil and gas.

DOMESTIC ALTERNATIVES

The United States has the resources to provide its energy needs and to secure its economy and foreign policy against the hazards of insecure foreign dependency. For instance, the early 1972 report of the National Petroleum Council states: "No major source of U.S. fuel supplies is limited by the availability of resources to sustain higher production." The United States, although an energy-deficient country since the late 1960s, had not run out of energy in the early 1970s. Rather, by a complicated series of actions and inactions, it had implicitly chosen an increasing foreign dependency. When our country turned in late 1973 and early 1974 to a belated program of limiting foreign dependency, it had not run out of energy but, rather, had run out of time to establish an energy independence that had been considered too costly in terms of both money and policy adjustment. The Arab coercion, coupled with the price explosion of all foreign oil, forced to the forefront an appraisal of our energy jeopardy and what could be done about it.

According to the December 1973 report of the AEC, the United States has used only about 4 percent of its production for energy, which was comparatively cheap. Recognizing that energy will no longer be cheap, the United

States can now program new domestic energy development at significantly higher costs that are still acceptable. "The price of imported oil is now probably far above the long-run cost of supplying the United States from domestic production." (Council of Economic Advisors 1974, p. 50). The costs do, however, include policy changes, economic and social adjustments, and a sustained effort until at least 1985.

U.S. energy security considerations, however, include the energy security of other countries. Most other oil-deficient countries have little or no hope of reaching energy independence. A few may. For example, the Norwegians, sometimes referred to in international oil circles as the Arabs of the North, and the British may attain energy independence and more from their North Sea finds.

According to the AEC report, Western European countries and Japan were already using 8-12 percent of their production for energy before the suppliers more than tripled the FOB price of most of their oil in late 1973. The clear implications were severe inflationary pressures and a possibly disastrous balance-of-payments situation. The price hikes are so huge for Japan as to be almost as grave as being defeated in war, a Tokyo newspaper declared.

Even in 1950, and perhaps later, the situation would have generated at least alarms of overt force, if not the use thereof. In the continuing international interplay concerning the critical energy resource of oil, force will be part of the backdrop, indelicate as this point may be. The realities should be recognized.

The United States, with a past low cost for energy as a proportion of gross national product and a potential for developing domestic resources toward self-sufficiency, has more acceptable options than most other energy-deficient countries. The economic health of those countries is still a vitally important U.S. interest. That economic health would be aided if the United States were less, rather than more, of a competitor among buyers of fuels, principally oil. The energy independence of the United States would add an important element of economic, political, and other stability in international affairs. Hence, both conceptually and specifically, the announced U.S. Project Independence is both a foreign and a domestic policy.

Three significant proposals for narrowing the future U.S. energy gap between demand and domestic supply were made between late 1972 and early 1974, two before the President's energy message outlining Project Independence. The first, made during the era of complacency concerning our growing energy dependency on insecure sources, is in published studies of late 1972 and of January 1973 by the Office of Emergency Preparedness. These studies outline ways to a reduction in projected demand by 1980 equivalent to approximately 7 million b/d of oil and a further shift of electricity production from scarce oil and gas to coal equivalent to 2 million b/d of oil. The suggestions, which include emphasis on insulation, shift of freight and passenger traffic toward more economical transport, and emphasis on mass transit, appeared drastic to the point of impracticability at the time—but not a year later.

The Atomic Energy Commission study of December 1973 tackled both the demand and supply sides of energy. It proposed five avenues of action: conservation, increased oil and gas production, use of coal instead of oil and gas, validation of the nuclear option (meaning acceleration of nuclear power), and exploitation of renewable resources (solar, geothermal, fusion, hydroelectric). The AEC study, while projecting a way to self-sufficiency by 1985, did not see a way to freedom from foreign oil by 1980 except by "imposing administrative restrictions on consumption and/or taking extraordinary measures to stimulate a sharp increase in domestic production." The study's primary objective, however, was to outline a research and development program for which the significant payoffs inevitably have long lead times beyond 1980 and even 1985. We must rely primarily on other measures to narrow or close the energy gap in the shorter run.

The unpublished background paper of the administrator of the Federal Energy Office (Feb. 11, 1973) presented "a highly ambitious program for achieving U.S. energy independence by 1980" to the 11-nation Washington Energy Conference. The paper suggested a drastic reduction in future U.S. energy demand growth from the commonly projected 3.6 percent annually to 2.0 percent per year, although consumption had increased 5 percent in 1972 and 4.8 percent in 1973. This reduction would be achieved, in part, through administrative actions encouraging conservation, through the disincentives to consumption of higher energy prices, and through the shift of the U.S. public's attitudes from the traditional, ever-expanding consumption ethic toward an emphasis on conservation.

On the supply side, the background paper recognized the incentives of higher energy prices and outlined a program including massive shift toward coal (increasing production by 60 percent by 1980), increased oil and gas production, government assistance in financing, and acceleration of nuclear power plants.

The proposal to delay for five years the imposition of the secondary air-quality standards—those designed for plant life, animals, property, and the general environment—while continuing the primary (health) standards illustrates the interpenetration and, sometimes, conflicts among fundamental programs.

By a month after the background study, the Federal Energy Office staff had concluded that even a program of maximum energy resource development and conservation would still leave the U.S. dependent on imports in 1980 for 4.4 million b/d of oil and for 1.5 million b/d in 1985 (*Oil and Gas Journal,* Mar. 18, 1974, p. 42). Also, this program would require a capital input of $190-225 billion. The staff, in reaching this estimate, used an annual demand increase of 2.6 percent while recognizing that the increase might be higher, with consequent greater dependency. They assumed a saving through conservation equivalent to 4.6 million b/d of oil by 1980. One of the major problems lies in effecting the transformations required to substitute fuels we have—principally coal—for oil and gas in our highly petroleum-oriented economy. While satisfactory energy independence is not in the cards by 1980, or even perhaps by 1985, the U.S. executive branch was committed to pressing both energy conservation and domestic energy expansion.

While Project Independence was called a program of self-sufficiency, the top U.S. energy official, William Simon, made clear, in a paper presented to the Washington Energy Conference in February 1974, that the direction and content of the new U.S. programs "do not mean that the United States will terminate all imports. Rather the U.S. objective is to be [in] a position by 1980 where it can go without imports, if necessary, without serious damage to the U.S. economy." This definition of self-sufficiency implicitly recognizes the historic energy relations with Canada and the Caribbean. Canada, for instance, supplies over a trillion cubic feet of our natural gas annually, or about 4 percent of our consumption. A domestic substitution for all oil and gas supplies from these areas would necessitate drastic adjustments indeed.

Further, the envisaged energy independence program leans heavily on energy conservation. Conservation will be influenced by the increased prices, but this market force of price normally operates gradually. Governmental actions, such as legislating a mileage minimum on car gas consumption and accelerated mass transit programs, will be required.

Moreover, if such a program were to be successfully implemented, the margin for retrenchment existent in 1973 due to lavish use of energy would not be available by 1980 and beyond in case of a boycott similar to that of 1973-74.

The proposals for energy independence by 1980 or even 1985 outlined above aroused some skepticism among those informed concerning energy matters. The premises, along with the conservation targets, included great reliance on Alaska and offshore production for oil and gas and a great expansion of coal consumption. Both these expansions are critically dependent on laws and administration, capital availability, and reconciliation with environmental programs. Also, the United States faces another potential setback for secure oil when Canada completes a pipeline to eastern Canada and switches a substantial part of western Canadian production, now going to the U.S. Midwest and west coast, to substitute for Canadian imports from Venezuela and the Middle East. Furthermore, with the rise in price of foreign oil, U.S. coal, which has been an important earner of foreign exchange, may be in greater foreign demand, leading to suggestions of export limitation on this resource that contributes significantly to the plus side of our balance of payments. Finally, among the major reasons for skepticism, the United States has not in the past, except for war and the New Deal, acted, if at all, with the needed alacrity on essential legislation. The method and direction of action for Project Independence did, however, seem clearly outlined.

An energy independence program has to take account of fuel transportation and processing as well as of energy production capabilities. Here there is a dilemma caused by both forecasting uncertainties and the long lead times and capital costs of tankers and refineries. In the short run, imports will continue at a high rate, as will consumption of petroleum products. But the world price rise may cause a sufficient decrease in demand that previous forecasts of tanker and refinery needs may prove significantly invalid. As an example of the swings in projections of needs, consider the U.S. case. If the 1970 projections of the Cabinet Task Force had proved correct, the United States would have had adequate refining capacity for the mid-1970s, taking into account the policy of permitting import of residual heating oil for the east coast. Yet by 1972, with the surge in demand, it appeared that a serious shortage of domestic refining capacity might occur. The Arab boycott, the initiation of an energy conservation program, and some unforecasted refinery expansions resulted in a shift, at least temporarily, to a more optimistic refinery outlook. And finally, the proposals of Project Independence, if executed, would significantly decrease previously projected petroleum processing requirements. Both the policy-maker and the energy business executive will view the future of transportation and processing with interest and apprehension.

Supertankers of 250,000 dead weight tons and more are the norm for the future, but the United States has no ports capable of accepting them. If we belatedly start port development tomorrow, it will be some years before a port can be operational; and until these ports are provided, an increasing proportion of crude oil is likely to be transshipped at increased cost or—more likely—processed in offshore refineries and the finished products shipped in smaller tankers. Closer offshore refining locations include eastern Canada, the Bahamas, and the Caribbean. The twelve Oil Producing and Exporting Countries (OPEC), other than Venezuela, have been slow to generate their own refineries. Libya, however, is building one medium refinery and is reported to be considering a large one.

According to the oil industry, U.S. refining capacity lagged after 1970 because of low profit margins. The industry has also alleged siting problems due to environmental objections, uncertainty of crude oil supply, and the lower costs of offshore construction and operation. The hazards of forecasting demand have been mentioned above. If the targets of Project Independence are approached, there may be adequate, or more, U.S. refining capacity, again confuting the forecasters; and this situation could apply worldwide with a decrease in projected demand resulting from increased prices.

Dependence on an offshore refinery, which might be in the oil-producing country, is both a balance-of-payments problem and a national security problem. Such foreign refining means higher costs of oil imports and may mean exported capital, with a consequent adverse impact on our balance of payments.

More important, the dependence on foreign refining, coupled with dependence on foreign sources for crude oil, is a double security jeopardy and a double leverage on our foreign policy.

PRICE, COST, AND CAPITAL

Over the long run, price is the major arbiter of supply and demand—other things being equal. "Other things" have certainly not been equal in the U.S. energy scene, with special tax arrangements, restrictions on oil imports that served as a partial floodgate until a few months before the shock of the Arab boycott, a ridiculously low regulated price of natural gas compared with other fuels, and other arrangements limiting the operation of market forces. Nor will other things be equal in the future, since the United States will undoubtedly continue to have many special laws and administrative controls pertaining to energy. One of these restrictions will need to be a reconstituted oil import control program of some sort if Project Independence begins to succeed. Otherwise, U.S. entrepreneurs will happily help the Middle East to undersell U.S. production of higher-cost energy fuels, such as oil from shale, thereby checking the commitment of capital and progress toward energy independence. With production costs on the order of a dime a barrel and their competitors' costs in a free market measured increasingly by the costs of synthetic fuels (such as shale oil) and of coal, the oil-surplus states have a very advantageous trading position, the more so if they can maintain their cartel.

Energy independence means much higher energy costs than in the pre-1974 era. This unpalatable fact would almost certainly have prevented the United States from following a course insuring adequate energy security if the world price of oil had not been raised massively at the same time as the October 1973 Middle Eastern war and the Arab boycott. The new price may not continue, but certainly prices will not again approach their old levels. Previously, the objective of the oil-surplus states was to press their prices toward the protected price of U.S. oil. Over a period of a few weeks, the petroleum price situation was reversed; and U.S. energy producers, price-controlled, were hoping to move toward the prices of foreign oil. Those foreign prices made development of domestic energy vastly more attractive, but it would take a while. The State of the Union message of January 1974 mentioned a need for a $200 billion investment by 1980, and estimates of a need for around $500 billion investment by 1985 were common. The problem of obtaining such vast amounts of capital was severe. Business naturally saw the need as justifying higher earnings; others suggested persuading the Middle Eastern states to invest the vast earnings from their higher-priced oil in development of U.S. energy resources. While the latter course would certainly keep these rapidly expanding balances out of mischief on the international scene, as more than one wag suggested, the course might eventually build to a situation where Middle Eastern sovereign investors could be concerned over expropriation (or "participation" demands) by the United States.

One of the wrenching adjustments to the U.S. economy may be a shift toward pricing energy fuels on the basis of energy content (by Btu rather than by barrel, ton, or cubic foot), which would mean a major increase in natural gas prices. This natural gas price rise may be on the way anyhow, with coal gasification and imported liquid natural gas. Another possible wrenching adjustment, suggested by some Middle Eastern officials, is to price internationally traded oil as equivalent to the cost of trade-off substitutes, such as oil from shale, which should begin to come into production in the late 1970s. Still another suggestion by Middle Eastern leaders is that price be related to inflation and to currency devaluations—a course of action inevitably levering the price of export oil continually upward while contributing to further inflation.

When the cost of Middle Eastern oil was approximately $2.20 a barrel FOB, as it was in early 1973, many in the United States, including some executive and Congressional leaders, viewed with equanimity an annual foreign dependency of slightly over 2 billion barrels of oil, with a prospective increase of imports of around 5 percent (or 1 million b/d) a year in total oil demand. Practically all of that increase would come from the Middle East, in addition to the existing 2.4 million b/d Middle Eastern dependency. True, most of those "viewing with equanimity" were activated by economic motives (yearning for "cheap" foreign oil) coupled with a traditional opposition to oil import controls. Conversely, most of the people and leadership of the energy-producing states of the Southwest and Rocky Mountains had an economic incentive for supporting oil import controls and programs for development of U.S. domestic energy resources, as well as standing for energy security. The world price explosion gave a common economic incentive to both sides to close ranks on an independence/energy security program.

Quite aside from any coercion by boycott, the measure of our foreign economic problem is sobering. Using a stabilized landed crude oil price of the first part of 1974, the cost of 1973 U.S. ($9-11 a barrel, depending on source and quality) imports would have been around $25 billion. The increase per year, at approximately 5 percent growth of petroleum consumption of 1973, would be initially over $3 billion a year. Using a pre-boycott and pre-Project Independence estimate of 12 million barrels a day imports, by 1980 the balance-of-payments cost to the United States would then be, assuming no increase in early 1974 import price, on the order of $50 billion unless we progress toward energy independence, or the oil suppliers are persuaded to restrain prices, or both. As a yardstick to help with these mind-boggling figures, the manufactured goods exports of the United States in 1973 were $45 billion and total merchandise exports were $70 billion (*International Economic Report of the President* 1974, pp. 99, 107). Trade deficits, threatened devaluations of the dollar, and a significant part of the economy working to pay the Arab states would be the outcome. The latter outcome is certainly worrisome from the energy security standpoint but might be acceptable from a purely economic standpoint if cheaper energy arrangements are not possible domestically. They should be available (Council of Economic Advisors, *Annual Report to the President* 1974, p. 122).

It can be argued that the Arabs cannot drink their oil; they have to find customers. But the hard facts are that by at least tripling the price of oil in 1973, the oil-surplus countries made themselves much less dependent on any one, or several, oil-deficient customers for needed income. While being able to sell less oil for more money, several of them were also building huge reserves of foreign exchange. They thereby moved to a very comfortable, if not dominant, negotiating position.

The less developed countries have a special energy situation. They are generally oil-deficient and dependent on oil for development. They have become very dependent on fertilizer for producing their food supply. Fertilizer requires either foreign exchange for purchase or energy for its domestic production. These countries rely heavily on import capital, much of it from international lending institutions, for their continuing development. The increases in the price of oil in late 1973 and early 1974 cost the developing countries more than their 1973 capital imports. Put another way, the lenders to developing countries would be providing funds to transmit to the oil-surplus—principally Arab— countries, which certainly did not need development funds. There have been suggestions of a two-tier pricing system benefiting less developed countries, but the outlook is bleak. "The developing countries are in danger of being left high and dry. Their very existence is threatened by increasing oil prices because they do not have as high a net product as the industrialized countries to draw upon" (Schmidt 1974b, p. 449).

While the Shah of Iran did point a way by promising $1 billion a year to help development, the promise was for a loan, not a grant, necessitating interest and principal payments from countries already heavily committed to use foreign exchange to handle their debts.

Laying aside the fact that non-Communist world oil consumption rose by over 9 percent in 1973, and assuming no increase in 1974 consumption over 1973 and no increase in early 1974 prices, the costs to oil-importing states rose from $45 billion in 1973 to approximately $120 billion in 1974 (*International Economic Report of the President* 1974, p. 107). Such a massive shift in the cost of imported energy, with a possible continuing increase, is certain to provide a major puzzle to international economic forecasters. Price increases have a dampening effect on demand. But oil, being an essential resource, has a low demand elasticity. Massive price increases of oil and other energy make for inflation, increased unemployment, and serious readjustment of international economic affairs. The tendency is likely to be a scramble to increase exports to pay for the essential imported oil and to reduce foreign expenditures to gain foreign exchange for oil, all seriously affecting the previously normal pattern of world trade (Pollock 1974, pp. 452-71).

The disposition of their earnings by the oil-producing states is part of the forecasting puzzle. A cumulative OPEC surplus of $350-550 billion, with its implications for monetary instability, might occur by 1980—a useful comparative figure is total 1972 world export trade of $417 billion (Pollock 1974, p. 461; *International Economic Report of the President* 1974, p. 92). Decisions on the disposition of oil earnings are certain to have a major political and economic (sometimes including military) component. The petropowers, for example, have the resources to buy all the arms they want. There are plenty of eager salesmen of those arms. Some states (such as Venezuela and Iran) can absorb a great part of earnings in internal development. Others do not have such domestic absorption capability for some time, if ever. Saudi Arabia, with a population of 6 million people, might receive over $20 billion in oil payments in 1974. Abu Dhabi, receiving over $20,000 per capita in oil payments in 1973, might quadruple this amount in 1974. Commitment of the capital to indigenous oil-based industry, such as refineries and petrochemical plants, takes time and results in making the oil-deficient countries even more energy-insecure, with even greater adverse balances of payments. The suggestion that funds be invested for energy development in energy-deficient countries has been mentioned. The funds could be used as liquid balances, creating a threatening bloc of petro-dollars, petro-yen, petro-marks, and so on in the international monetary system. Jiddah, or perhaps Beirut, may one day be a financial center vying with New York, London, and Zurich.

THE RISKS OF DEPENDENCY

The scope of energy security, or lack thereof, has economic, political, and some important military aspects—all generally closely intertwined. The United States is a world superpower with concerns over both cost and coercion of policy. While most other states are primarily concerned with cost, the shadow of coercion is still a concern—witness the boycotting of the Netherlands and Denmark and the strong pressures by the Arabs on all Western European countries and Japan in late 1973. The Organization of African Unity formally asked the Arab states to extend the oil boycott to South Africa and Rhodesia in

November 1973, bringing additional pressure on the white minority governments of these states; their need for Arab oil, however, was limited—South
Africa obtains a great part of its energy from coal and maintains a petroleum
stockpile.

A shortfall from demand in world oil production need not, however,
necessarily be due to coercive intent. The oil-surplus countries are aware that
their oil resources are finite. Canada, Venezuela, Kuwait, and Libya have already restricted production and/or exports for reasons of domestic policy.
Production might be restricted to conserve reserves for the next generation, because of lack of absorptive capacity for the income, or for other reasons than
coercion. Now that decisions on production are moving from private companies to governments, the oil-deficient states have a concern that the oil-
surplus states have sufficient incentives to produce the needed oil for the world.

With energy production and export controls passing to governments and
prices so high as to dull economic incentives for some important oil-surplus
states, production and distribution decisions will inevitably be heavily tinged
with political considerations. The most sensitive of these considerations has to
do with security generally and extends to military power as a policy instrument.

The U.S. military requirement for energy fuels, principally petroleum, is
not high and is not estimated to be unmanageable from the standpoint of
quantities needed in case of a significantly increased state of defense readiness
or actual military action. Using Department of Defense data, military petroleum
demand was 4.7 percent of U.S. total consumption in 1972 and had been only
7.6 percent of U.S. consumption in 1969, at the peak of Vietnam operations.
One can speculate, however, about what would have happened had the Arab
boycott of 1973 been applied during that peak period in 1969, when most
fuels for Vietnam were shipped directly from the Persian Gulf. This might have
been a much more effective "Stop the War" effort than all the student and
other public demonstrations in the United States at that time. For instance, the
U.S. fleet in late 1973 was unable to continue its usual refueling from Saudi
Arabia and was refused refueling in Hong Kong, which was supplied by Arab oil.

It is interesting to compare the current small proportions of consumption
for military programs with World War II, when military use represented one-
third of the U.S. petroleum consumption. In sum, the energy security threat,
through coercing the economy and the U.S. way of life and inhibiting freedom
of foreign policy, is now much greater than a threat to inhibit the capability for
operation of U.S. armed forces. Those forces, noting the Arab embargo lesson,
may need special reserves and may now need more tankers and assuredly cooperative overseas refueling stations.

Those concerned with peaceful settlement of disputes traditionally argue
that if the makers of arms would refuse to sell their products, such a policy
would have a very useful effect in preventing armed conflicts. Oil is an essential

supply for any significant conventional war. It is impractical and misleading to separate oil used by the military forces from oil used in operating the economy of any combatant country. A state with a significant dependence on oil imports has to consider the reliability of its import sources for oil as seriously as the military capability of a prospective foe if the conflict is likely to be prolonged. Concern over political permissiveness of governments at the source of needed oil is now added to the traditional concern over security of sea-lanes—a point well illustrated by the refusal of Aramco (under the thumb of the Saudi Arabian government) to supply oil for the U.S. Navy in late 1973. Some may wish to speculate whether this situation tends more toward a peaceful world or more toward nuclear weapons—a speculation beyond the scope of this discussion. Another speculation—will the Arabs' increasing wealth lead toward peace (a desire not to risk their new wealth) or away from it?

There is a little-discussed coercion capability in third-party control of sensitive points on oil transport routes. The interruption in 1970 of the pipeline from Saudi Arabia to the Mediterranean across Syria is a minor example. The Strait of Hormuz, at the entrance to the Persian Gulf, with a tanker passing every 11 minutes, the Cape of Good Hope, with a tanker passing every 20 minutes, and the Malacca Straits are examples of highly strategic spots in the new geopolitics of energy supply. Parenthetically, the Suez Canal is no longer oil-strategic, since its reopening would be equivalent to only 9 percent addition to the world tanker fleet, which has been growing at over 13 percent a year (Adelman 1972-73, p. 92). Finally, whether a situation is one of coercion, or of using the principal national resource to achieve legitimate national objectives, is a matter of judgment and is bound to be the subject of controversy.

CONCLUSION

The Arab overt coercion program against the United States was bound to be transitory; but it showed that oil power is power indeed, particularly when it can be exercised in the benign shadow of Soviet power. The precedent will temper international affairs for a long time.

The OPEC members are Ecuador, Indonesia, Gabon, Nigeria, Venezuela, Iran, Abu Dhabi, Qatar, Iraq, Libya, Algeria, Kuwait, and Saudi Arabia. The last seven are Arab states, which as the OAPEC (which also includes Bahrein, Egypt, and Syria) imposed the boycott against the United States and the Netherlands. It is noteworthy that only four of the OAPEC states (Libya, Kuwait, Abu Dhabi, and Saudi Arabia) took action to reduce production during the boycott (Krasner 1974, p. 69). Two of these (Libya and Kuwait) already had production restriction policies in effect. All 13 members of OPEC, however, operating as an effective international cartel, joined in the explosive price increase, as did Canada and the USSR, the principal non-OPEC oil exporting countries. The limited number of countries actually restricting production indicates the concentration of oil power (Akins 1973, pp. 468-69), and is disturbing rather than heartening, in view of the effectiveness of the boycott.

The worldwide revolution in energy includes a newly developed awareness, on the part of energy-surplus countries, of the importance of energy resources and their effectiveness as political and economic instruments in world affairs. Furthermore, these oil-surplus states, realizing a responsibility to their own future generations and recognizing that energy resources are exhaustible, cannot always be assumed to produce as much as the consuming states might desire. The oil-deficient states share a dependence on imported oil and a concern over price that is primary for most countries. There can be a unilateral "every man for himself" approach to dealing with the oil-surplus countries. The outcome would be bilateral deals disrupting the normal pattern of world trade and destabilizing the price of oil. Alternatively, the oil-deficient states can act by coordination and cooperation, including consultation with the oil producers, to build and maintain a world energy system essential to guard against world depression and to undergird world prosperity. The oil-surplus states, with their new-found power and prospective wealth, certainly do not gain from a depressed world—killing the goose that lays the golden egg—and lose even more if they are blamed for international economic disruptions.

Late 1973 and early 1974 saw the United States cross a divide in foreign-policy areas of emphasis, with energy suddenly moving to center stage of both foreign and domestic policy. Energy, principally oil, also moved center stage for most of the other energy-deficient countries.

There will continue to be a U.S. "energy gap" at least for a while. That gap will have to be filled by imports and/or drastic measures, such as allocations and rationing. The interpenetration of domestic energy programs—those that expand domestic production and those that deflate demand—and of foreign affairs—both policies and substantive import programs—should be clearly apparent. The more we produce and conserve, the less we are dependent on insecure foreign sources of supply, and hence the less subject to political coercion and balance-of-trade problems. There is no more important question than whether the U.S. body politic, from President and Congress to grass-roots electorate, has the resourcefulness and the commitment to take the actions necessary to eliminate our energy jeopardy and to regain energy security.

Energy will long be the primary component of the international economic scene and will heavily condition other areas of foreign policy. The oil-producing countries now do not need to possess nuclear weapons or other indications of power to be noticed in international councils. Oil is power enough.

As for the United States, the post-World War II focus on the Cold War and Communism waned just in time to be replaced by a central and acute concern in both domestic and foreign policy over the long-term energy problem.

3

THE GENESIS OF THE
U.S. OIL CRISIS
Richard B. Mancke

The prognostications of petroleum pessimists came true in late 1973. Following the resumption of full-scale armed warfare between Arab and Jew, members of the Organization of Arab Petroleum Exporting Countries (OAPEC) agreed to reduce or, in some cases, entirely eliminate oil exports to all countries failing to adopt a pro-Arab foreign policy. This reduction in Arab oil exports precipitated a severe worldwide energy crisis. By January 1, 1974, the price of a barrel of crude oil at the Persian Gulf had more than doubled to about $8, and small quantities of previously uncommitted "participation" crude sold for more than $20. Moreover, high government officials—most notably, Secretary of State Kissinger—publicly expressed the fear that continued oil shortages and "ruinous" high oil prices could cause worldwide depression.

The Arab embargo was the proximate cause of the 1973-74 U.S. energy crisis. Was it the root cause? Many Americans think not. Instead, they have believed charges placing the blame on alleged selfish (or sometimes merely incompetent) actions by various convenient scapegoats. Any litany of scapegoats must include the large "monopolistic" oil companies that reaped higher prices and huge profits as a result of the worldwide shortages and therefore took steps—usually unspecified—to exacerbate those shortages; the Nixon administration, which failed to take any of the "hard" steps necessary to forestall this crisis, and which actually may have encouraged it in order to help its "big oil" political allies; "fuzzy thinking" environmentalists who made crisis inevitable by stubbornly thwarting most attempts to increase U.S. energy supplies; and greedy consumers, whose insatiable energy demands made shortages inevitable.

The first part of this paper recounts the roles these scapegoats played in molding several of the more important policy decisions made prior to the 1973-74 energy crisis. Given their legitimate strong interest and involvement in energy matters, it was inevitable that their roles be important. Nevertheless, while each of these groups took steps to advance its own interests, they neither caused our energy problems nor precipitated the frequent failure of policies designed to remedy them, in the sense implied by their accusers. Indeed, sophisticated analysis suggests that the charge of conspiracy by the oil companies is false even though earnings of the 25 largest oil companies rose 53 percent in 1973, primarily in the fourth quarter (Mancke 1974b). Similarly, it seems implausible, on balance, that the Nixon administration could have thought that the political gains from sharply higher profits for "big oil" would offset the political costs incurred as a result of the huge losses suffered by consumers and many businesses in the 1973-74 energy crisis.

Instead, when viewed in toto, two other factors prevail: a widespread misperception of both the magnitude and, more important, the true nature of our energy problems, and the fact that the policies actually implemented were almost always too rigid and, frequently, were designed to achieve contradictory goals. I believe that the search for scapegoats exaggerated both themes. The second part of the paper argues that these two factors of misperception and contradiction also characterized the U.S. response to the 1973-74 energy crisis. The last part discusses why misperception and contradiction were so widespread.

PRELUDES TO THE 1973-74 ENERGY CRISIS

If one can believe the accompanying rhetoric, most important U.S. energy policies have been aimed at achieving one or more of four valuable goals: insuring the discovery and development of low-cost energy supplies adequate to meet our growing needs; preventing growing dependence on energy from militarily or politically insecure sources; reducing the environmental pollution that is a by-product of most production, distribution, and consumption of energy; and reducing the arbitrary transfers of billions of dollars annually from oil consumers to oil producers and owners of oil lands. Since the end of World War II, Americans have spent billions of dollars annually attempting to achieve these worthy goals. Unfortunately, the evidence summarized below documents their failure.

Oil Glut: The U.S. Energy Problem in the 1930s

Crude oil prices plummeted during the 1930s because the Depression led to a sharp fall in oil demand at the same time that the discovery and speedy development of the giant East Texas field led to a sudden surge in supply. In the

United States oil is owned by whoever "captures" it from the ground. When the land overlying a specified oil pool has many owners, each has an incentive to produce the oil as quickly as possible in order to prevent a neighbor from "capturing" it. In sum, overdrilling is encouraged. (For elaboration on the costs of prorationing, see Adelman 1964; Lovejoy and Homan 1967; McDonald 1971). Prices fell so low that a few Texas producers allegedly found they could cut their losses by dumping "surplus" crude oil into nearby creeks. Faced with this "conservation" crisis, the major oil-producing states of the U.S. Southwest (Texas, Louisiana, New Mexico, Oklahoma, and Kansas) adopted a policy—called market-demand prorationing—designed to give each state control over the total supply of oil produced by firms doing business within it.

The mechanics of market-demand prorationing are simple. First, the state sets each well's maximum allowable daily production. The size of this "basic allowable" depends on two parameters: the well's depth and the number of acres it drains. Concern with cost rather than productivity provided the rationalization for the "basic allowable" formula. Specifically, because deep wells are more costly than shallow wells and costs rise when more wells are drilled on a tract, the states were persuaded that it would be "fair" to give higher "basic allowables" to oil fields with deeper wells and/or densely drilled tracts. The "basic allowable" formulas were not geared to engineering constraints. Some large fields could have been operated at a rate several times higher than the "basic allowable."

Promoting conservation provided the official rationale for prorationing. Nevertheless, it was not the chief concern of the oil states' prorationing commissions. Instead, they acted as if their principal assignment was to use prorationing to maintain or raise crude oil prices by restricting available supplies. Because monthly oil demands fluctuated widely and producers could always raise their "basic allowables" by drilling more or deeper wells, successful performance of this assignment was not easy. In addition, problems arose because oil produced in any specified state faced competition from oil produced in other states. To solve these problems, two additional tools were necessary.

The problem caused by fluctuating demands and growing supplies was solved by refusing to let each well produce its "basic allowable." Instead, each of the major prorationing states asked the major crude oil refiners how much they expected to buy in the following month. With this information, any oil state could estimate quite accurately the monthly demand for its oil. The prorationing states then calculated the forthcoming month's "market-demand factor" by dividing the estimates of the total demand for their oil by the total of all "basic allowables." Finally, each prorationed well's actual output during the next month was restricted to the product of its "basic allowable" and the state's market-demand factor.

Use of market-demand prorationing gave oil-producing states a precision instrument for controlling their producers' total outputs. However, failure to coordinate their prorationing policies could have resulted in interstate competition for higher oil sales and, hence, lower prices. In order to forestall this possibility, the major oil-producing states coordinated their prorationing activities through the office of the Interstate Oil Compact Commission. The U.S. government also provided assistance. For example, the Connally Hot Oil Act prohibited the interstate sale of oil above the "allowables" set by state prorationing boards.

Until 1970, the supply restriction due to prorationing was severe. To illustrate, from 1960 through 1965 Texas wells were always restricted to producing less than 30 percent of their "basic allowables." By 1973, however, most fields were allowed to produce at 100 percent of their "basic allowable." Many proved unable to produce at this level; hence, prorationing no longer really constrained their output. A few fields (notably Yates) could have produced more than their "basic allowable"—prorationing still restructed their output.

The oil states' enforcement of market-demand prorationing did help to reduce the problems of overproduction plaguing the American oil industry during the 1930s. Unfortunately, the remedy ultimately proved far more costly than the illness it was designed to cure. The costs were of two kinds. First, since oil fields with deeper, more closely spaced wells were rewarded with higher "basic allowables" and since inefficient stripper wells (wells producing less than 10 barrels per day) were exempted from all output restrictions, prorationing created strong incentives for wasteful overdrilling. Second, by using prorationing, the large oil-producing states could severely restrict total crude oil output and thereby succeeded in keeping prices for U.S. crude oil far above the competitive level until the late 1960s.

Consumers of American oil were the principal victims of market-demand prorationing. The principal beneficiaries included owners of oil lands, who reaped sharply higher rents (royalties and lease bonuses) because prorationing raised the value of any commercial oil found on their lands; the oil-producing states, which received higher rents from state-owned lands and also reaped higher severance taxes from all crude oil produced within the state; and domestic producers, who reaped windfall profits whenever prorationing was tightened so that they could sell their product at a higher price (Mancke 1974a, Ch. 4). The interests of these three groups have not always coincided. Indeed, disputes have sometimes raged between members of the same group. Nevertheless, because in most instances their interests have coincided (and still do), hereafter I shall refer to members of these three groups as the domestic oil interests.

The Danger from Rising Dependence on Insecure Foreign Oil

Prior to the late 1940s the United States was self-sufficient in crude oil;
the Gulf coast states actually exported large quantities to Western Europe. However, by 1950 rapidly expanding exports from lower-cost Persian Gulf sources
had nearly driven American oil out of European markets. Indeed, small but
growing amounts of Persian Gulf oil were beginning to be sold in the United
States. Rising U.S. oil imports could have only one consequence: undermining
the oil states' heretofore successful efforts to fix a high price for U.S. crude.
Specifically, in the face of increasing imports, American crude oil's high price
could be maintained only by continually tightening the oil states' prorationing
policies. But, even if this was successful, profits earned on U.S.-produced oil
would be reduced because of a fall in its market share.

The domestic oil interests sought to prevent any significant erosion of
their product's market share by persuading the federal government to restrict
oil imports. Obviously, it would not be politic to confess selfish motives. Hence
they offered the following national security justification for oil import quotas:
If the flow of oil imports was interrupted, the United States would face severe
energy shortages until alternative supplies could be developed and/or steps
taken to reduce demand. This could take several years. During the interim, the
cost to the economy would be high because of the absence of short-run substitutes; even after the short-run shortage was over, costs would continue higher
because the newly developed energy supplies would be more expensive.

Until the 1970s the national security justification for oil import controls
rang false. The United States imported relatively small quantities of oil, and
virtually all came from what were (before 1970) militarily and politically secure
Caribbean or Canadian sources. Prolonged interruptions from either source
were unlikely. Moreover, even if they did occur, the United States had ample
reserves of domestic supplies. Nevertheless, accepting the then false national
security rationale in toto, President Eisenhower established mandatory oil import controls in 1959. In a decision that was to have major political ramifications, he decided that the valuable rights to import the limited amount of
foreign oil permitted under the quotas should be allocated to refiners and (later)
petrochemical producers.

Enforcement of import quotas encouraged higher domestic crude oil outputs by restricting the price competition offered by foreign oil. More precisely,
by restricting imports, the demand for domestic crude oil was effectively raised;
and this higher demand could be satisfied only by a rise in domestic output.
The enhancement of national security attributable to this higher domestic output was the alleged benefit from an oil import control policy. Its cost was the
higher prices necessary to persuade domestic producers to raise their output.

President Nixon's Cabinet Task Force on Oil Import Controls estimated that the higher prices cost U.S. consumers roughly $4.8 billion in 1969 (Cabinet Task Force 1970, Appendix G). A large part of these higher consumer costs represented higher incomes for the oil interests.

Arguments over the legitimacy of the high income transfers resulting from the enforcement of oil import quotas were inevitable. They were of two types. On the one hand, those living in regions of the United States producing little or no oil complained that the prices they paid for refined oil products were unfairly high; the oil interests strongly disagreed. On the other hand, recipients of the valuable rights to import cheaper foreign oil repeatedly offered reasons why each deserved a higher share. These two arguments were merged after what became known as the Machiasport controversy.

Because of their distance from the petroleum sources near the Gulf coast, residents of New England have always paid relatively more for both refined oil products and natural gas than residents of other parts of the country. Also, not owning any oil lands, they do not receive any of the oil rents. As a result the New England Congressional delegation consistently spearheaded the attack against oil import quotas. In 1968 Occidental Petroleum proposed a plan that it claimed would reduce New England's heating oil prices by 10 percent: Occidental would build a 300,000-barrel-per-day refinery at Machiasport, Maine, if it were granted rights to import 100,000 barrels of crude oil daily. Under the 1969 quota allocation formula, Occidental's proposed Machiasport refinery would have been allowed to import less than 30,000 barrels of crude daily. Since the right to import one barrel of oil was worth about $1.50 in 1969, acceptance of Occidental's request would have rewarded it with an additional daily subsidy worth in excess of $100,000. But because total oil imports were strictly limited by the quota, Occidental could have been granted more import rights only if other refiners received less. Thus, the entire additional subsidy requested by Occidental would have been at the expense of competing refiners.

After Occidental made its Machiasport request, the battle was joined: New England supported Occidental's proposal, the oil states and competing refiners were strongly opposed. In an effort to resolve this ticklish battle, President Nixon established a prestigious Cabinet task force to undertake a comprehensive review of U.S. oil import restrictions. Reporting to the President in 1970, the Oil Import Task Force concluded that the quota bore "no reasonable relation to current requirements for protection of either the national economy or of essential oil consumption" (Cabinet Task Force 1970, p. 128). To remedy this problem, the task force recommended that oil import quotas be phased out and replaced with a high, but over time declining, tariff. After studying this recommendation for several months, the President rejected it. As his critics delighted in pointing out, this decision undoubtedly reflected political considerations. After all, the "oil lobby" could provide useful aid both to an incumbent

President pursuing a "Southern strategy" and to a likable Republican—George Bush—in the midst of a run for the Texas Senate seat. Also, abolishing the quota would reward Senators Kennedy and Muskie, two leading contenders for the 1972 Democratic Presidential nomination. These political considerations were strong. However, the President did have valid nonpolitical justifications for his decision. In particular, because of delays in constructing the Alaska pipeline and above-average growth in oil demands induced by worsening natural gas shortages, it was already evident by mid-1970 that the Oil Import Task Force's projections of U.S. oil import dependence in the near future were far too low and, therefore, that it had underestimated the possible damage from oil import interruptions.

The battle over oil import quotas continued to rage until they were abolished by a Presidential executive order issued in April 1973. In retrospect there can be no doubt that controls restricting U.S. oil imports were bad throughout the 1960s. They cost consumers billions annually; and whatever security they provided was superfluous because, prior to the 1970s, the United States never faced a valid oil security threat. However, by 1970-71 the situation had begun to change. U.S. dependence on oil imports was beginning to grow rapidly, and there were no longer ample domestic reserves that could be brought on stream within a short time. Even worse, because of improved co-ordination among members of the Organization of Petroleum Exporting Countries (OPEC)—a cartel composed of all large oil-exporting countries except Canada—sizable interruptions in the flow of oil imports became a real and growing possibility.

Upon its formation in 1960, OPEC's announced purpose was to prevent further falls in world oil prices. Throughout the 1960s the cartel failed to achieve its goal. However, at the Teheran Conference in January 1971, OPEC's prospects suddenly improved. At Teheran, after threatening to cut off all oil exports, OPEC succeeded in negotiating a 50-cent-per-barrel price rise. In return it agreed to guarantee stable and predicatable oil prices for five years. This guarantee remained in force for about four months. Then OPEC reopened negotiations to demand more money, a blackmail scenario subsequently repeated.

After OPEC's Teheran success, the United States faced a very real oil security threat. Unfortunately, primarily because of the virulence of the oil import quota debate, few realized the possible dimensions of this threat prior to the Arab embargo in October 1973. Hence, it proved politically impossible for the President to take any of the difficult steps necessary to alleviate what had become an increasingly dangerous dependence on oil imports. Indeed, responding to strong pressure from oil consumers and Senate critics, from 1970 to 1973 he periodically relaxed the oil import quotas in order to prevent what he regarded as politically untenable rises in domestic crude oil prices. As a result U.S. dependence on oil imports soared during the early 1970s, and we were ill prepared to deal with the 1973 Arab oil embargo.

Running Out of Natural Gas

Natural gas has been the United States' fastest-growing major energy source since the end of World War II. It satisfied about one-eighth of total U.S. energy demands in 1945, and roughly one-third of our much higher 1970 demands. Unfortunately, U.S. production of natural gas had virtually stopped growing by the start of the 1970s. Even worse, it began to decline in 1972. As a result of our worsening natural gas shortage, the annual rate of growth in U.S. demand for oil products—natural gas's closest substitute—soared to roughly double its pre-1970 level. By 1974 the average daily excess of natural gas demand over supply was equivalent to around 3 million barrels of crude oil. Since U.S. production of crude oil has also peaked at about 9-9.5 million barrels daily, at least until the late 1970s, when new production from Alaska's North Slope and soon-to-be-leased federal offshore lands should begin to come on stream, rapidly rising oil imports are the only option.

The present natural gas shortage is not due to nature's stinginess; it is man-made. Its proximate cause has been the Federal Power Commission's (FPC) enforcement of low ceiling prices on all interstate sales of natural gas. Because they have been too low, these price ceilings have discouraged firms from exploring for and developing new natural gas reserves. The best available evidence suggests that natural gas would remain much cheaper than its nearest substitutes even its price were allowed to rise high enough to eliminate this shortage (MacAvoy and Pyndyck 1973). In view of this fact, are there any reasons justifying the FPC's wellhead price regulation?

The Natural Gas Act of 1938 authorized the FPC to regulate interstate pipelines in order to "protect consumers against exploitation at the hands of the natural gas [pipeline] companies." This was thought to be necessary because of the "great economic power of the pipeline companies as compared with that of communities seeking natural gas." Since a single interstate pipeline is typically the sole supplier of natural gas in most markets, protecting its consumers from possible monopoly exploitation is a valid policy goal.

The scope of the 1938 act was ambiguous. Until the early 1950s the FPC maintained that it was not empowered to regulate the prices that pipeline companies paid gas producers; instead, the Commission held that it could regulate only the prices charged for interstate pipeline services. As long as natural gas wellhead prices stayed near their Depression levels, there was no consumer opposition to the FPC's ruling. This consumer indifference soon evaporated after the rapid expansion of interstate pipeline capacity led to huge postwar increases in natural gas demand. As demand increased, so did the wellhead price. Consumer representatives reacted to these higher prices by asking the FPC to reverse its decision not to control them. Two justifications were (and continue to be) offered. Most frequently heard (initially) was the justification that such price controls were necessary because natural gas producers were exploiting their monopoly power. In its 1954 *Phillips Petroleum Co. vs. Wisconsin* decision, the Supreme Court implicitly accepted this justification and ruled that the Natural Gas Act did require the FPC to regulate wellhead prices. Commenting on this justification, Paul MacAvoy, perhaps the nation's leading academic authority on natural gas, wrote:

> Regulation is generally conceded to be of doubtful propriety if the reasons for imposition of controls were fallacious. Regulation was advocated in the courts and Congress to prevent monopoly prices in the Southwest. Studies of most field and supply markets in Texas, Louisiana, Oklahoma, etc., indicate the presence of systematic competition . . . throughout the period in which regulation was proposed. The problem to be solved by regulation seems not to have existed, so that the court mandate was given for "wrong" reasons. The necessity for Federal Power Commission regulation is doubtful. (MacAvoy 1962, p. 4)

The second justification offered for FPC regulation of natural gas wellhead prices was that higher prices would not lead to appreciably higher outputs; rather, they would only lead to windfall profits for owners and producers of natural gas. As already noted, most available evidence does not support the assumption that gas supplies are not price-responsive. This evidence has been conveniently ignored by those favoring natural gas wellhead price regulation. Instead, they have preferred to offer populistic arguments like the following:

> Reduced to its simplest terms, the issue is whether Mr. Getty shall buy a yacht . . . or whether thousands of New Jersey commuters shall enjoy an extra evening "on the town" in Manhattan once a year. (Dirlam 1958, p. 491)

The FPC's initial attempt to regulate wellhead prices proved unsuccessful. Between 1954 and 1959 natural gas wellhead prices nearly doubled. Faced with this fact, the Supreme Court ruled in the 1959 CATCO case (*Atlantic Refining Co. vs. Public Service Commission*) that the FPC's wellhead price regulation procedures were inadequate. The FPC responded to the CATCO decision by adopting areawide wellhead price regulation in September 1960. This regulation proved effective. Natural gas wellhead prices hardly rose throughout the 1960s, even though demand continued to grow rapidly. Initially these price controls had no adverse consequences. However, by the mid-1960s this was no longer true. Buyers of interruptible supplies, the first victims of natural gas shortages, found their supplies terminated in the midst of winter. Since the late 1960s, another rationing device has been increasingly used: the blanket refusal to provide service for broad classes of potential consumers. Those unable to get natural gas service have suffered high costs. To illustrate, during the winter of 1973-74 it cost only one-third to one-half as much to heat the typical home with natural gas as with distillate fuel oil, its closest substitute.

To summarize, the FPC's enforcement of stringent wellhead price ceilings has led to a large, fast-growing shortage of natural gas. As time passes and the shortage worsens, it becomes less likely that the monetary savings reaped by those fortunate consumers who can obtain all (or most) of the gas they desire at the low ceiling price offset both the larger monetary losses suffered by gas suppliers and consumers denied gas service and the high costs suffered by the entire nation because worsening shortages of natural gas mean both increased reliance on insecure foreign oil and greater environmental pollution. Unfortunately, because Congress faces strong pressure from those fortunate consumers who currently benefit from "low" natural gas prices and because the myths that natural gas supplies are price-inelastic and that its production is monopolized continue to persist, legislation abolishing FPC wellhead price regulation remains unlikely.

Alaskan Oil: Where Was It?

In 1967, Atlantic-Richfield and Humble Oil (now Exxon U.S.A.) discovered the Prudhoe Bay oil field on Alaska's North Slope. Prudhoe Bay's 9.6 billion barrels of currently proved reserves make it the largest oil field known in North America. In 1969 its owners decided that the cheapest way to deliver this oil would be to pipe it 900 miles across Alaska to Valdez, an ice-free but earthquake-prone port on the Gulf of Alaska. At Valdez it would be transferred to large tankers destined for the west coast. The producers planned a pipeline throughput of 2 million barrels daily and initially expected to start delivering this oil in late 1972. But these expectations were not realized—primarily because a coalition of environmental groups obtained an injunction preventing the U.S. Interior Department from issuing the necessary construction permit until it had evaluated the adverse environmental effects attributable to the pipeline and had examined the environmental impact of alternative means of supplying American consumers with similar quantities of energy. In late 1973 Congress passed special legislation aimed at shortcutting the seemingly interminable litigation. Oil should begin flowing through the Trans-Alaskan Pipeline (TAPS) in mid-1977. Daily throughput should reach 2 million barrels no later than 1979-80.

Large shipments of Alaskan oil would have been very useful during the

1973-74 Arab embargo. Benefiting from hindsight, many have chosen to blame environmentalists because of their opposition to TAPS. Such criticism would be appropriate if the TAPS opponents had adamantly opposed all plans to deliver Prudhoe Bay's oil. This was not the case. In fact, their contributions were intended to be constructive. Specifically, they pressed for two things: that the pipeline be built through Canada and that additional environmental safeguards be required. Because of the huge volumes of oil to be shipped from the North Slope and the unusually rugged but ecologically fragile terrain that it must traverse, both the Interior Department and the pipeline's developers eventually conceded that additional environmental safeguards were desirable.

The environmental reasons for preferring a trans-Canadian route were strong. Three benefits were promised: TAPS would traverse earthquake-prone regions; the Canadian route was not as seismically active. Oil shipped via TAPS must be transshipped via tankers to the West Coast and some oil spills would be inevitable, whereas the flow of oil through the Canadian pipeline would be uninterrupted between the North Slope and Midwest refiners. Because of the large quantities of oil and gas known (or supposed) to be in northwestern Canada and the Alaskan North Slope, there were already plans to build both natural gas and crude oil pipelines across Canada to the United States. It seemed certain that one or both of these pipelines would be built during the 1980s, whether the TAPS was built or not. The damage to wildlife nesting patterns and migration flows, arctic permafrost, and virgin wilderness could be greatly reduced if all arctic pipelines traversed a common corridor. Since at that time it was believed that these other pipelines must go through Canada, the huge environmental savings were possible only if the Alaskan pipeline was not built.

Choice of the trans-Canadian route probably was also preferable when judged by either economic or national security criteria. Admittedly the Alaskan pipeline would be cheaper and could be constructed more quickly. However, these advantages were probably more than offset by two factors: Alaskan oil was more valuable (would command a higher price) in the Midwest than on the West Coast, and choice of a Canadian route would have accelerated the rate of commercial development of much-needed new oil sources in both arctic regions and the southern Gulf of Alaska.

The unfortunate delays in delivering Alaskan oil illustrate a real problem. However, that problem was not obstructionism by environmentalists. They merely chose to use the only tools available to try to persuade the federal government to impose more stringent environmental safeguards and to force it to seriously consider adoption of the seemingly preferable trans-Canadian route. Rather, the real problem was an inflexible administrative review process that on the one hand was unable to accept useful input from concerned citizens who had a legitimate interest in this matter and, on the other hand, was unable to prevent interminable delays before a "final" decision could be reached.

The four examples just discussed illustrate important instances when U.S. energy policy failed and are by no means exhaustive (Mancke 1974a). Nevertheless, they suffice to illustrate that the twin themes of contradiction and misperception, rather than deliberate malfeasance, lie at the heart of the failure of U.S. energy policy.

THE U.S. RESPONSE TO THE ARAB OIL EMBARGO

The Arab decision to embargo oil sales precipitated worldwide panic. Americans sought explanations for the horrible fact that their mighty economy was in danger of being brought to its knees by "mere" Arabs. In the resulting environment of exaggeration, fear, and retribution, good policy-making proved impossible. Analysis of the high economic and environmental costs that would result from each of the several policy choices aimed at changing post-embargo conditions—especially those designed to achieve the recently proclaimed goal of energy self-sufficiency sometime in the 1980s—is beyond the scope of this paper. Rather, this section takes aim on a more modest goal: analyzing a few of the problems that plagued federal attempts to alleviate the recent embargo-caused oil shortages.

On the eve of the Arab decision to totally embargo oil sales to the United States, the latter was thought to be consuming roughly 3.5 million barrels per day of crude oil (or refined product equivalents) from Arab sources. The Federal Energy Office (FEO) was created and given broad powers to get the United States out of the immediate crisis resulting from the cessation of these Arab imports. The FEO responded by implementing an allocation program designed to force Americans to reduce their daily oil consumption by the full 3.5 million barrels (roughly 17 percent). This program worked by mandating sharp cutbacks in the quantities of oil products (especially gasoline) that could be sold. The long lines, panic buying, and general economic dislocations that accompanied these cutbacks are well known. Not known is the fact that evidence available shortly after the embargo began showed that the FEO's allocation steps were far too strong. In fact, far too stringent rationing, rather than oil import shortfalls, was the real cause of most of the economic dislocation suffered by Americans during the Arab oil embargo.

The full effects of the Arabs' "total" oil embargo should have been felt first in December because the trip between the Persian Gulf and the United States takes about six weeks. Hence, even a perfectly effective Arab embargo of oil sales to the United States would probably not have caused a sizable reduction in U.S. oil imports before December. The average monthly fall in U.S. oil imports was calculated by computing average daily oil imports during each month and subtracting from this total average daily oil imports during October 1973. The import figures are those compiled by the American Petroleum Institute and published in weekly issues of *Oil and Gas Journal*. Compared with pre-embargo levels, the actual daily fall in total U.S. oil imports averaged 465,000 barrels in February and 1.234 million barrels in March. The reductions in our oil imports proved to be far less than estimated because some Arab oil continued to leak into the United States and some non-Arab oil that would have normally been shipped to Europe or Japan was instead diverted to U.S. markets.

Besides underestimating U.S. oil supplies during the Arab embargo, the FEO (along with most "experts") ignored the sizable oil savings due to reduced demands for other (nonoil) kinds of energy. Specifically, they failed to recognize that because other types of energy supplied more than half of the United States' total needs and because they were close substitutes for oil products (except gasoline and lubricants) in most uses, a given percentage reduction in U.S. demands for these oil substitutes had roughly the same effect as an equal increase in available oil supplies. During the embargo Americans voluntarily reduced their demands for nonoil energy by about 10 percent below predicted nonembargo levels. The indirect oil savings attributable to this ignored factor appear to have offset roughly the entire shortfall due to the Arab embargo.

Table 1 presents data on year-to-year changes in U.S. stocks of crude oil and refined products. These data established that U.S. energy policy-makers overreacted to the Arab embargo. Specifically, it shows that on the embargo's eve (October 5, 1973), U.S. stocks of crude oil and all refined products except gasoline were slightly less than the year before (October 6, 1972). Ideally the FEO would have allocated products throughout the embargo so that stocks stayed at or slightly below levels of the comparable time a year earlier. Unfortunately, Table 1 shows that stocks of every product except gasoline registered steady improvement relative to the year before as the embargo ran its course. Thus, column 7 shows that, compared with one year earlier, total stocks of crude oil and refined products rose by about 11 percent from early October through early March. This massive inventory buildup, during precisely those months when the United States was victim of a "total" Arab embargo, was the major cause of the economic dislocation suffered by Americans during the Arab embargo.

the FEO believed that it would be less disruptive to reduce gasoline consumption proportionately more than consumption of other refined products, especially distillate fuel oils, which are used primarily for industrial and home heating. Hence, it ordered oil refiners to produce more heating oil and less gasoline. Table 3.1 confirms that by early December, distillate fuel oil stocks had soared far above levels a year earlier—they were not in short supply. But at the same time, long lines for gasoline were beginning to form. Obviously the FEO had overestimated likely fuel oil supply problems and underestimated those for gasoline. Two factors explain this mistake.

TABLE 1

Year-to-Year Change in U.S. Stocks of Crude Oil and Refined Products, 1972-74 (million barrels)

Absolute and Percentage Changes from	1 Crude Oil	2 Gasoline	3 Jet Fuels	4 Kerosene	5 Distillate Fuel Oils	6 Residual Fuel Oils	7 Total Crude Oil and Products*
Oct. 6, 1972 to Oct. 5, 1973	-10.798 (-4.2%)	+1.278 (0.6%)	-5.948 (-19.7%)	-0.729 (-3.3%)	-0.286 (-0.1%)	-7.904 (-12.3%)	-26.866 (-3.1%)
Nov. 3, 1972 to Nov. 2, 1973	-10.961 (-4.3%)	2.919 (1.4%)	-4.384 (-15.2%)	1.864 (8.8%)	6.806 (3.5%)	-6.889 (-11.0%)	-13.671 (-1.5%)
Dec. 8, 1972 to Dec. 7, 1973	0.643 (0.2%)	-6.718 (-3.1%)	0.599 (2.2%)	4.795 (24.1%)	29.892 (16.8%)	-0.825 (-1.5%)	28.907 (3.4%)
Jan. 12, 1973 to Jan. 11, 1974	1.225 (0.5%)	-9.776 (-4.5%)	3.354 (12.7%)	4.201 (24.0%)	44.657 (29.9%)	-2.879 (-5.2%)	43.688 (5.5%)
Feb. 2, 1973 to Feb. 1, 1974	-4.960 (-2.1%)	-3.830 (-1.7%)	3.386 (13.4%)	4.409 (27.5%)	50.641 (38.4%)	-2.854 (-5.8%)	52.637 (6.8%)
Mar. 2, 1973 to Mar. 1, 1974	0.889 (0.4%)	9.786 (4.5%)	4.420 (17.8%)	2.161 (14.2%)	36.538 (31.5%)	-1.146 (-2.5%)	58.215 (7.8%)

Source: Raw data is from the American Petroleum Institute's weekly reports on stocks of crude oil and refined products.
*In addition to the products listed, the total figures include aviation gas and unfinished oils. Thus, they differ slightly from those obtained by adding columns 1 through 6.

First, in our car-dependent society, most motorists found large immediate reductions in car miles traveled were possible only if they made substantial lifestyle changes. Also, changing long-ingrained high-gas-consumption driving habits was not easy—constant vigilance was needed. In contrast, quite large reductions in distillate fuel demands followed directly from some very easy decisions. Most obvious, use of fuel oil for heating could be cut back 6 to 10 percent in northern climes merely by turning thermostats down 6 degrees.

Second, both coal and natural gas are substitutes for distillate fuel oils. As a direct result of reduced demands for these substitutes, less distillates were needed. To illustrate, U.S. natural gas supplies are unable to fully satisfy winter heating demands. Hence, those buying natural gas on interruptible contracts expect their supply to be stopped during winter. When this happens, they usually substitute distillate fuel oil. The voluntary cutbacks by natural gas users during the winter of 1973-74 reduced the magnitude of natural gas interruptions. This led directly to reduced distillate fuel oil demand. Because gasoline has no good substitutes, the reduced demands for other fuels did not lead to similar reductions in demand for it. In sum, the FEO's decision to emphasize distillate fuel oil production at the expense of gasoline was unnecessary. Moreover, it actually created the long gasoline lines that caused so much havoc during the embargo.

There are large differences in the degree to which American oil refiners process Arab crude. Obviously, those most dependent on Arab crude at the embargo's onset faced the severest shortages. They persuaded Congress that this was not equitable. Congress, in turn, instructed the FEO to establish a program requiring relatively crude-rich refiners to share supplies with their less fortunate crude-short competitors. To implement this directive, the FEO ordered (beginning February 1, 1974) those refiners with above-industry-average crude supplies to sell some of their "surplus" to crude-poor competitors. The maximum price a refiner could charge for "surplus" oil was set equal to the weighted average of its total crude oil costs from all sources. Because most price-controlled domestic crude cost several dollars less per barrel than foreign crude, crude-poor refiners realized that they could reduce their costs by reducing their own imports of non-Arab oil and, instead, buying "surplus" from crude-rich refiners. For the same reason, crude-rich refiners realized they would lose several dollars on every barrel of oil imported and then sold at the allowed maximum "average" price. In sum, because of this FEO regulation, both crude-short and crude-rich refiners were encouraged to cut back crude oil imports. Reports circulated in industry trade journals suggest that the net effect of this well-intentioned but badly designed regulation was to reduce U.S. crude oil imports by up to 1 million barrels daily in February and March (*Oil and Gas Journal,* March 4, 1974).

WHY ENERGY POLICIES FAIL

This discussion has suggested that most U.S. energy policies have failed either because of poor design or, more fundamentally, misperception of the real nature of the underlying problem needing solution. Rather than buttress this thesis with additional examples, it is probably more useful to search for general causes. I believe there are two: the inability or unwillingness to coordinate existing policies and the failure to adopt flexible policies responsive to the ever-changing factual scenarios that we face.

Poor Policy Coordination

U.S. energy policy emanates in bits and pieces from various power centers. Below I present highly capsulized synopses of the principal interests and activities of a sample of the most important federal sources: five executive departments—Interior, Treasury, State, Defense, and Commerce—and four administrative agencies or regulatory commissions—Atomic Energy Commission, Federal Power Commission, Environmental Protection Agency, and Federal Energy Administration. The reader is forewarned that these synopses are far too simplistic. In particular, they fail to adequately reflect the diversity of opinion and approach that exists within any department or agency. Within many there are several competing subpower centers and all are subject, in varying degrees, to input from a plethora of concerned Congressional committees (especially Senator Henry Jackson's), Presidential assistants, the Office of Management and Budget, courts, concerned industries, mineral landowners, state governments, and the general public. Nevertheless, these synopses do show that by deliberate design as much as by mere neglect, each of these power centers (with the possible exception of the recently created Federal Energy Administration) sees only a part of our total energy problem and typically represents only a few of the interests legitimately concerned.

Interior Department

Until public interest in energy policy questions began to explode in the late 1960s, the Interior Department was the most important source of U.S. energy policy. Its line divisions, such as the Bureau of Mines, U.S. Geological Service, Bureau of Land Management, and Office of Oil and Gas, held responsibility for implementing and monitoring federal policies with regard to promoting fossil fuel energy research, leasing federal lands for energy production and transmission, and regulating oil imports.

The chief criticism of the Interior Department has always been that it is tied too closely to the domestic fossil fuel interest. The evidence summarized in the earlier discussion of the controversies over the administration of oil import controls and the construction of the Alaskan pipeline supports this criticism. One way of promoting this tight community of interests has been an oil industry practice of persuading some of its most promising younger executives to take lower-paying jobs as Interior Department top-staffers. After a few years of government seasoning, these executives typically return to top management slots with their former private employer.

Because of its long-time involvement in energy matters, the Interior Department was the obvious choice to play a lead role in formulating and implementing the new policies needed to solve our post-1969 energy problems. However, in order to get major changes in existing energy policies, it has become necessary to get a reasonably broad-based public support. Because of Interior's close identification with domestic energy interests, it was not realistic to assign it the politically sensitive task of formulating new energy policies. For this reason, the Interior Department's dominance over U.S. energy policy has continuously eroded since 1969. Interior first began to lose some of its dominance over U.S. energy policy-making when President Nixon assigned the job of reviewing U.S. oil import policy to a Cabinet Task Force chaired by then Secretary of Labor George Shultz. Washington rumors said that Shultz was awarded this honor because of his impartiality. Today most important energy policy decisions are made elsewhere. However, because of its expertise and experience in administering energy policies, the Interior Department continues to play a key role in implementing those policies that are adopted.

Treasury Department

Historically the Treasury Department has been concerned with three energy policy problems: the balance-of-payments implications of the United States' rising energy imports, the efficiency and equity effects of the special tax benefits given to domestic energy companies (principally the oil depletion allowance), and the implications for federal revenues of additional federal sales of mineral land leases. Under the leadership of George Shultz, Treasury's authority over U.S. energy policy decisions ranged far beyond these traditional areas. To illustrate, in 1973 Treasury took the lead in molding the Nixon administration's positions on such key issues as what should be the United States' new oil import policy, whether or not rationing should be used to circumvent the oil shortages due to the Arab embargo, and the administration's response to charges that the nation's oil problems were the result of a conspiracy among oil companies (Mancke 1974b). In addition Shultz, in his role as Presidential counselor, had considerable influence over the policy decisions of Interior and

Commerce. Moreover, through his assistant William Simon, he influenced the positions of the newly created Federal Energy Office. With Shultz's departure it is inevitable that Treasury will lose some of its recent dominance over U.S. energy policy-making. Nevertheless, I suspect that for at least the next several years this department's responsibilities will transcend its historical assignments.

State Department

Rising U.S. oil imports from economically, militarily, and politically sensitive Arab Persian Gulf countries have guaranteed that the State Department will play a growing role in setting U.S. energy policy. This accretion of power to State has been enhanced by Secretary of State Kissinger's immense personal power within the administration. It is obvious that Kissinger's success or lack of it in establishing and maintaining some semblance of peace in the Middle East will be of vital importance in determining what should be the nature and scope of the United States' long-run energy policies. Perhaps less obvious, the economic and political concessions to which he commits the United States in order to obtain Middle East "stability" will also shape the dimensions of our future oil security problems. Nevertheless, in large part because the State Department is now a highly individualized operation that lacks an experienced staff capable of properly analyzing the economic consequences of future energy policies, I predict (and hope) that State will continue to be less important than Treasury in the energy area.

Defense Department

The goal of reducing threats to the security of the United States has provided the principal justification for many of the United States' energy policies. As a corollary, it would appear to follow that the Defense Department would play a key role in setting U.S. energy policy. In fact, this has not been the case. Though justified on national security grounds, such glamorous and important energy policy decisions as those involving determination of the desirable level of U.S. dependence on oil imports or the decision to press construction of the trans-Alaskan pipeline were never made in the Defense Department. Instead, they were made by others and Defense was merely asked to add its prestigious endorsement. It is doubtful that Defense has either the inclination or the expertise for this state of affairs to be very different in the near future. Hence, Defense's real energy policy decisions will center on such less important matters as whether to accede to the rising number of requests for the Navy to allow production of oil and gas either known or thought to be available in its petroleum reservations in the western United States and northern Alaska.

Commerce Department

The Commerce Department views its mission as promoting improved efficiency for all American commerce and industry. In general, this has meant that American business has been able to rely on Commerce to press its interests within the Executive branch. In energy policy matters Commerce is most closely identified with two positions. First, since the interests of energy producers and landowners are already well represented by the Interior Department, Commerce seeks to represent the interests of industrial energy consumers. In practice, it has been an especially strong supporter of all efforts by petrochemical companies to get cheaper petroleum feedstocks. Second, Commerce has been an active proponent of increased trade with the Soviet Union, believing that crude oil and liquefied natural gas are potentially two of the Soviet Union's most valuable exports. In sum, Commerce plays a subsidiary role in shaping U.S. energy policy. Because of the narrowness of its political base in the energy area, it is unlikely that the nature of its role will soon change.

Atomic Energy Commission

The Atomic Energy Commission has the dual role of promoting peaceful applications of nuclear power and of protecting the public interest. Presently promoting increased use of nuclear power—in particular the breeder reactor—appears to be almost its sole concern. Because its influence grows larger as peaceful uses of nuclear power proliferate, there is good reason for suspecting that environmentalists are justified when they assert that the AEC's two roles of promotion and protection are contradictory and that protection of the public has received short shrift (Mancke 1974a, Ch. 9).

Federal Power Commission

The Federal Power Commission's principal energy assignments are regulating interstate shipments and sales of natural gas and electricity. At present its power over natural gas is unchallenged by any other government body. The unfortunate results of its court-ordered wellhead price regulation do not need additional discussion. The FPC is the principal setter of federal policy concerning electricity. However, in this area it shares some power with the Atomic Energy Commission and the Environmental Protection Agency. The FPC shares with the AEC the questionable premise that the electricity-generating capacity of the United States needs to be expanded as quickly as is economically possible.

Environmental Protection Agency

The environmental Protection Agency was created in 1970 to implement recent environmental legislation. EPA, beneficiary of an overwhelming Congressional mandate, responded by issuing controversial mandatory emission standards for automobiles and stationary power sources. Nevertheless, EPA must be viewed as at best a peripheral source of U.S. energy policy. It is seldom seriously consulted by other federal agencies on energy matters; and there is a rather strong possibility that, because of the public's fear of worsening energy shortages, its power to combat energy-related polluting activities will be curtailed.

Federal Energy Administration

The Federal Energy Administration is the just-established successor to the Federal Energy Office—the office created by Presidential executive order in late 1973 to coordinate efforts to alleviate the immediate Arab oil embargo crisis. FEA's assignment is to pull together the nation's energy resource management. Such coordination is certainly needed. Fragmented decision-making has worsened most of our energy problems. Unfortunately, because each source of U.S. energy policy-making jealously guards its prerogative to set policy in its historical bailiwick, the mere creation of the FEA will not guarantee an end to our coordination crisis. This will happen only if the FEA has a strong administrator who enjoys secure job tenure, commands the strong backing of the President, and on most matters has the sympathy of a majority of the Congress. Presently the FEA lacks such leadership, and it may never have it in a noncrisis period. Hence, U.S. energy policy is likely to continue to suffer from too little coordination.

Inflexible Policies and Ambiguous Facts

The other cause of energy policy failures has been the adoption of inflexible policies that cannot adjust to the inevitable changes in the fundamental "facts" upon which they are based. At any time these facts are ambiguous because of the lack of "hard data" on such important parameters as the long-run price responsiveness of demand and supply for the major kinds of energy, the speed with which secure domestic energy supplies can be expanded, and the security of energy supplies from various foreign sources. The ambiguity of such facts is directly attributable to underlying geological, technological, and political uncertainty. It can be alleviated only as better knowledge accumulates. As the costly failures of such policies as natural gas wellhead price ceilings and mandatory oil import controls illustrate, whenever there is considerable uncertainty about future conditions affecting a regulated industry, it is poor strategy to blindly adhere to an inflexible policy whose success depends on the occurrence of a specific, and frequently unlikely, chain of events. Instead, a flexible groping strategy is advisable: initially a great many of policy options should be pursued; more resources should, of course, be devoted to those initially judged most promising or least costly; as time passes and we are able to evaluate how well the different policies have worked, the failures should be cut back and, at some point, eliminated; the successes should receive a growing share of the government's total resource commitment (Mancke 1974a, Chs. 10, 11). Unfortunately, such recent events as the sudden adoption of Project Independence after the start of the Arab embargo, suggest that U.S. energy policy-making will continue to be both uncoordinated and inflexible. Unless there is a fundamental change in this approach, I suspect that the United States will suffer the enervating costs of repeated energy crises.

4

THE INTERNATIONAL
OIL INDUSTRY
Bernhard J. Abrahamsson

Demand for power in industry and transportation, coupled with need for raw materials in the petrochemical industries, has made oil the most important energy source and the paramount commodity in international trade. While supply has grown to more than match demand in the post-World War II period, serious disruptions and dislocations have occurred in the last quarter century— the latest being the Arab oil embargo and the production cutbacks resulting from the fourth Arab-Israeli war in October 1973.

While the war undoubtedly served as a catalyst and precipitated events, the Arab-Israeli conflict is not a basic factor in the long-term oil situation; rapidly changing demand and supply conditions are at the root of the problem. The emergence of the United States as a major oil importer in the last few years added substantially to the competition for world oil resources. The tight supply situation, while evident for several years, was precipitously exploited by the producing countries toward the end of 1973. First, the members of OPEC, excluding Iraq, stopped all shipments to the United States and the Netherlands, and reduced supplies to the other consuming nations by cutting back on production. Second, OPEC, which includes among its members most of the OAPEC countries, took advantage of its monopoly situation and, by the end of December 1973, succeeded in nearly quadrupling the price of crude oil (*International Economic Report of the President,* 1974, p. 45).

To better understand the complex interplay of economic and political forces, it is necessary to have at least a rudimentary overview of the international oil industry—which is the purpose of this chapter. The intention is to focus on the general characteristics of world demand for and supply of oil, and to review developments that have affected the relationships between international oil companies and the governments of the producing nations in such a way as to facilitate the recent course of action pursued by those governments.

OIL DEMAND AND SUPPLY

The outstanding feature of the international oil industry is that, with a few exceptions, the areas of consumption and production do not coincide. From this, several things follow: a heavy dependence of most nations on non-domestic oil resources, problems pertaining to control of and access to oil supplies, and a situation where oil accounts for a high proportion of volume and value of international trade. All this tends to make oil "a political commodity *par excellence* (Enrico Mattei, quoted in Hirst 1966, p. 28). Apart from North America and the USSR, none of the major consumers of oil produces enough to meet its demand. The converse is also true: no major producer, again with the exception of the USSR and North America, has sufficient domestic demand to absorb its output capacity. Thus a strong relationship of dependency exists between producing and consuming nations.

In 1972 the United States produced about one-fifth of the world's oil output but consumed somewhat more than a third of that output. Its import needs were filled mainly from the Caribbean and Canada, with a minor but increasing part coming from the Middle East. The Communist bloc, on the other hand, produces more than it consumes and for some time has exported crude, mainly to Western Europe. Given the growing demand in the USSR and other Eastern European countries, and the fact that most new domestic Russian oil sources are in eastern Siberia and difficult to develop and exploit, the status of the USSR as a net exporter may change in the near future.

Western Europe and Japan, the major consumers of surplus oil production, absorb, respectively, almost a third and a tenth of total world oil production, yet neither area produces any significant amount to meet this demand. As a consequence, both are heavily dependent on the surplus-producing nations. Western Europe depends on imports for about 95 percent of its oil consumption, while the dependence of Japan is virtually total.

The largest source of these imports for Western Europe is the Middle East, which supplied about half of its needs in recent years. North Africa accounts for a third, while Western Africa and the USSR supply about 7 percent each. For Japan, dependence on Middle East oil is somewhat over 80 percent, with another 14-15 percent coming from Southeast Asia, mainly Indonesia. In both Western Europe and Japan, oil provides more than half of all energy used (57 percent for Western Europe, 55 percent for Japan); and before the events of

1973, oil's share was forecast to increase substantially throughout the 1970s (to 62 percent and 73 percent, respectively, by 1975). The historical unreliability of predictions, mentioned in Chapter 1, should be noted, however.

The heavy dependence of these two areas on the Middle East is, of course, a reflection of that region's relative abundance of oil. Of the world's total *proven oil reserves,* the Middle East accounts for 56 percent (Saudi Arabia, 21 percent; Kuwait, 10 percent; Iran, 10 percent; Iraq, 5 percent; others, 10 percent), followed by the Communist countries (16 percent), the Western Hemisphere (12 percent), Western Europe (2.5 percent), and the rest of the world (2.5 percent) (Ford Foundation, 1974). The reason for emphasizing the relative figures is that the concept of "proven reserves" is equivocal. According to the definition given by the American Petroleum Institute, proved reserves are "the estimated quantities of crude oil which geological and engineering data demonstrate with reasonable certainty to be recoverable from known reservoirs under existing economic and operating conditions" (American Petroleum Institute 1972). On the rather bold assumption that economic and operating (technological) conditions affect all areas equally, the relative distribution of proved reserves gives a better picture of the location of oil resources than do absolute amounts. It should be noted, however, that even a small relative share may mean sufficient absolute amounts to provide self-sufficiency for a country (see Abrahamsson and Steckler 1973, pp. 6-21; Hartshorn 1962, Ch. 3; Odell 1963, Ch. 1; Adelman 1971, Ch. 1).

While the dependence of Western Europe on the Middle East is substantial, it was still greater in the 1950s and 1960s. The reasons for the relative decline are primarily the disruptions of the oil flow caused by the closing of the Suez Canal in 1956 and 1967. These closures, together with various political events that will be related presently, set in motion efforts to lessen the dependence on the Canal and, in the long run, on the oil of the Middle East. Oil explorations expanded on a large scale, interest in new forms of energy was renewed, and rapid technological progress occurred in the transportation of crude oil.

Major oil fields were found in Algeria and Nigeria, and both began production in 1958. Libya followed in 1961, and Tunisia in 1966. These areas became prominent in Western Europe's supply picture after the 1967 closing of the Suez Canal. By 1970 the Middle East supplied some 48 percent of Western Europe's needs, compared with 62 percent in 1965. On the other hand, dependence on African oil rose from 24 to 41 percent. Further explorations focused on the North Sea, where a major strike was made in April 1970—the Ekofisk field in the Norwegian sector. Since then Norway not only has attained self-sufficiency in oil but also has made a modest beginning as a net exporter. Significant deposits have also been found in the British, Dutch, and Danish sectors. The potential seems sufficiently high to warrant the expectation that

England also may attain self-sufficiency in the near future, becoming the second European country other than the USSR to achieve that status. The discovery of what appears to be a major field in the Aegean Sea may also confer self-sufficiency on Greece (*Petroleum Intelligence Weekly*, April 22, 1974). There are enough other promising areas in the Mediterranean and various parts of the Atlantic to justify the long-term expectation that Western Europe has the potential to achieve a relatively high degree of independence from non-European, or Middle Eastern, oil sources.

For Japan the picture is less bright. New fields have been found in Australia, on Sumatra and Borneo, and in the South China Sea. The new supplies so far have not appreciably affected Japan's dependence on the Middle East. The most promising prospect for Japan is the Senkaku Islands in the Ryukyu chain—where, however, mainland China also claims sovereignty. Considering the apparent ubiquity of oil, intensified explorations may well change the situation for Japan as for Western Europe. Meanwhile, Japan is attempting to diversify its sources. Contracts have been signed with China for delivery of modest amounts of crude (1.5 million tons, or 30,000 b/d) during 1974 (*Oil and Gas Journal*, February 11, 1974), and discussions are in progress for possible Japanese-Russian joint ventures to develop eastern Siberian fields.

For the United States the outlook is quite different. The United States can, if it so chooses, supply domestic demand entirely from sources within its national borders. However, for both political and economic reasons, this has not been the practice in the past. As mentioned earlier, part of U.S. oil consumption has been supplied by imports from the Caribbean, Canada, and, to some extent, from the Middle East. The question of whether imports of crude and refined petroleum should be allowed a greater or smaller share of the U.S. market has been argued in the political arena for many years. However, recent developments in the country's energy situation have put this question into a new perspective. For the first time the United States faces the prospect of an energy shortage.

Demand for oil and natural gas has been increasing at a faster rate than new discoveries; and unless countermeasures are taken, the country probably will be heavily dependent on imported supplies. Indeed, imports provided 35 percent of U.S. oil consumption even in 1973. The crux of the matter does not appear to be that there is an acute scarcity of fossil fuels per se but, rather, that cheap domestic fuel sources are scarce. With increased oil prices, both worldwide and domestic, proved oil reserves in the United States are believed to be at least double the amount given before prices rose early in 1974 (*Petroleum Intelligence Weekly*, April 15, 1974). Indeed, some estimate that, excluding new discoveries, the increase in potentially recoverable oil in the United States, resulting from the present price increases alone, would amount to 50 years' supply at present (1973) rates of production (Rose 1974). However, since even current demand is greater than current production, these reserves could not sustain self-sufficiency for that many years.

While recognizing that oil is a finite resource and, therefore, ultimately will be depleted, that time has not yet arrived. The current oil crisis is not one of physical existence. Rather, it is a matter of access to available worldwide supplies, and this is largely a matter of political and economic relationships. Before turning to these, and to complete the picture of supply and demand, a few words about refining capacity are necessary.

The distribution of refining capacity is shown in Table 2. The United States, the world's largest producer and consumer of oil, also accounts for the major proportion (46 percent) of the world's refining capacity. The Middle East and Africa, on the other hand—the largest surplus crude oil producers— have insignificant refining capacity (4.6 and 3.5 percent, respectively), while the opposite is true of Europe (31 percent) and Japan (15 percent). This distri- bution of refining capacity reflects relatively recent developments (*Oil and Gas Journal,* December 31, 1973).

In the early post-World War II period, markets for oil were small and the needs did not justify building refineries in these markets. Instead, large refiner- ies were constructed in the Persian Gulf, where the British presence provided the political stability for a good investment climate. The same favorable climate existed in Venezuela, and again refineries were built close to the source. In the 1950s several factors changed this picture: The Abadan crisis of 1951—caused by Iran's nationalization of the oil industry—shook the confidence of both con- sumers and oil companies in the security of Middle East supplies of refined products; the 1956 closing of the Suez Canal had a similar effect. At the same time, world oil demand was reaching levels that justified the development of market-located refineries and, somewhat later, economies of transport could be obtained by using very large tankers for crude oil.

Because per-unit transport costs can be significantly reduced when car- goes are shipped in large bulk quantities, there has been a tendency, over time, toward larger tankers. The growth in market-located refining capacity neces- sitated large-volume movement of crude oil. This, coupled with the uncertain- ties of the status of the Suez Canal after 1956, led to a very rapid growth in ship size. A big tanker, in the mid-1950s, had a carrying capacity of 30,000 to to 35,000 deadweight tons (dwt), or approximately 210,000 barrels of oil. At the end of the 1966 there were several 310,000 dwt ships on order; and in 1974 the largest ship afloat has a capacity of 477,000 dwt, or almost 3.5 million barrels of oil. These very large crude carriers are shortly to be surpassed by ultralarge crude carriers. Since ships above 200,000 dwt are not able to transit the Suez Canal, the main route for seaborne oil today is around Africa to Western Europe; but for reasons discussed below, the Suez Canal may again be of importance in the oil trade.

TABLE 2

World Refining Capacity (January 1, 1974)

	In 1000 barrels of daily crude throughput	In % of World Total (excluding Communist world)
Asia-Pacific	10,299	14.9
Europe	21,208	30.8
Middle East	3,159	4.6
Africa	2,390	3.5
Western Hemisphere	31,910	46.3
Total	68,966	100

Source: *Oil and Gas Journal,* December 31, 1973.

The trend toward larger tankers and market-located refineries has continued. Because the refining process creates more employment opportunities and has far greater linkage effects in terms of economic development, particularly as related to petrochemical industries, than does crude oil production, the location of refineries is one of the areas of friction between producing countries and oil companies.

For a long time there have been pressures by the governments of the producing countries in the Middle East for greater participation in refining and transport of their oil. The oil companies control about 75 percent of the world's tanker capacity—35 percent through outright ownership and the rest through long-term charters. The producing Arab countries, however, are entering this aspect of the industry through the formation of the Arab Maritime Petroleum Transport Company in January 1973 (Petroleum Press Service, February 1973).

Concerning refineries, though, the producing countries have not had the financial resources or the technological know-how to realize their plans. The oil embargo by OAPEC and the high prices engendered by OPEC changed the situation dramatically. High prices provided the financial resources needed, and the embargo gave political power to acquire technical assistance through bilateral agreements trading technology for oil. Aiding these efforts, environmental opposition to new refineries resulted in the "export" of refining capacity from the Western world to areas outside the main consuming markets. As a result, five of the largest refineries in the world are now planned in the Persian Gulf. Given the increase in refining capacity in this area, it is reasonable to expect that in a few years, the major part of the growth in Western Europe's demand for oil will be met by refined products from the Persian Gulf. This anticipated trade in products is likely to move in tankers smaller than very large crude carriers—perhaps 90-100,000 dwt. A marginally expanded Suez Canal could accommodate these ships, so the canal may again play a major role in international oil trade.

STRUCTURAL CHANGES

The role of the oil companies is peculiar and has direct bearing on the problems of control of and access to oil resources. While there is a very large number of oil companies engaging in one or more aspects of the oil industry— exploration, development, production, transport, refining, and marketing—the largest proportion (65 percent) of the Free World's production is in the hands of eight companies: Exxon, Texaco, Socal, Gulf, Mobil, British Petroleum, Shell, and Compagnie Francaise des Petroles (see Table 3). The first five are U.S. companies and, together with British Petroleum and Shell, are commonly known as the "Seven Sisters." These eight vertically integrated companies con- stitute the "majors," or internationals. Other, smaller companies, from virtually all consuming nations and with varying degrees of integrated operations, are the "independents."

The figures in Table 3 appear to support the popular view of the oil in- dustry as controlled by a handful of giant firms with perfect freedom of action, linked by worldwide supply and marketing arrangements and joint ventures. While this may have been true at one time, it is not the case today. Several de- velopments in the last few decades have altered the framework in which the international oil companies operate. It is beyond the scope of this paper to dis- cuss them in minute detail; only the broad sweep of events in the Middle East is given.

The concessions under which oil companies began operations in the Mid- dle East had two provisions of major importance for future events. First, the companies had the exclusive right to determine which areas within the conces- sion were to be explored and developed. Second, in return for a lump-sum con- cession bonus and royalty payments per barrel of oil produced, the host coun- tries waived their right to tax the concessions. The first provision meant that if major oil strikes occurred in one area of the concession, other areas might re- main unexplored—and this did happen. Payment of royalties per barrel had the effect of tying the producing country's income directly to the volume of pro- duction.

As long as production was at a high level and growing, this system posed

TABLE 3

Shares of Eight Major Companies in World Oil Production

	Exxon	B.P.	Shell	Texaco	Socal	Gulf	Mobil	CFP	Total Share
Percentage of Free World Production	13.0	10.6	10.2	9.1	7.5	7.4	5.0	2.4	65.2%, or 44,036,000 barrels per day

Source: Petroleum Economist, March 1974.

no problem. However in 1949 Saudi Arabia began negotiating with Aramco for higher payments. The proximate causes seem to have been the example set by Venezuela, which began taxing its concessions the year before, and the awareness that the U.S. government received more tax income from Saudi Arabian oil than did the host government from royalties (Stocking 1970, pp. 146-47). In 1950 a profit-sharing agreement was reached. In addition to royalties, it provided for the equal sharing of net operating profits—the "50-50 formula." Aramco is a producing company jointly owned by four U.S. majors (Socal, Texaco, Exxon, with 30 percent each, and Mobil, with 10 percent), so the oil produced by Aramco moved into these integrated companies at a "transfer price" established for accounting and tax purposes (Hartshorn 1962, pp. 130, 137, 138). The new profit-sharing formula required the establishment of a reference price (the posted price), determined by the oil companies. This agreement was duplicated with minor variations, and by the mid-1950s it was in use throughout the Middle East.

The system worked well as long as the world market for oil was stable; but by the end of 1952 the sharp demand pressures occasioned by the Korean War began to ease and, at the same time, supplies of crude oil expanded substantially. Excluding the impact of the Suez closure in 1956, the situation was one of oversupply with downward pressure on prices. The situation was aggravated in the next few years as the United States closed its market by means of import quotas in 1959, and the USSR pursued vigorous marketing in Western Europe—both policies at the expense of Middle Eastern oil (Frank 1966, Chs. 3, 4). The expansion of crude oil supply was not entirely the result of the activities of major oil companies. New concessions had been granted to independents in the Middle East, and were beginning production at this time.

The pressures on market prices increased; and in August 1960, Esso (Exxon) reduced the posted price, followed by the other major oil companies (Frank 1966, pp. 112-13). The immediate effect of the reduction was to decrease the revenues of the host governments—in effect, offsetting the gains of the 50-50 formula. This was followed in September 1960 by the formation of OPEC, the purpose of which was to gain political leverage and bargaining power vis-a-vis the oil companies in order to prevent decreases in prices and revenues. As stated in the first resolution of OPEC, and more explicitly in the June 1968 resolution, there are three main objectives of the organization: first, to obtain stable and, if possible, higher oil revenues for its members; second, and directly related to the first, to obtain higher prices for its oil; and third, to obtain a greater measure of control over production in its member states. (On the background of OPEC, see Schurr and Homan 1971, Ch. 1.)

OPEC has been successful. There have been no further price decreases. Revenues have increased steadily through increased production and, in some instances, favorable changes in the profit-sharing formula. The major turn in OPEC's favor in terms of prices came in 1971, when, after long and tense negotiations, agreements were signed in Teheran and Tripoli providing for agreed-upon price increases through 1975. Posted prices for Persian Gulf oil were to rise from $1.80 in 1970 to $2.83 in 1975—an increase of almost 60 percent. For Libyan oil, the corresponding figures were $2.53 and $4.20, an increase of 70 percent.

The hoped-for stability these agreements promised was short-lived. Devaluations of the dollar in December 1971 and February 1973 prompted compensatory increases in posted prices. Then, in the wake of the Yom Kippur war, OAPEC met in Kuwait on October 16. Two decisions were taken at that meeting—decisions of long-term, major impact on the oil industry. The Arab oil ministers unilaterally took the right to extablish the posted prices; and they decided to reduce production levels. While there had been instances of reduced production previously—notably in Libya and Kuwait—this concerted action shifted the control of prices and production unequivocally from the oil companies to the Arab host governments. In the ensuing months, other members of OPEC gained the same power, and OPEC's objectives of gaining control of prices and production were achieved.

The conditions for reaching these aims obviously were not created overnight. While OPEC was not able to force higher prices until 1971—though it was successful in preventing decreases—efforts to gain control of production were more favorable. The original concessions had relinquished all controls of oil exploration, development, and production in the areas to the concessionaire. Citing the doctrine of "changing circumstances," host governments set out to renegotiate the terms of the old concessions (Schurr and Homan 1971, p. 126). The aim was for host governments to participate as partners in the oil industry, not only in production but also in the "downstream" operations—refining, transport, and marketing. Through negotiation or nationalization, the host governments managed to recover the rights to unexplored and undeveloped parts of the old concessions. These areas have been offered for exploitation either to independents or to the host country's national oil companies as joint ventures. The terms of these new concessions differ from the old in that they provide for equity participation of the producing country. The agreement on which most such arrangements are based was the 1957 joint venture between the Italian state oil company, Ente Nazionale Idrocarburi (ENI) and that of Iran, the National Iranian Oil Company (NIOC) (Stocking 1970, pp. 404-05). In essence the two companies, through subsidiary corporations, were equal partners; but exploration costs would be borne by the Italians and refunded only if and when oil was found. Exploitation costs would be shared. Half of the joint venture's net profits would go to Iran as taxes. Since the remainder would be divided between the Italian and Iranian partners, the agreement gave Iran a total share of 75 percent, while Italy assumed all the risks of and capital investment in exploration. This type of participation, then, is the model of new explorations and supplies.

Where the oil companies still held control under the old arrangements, negotiations led to agreements at the end of 1972 in which the oil companies recognized the principle of participation. According to these agreements, producing countries would acquire a 25 percent interest by 1973, and this level would prevail until 1978. Thereafter, the interests of the producing countries would increase in stages until 1982, when they would attain controlling interests of 51 percent (Petroleum Press Service, February 1973). The oil companies' control thus appeared secure until 1982, but the agreements appear to be meaningless. Nigeria insisted on 35 percent interest by 1973, and Libya demanded majority control by the end of that year. By early 1974 Libya's demands were met; and a new participation agreement being negotiated between British Petroleum and Gulf, on the one hand, and Kuwait, on the other, would give the latter a 60 percent interest in 1974. This agreement, in all likelihood, sets the minimum terms for other agreements; and with Iran and others apparently intent on following suit, effective control of production by producing countries is a fact (Petroleum Economist, March 1974, 84-87).

These events have changed the structure of the international oil markets. Previously the majors owned, and therefore controlled prices and volumes of the input of, crude oil used in their integrated operations. Now the majors have not only lost control of the posted prices, which determine the actual cost of the crude input, but they have also lost, through participation, a measure of the integrated input itself. The share of the produced oil that goes to the host government—participation oil—is now beyond company control. In addition, most producing countries have the right to take royalty payments as 12 percent of either posted prices or oil production. With today's high prices, more is taken as oil than as money payments. Participation and royalty oil are sold by national companies either on the world market or to the oil companies. As of early 1974, the prices paid by the companies to buy back the participation oil have been 93 percent of posted prices (*Petroleum Intelligence Weekly,* April 15 and 22, 1974). It has been estimated that the amount of crude oil available to the majors from integrated production in 1974 will be 40 percent less on a world-wide basis than in 1972 (*Petroleum Economist,* March 1974, p. 84).

While this change in ownership and control would probably have occurred at some time in the course of events initiated by OPEC, the cataclysmic culmination of the process was precipitated by OAPEC, an organization that came out of the 1967 Arab-Israeli war. In April and May of that year, when tension was mounting in the area, Arab oil producers declared that oil supplies to any country extending aid to Israel in case of war would be cut off. The outbreak of the war resulted in a brief stoppage of both production and transportation of oil. Production was resumed in mid-June, but with an embargo on shipments to England, West Germany, and the United States. In August a conference of Arab producers rejected an Egyptian-Iraqi proposal for a three-month total embargo, and all restrictions were lifted. The argument for this course of action was that further oil revenues were needed by the Arab states to increase military strength and to accumulate sufficient reserves to allow a total embargo should the need arise. To plan for and coordinate possible future action in furthering the Arab cause against Israel, OAPEC was formed in 1968.

Although it is difficult to make a distinction between political and economic motives and means, it can be said that OAPEC's political objectives precipitated the achievement of OPEC's economic objectives. In the process the goal, in terms of prices, appears to have been exceeded. In view of the Teheran and Tripoli agreements of 1971, as well as the various participation agreements, oil prices were bound to rise; but no one could foresee the magnitude of increases under the combined impact of actions by OPEC and OAPEC in four months (October 1973-January 1974). OPEC, for all practical purposes, had achieved its objectives by early 1973. It seems, therefore, that the pricing policies effected by OPEC in the last quarter of that year were less the implementation of carefully formulated, predetermined objectives than the ad hoc exploitation of a unique situation. As a consequence the world economy is confronted by a new problem.

INTERNATIONAL FINANCIAL CONSEQUENCES

With higher prices, revenues of oil-producing countries will rise unless production is curtailed. The question, then, is whether production will be lowered, remain at the present level, or expand to meet growing demand—or whether new sources of energy and oil will provide a solution. Under any option there are problems. At one extreme, curtailed production will obviously have harsh effects on attained standards and ways of living, as well as on hopes for future enhanced living standards; but it may have little or no effect on international financial relationships. The burden on consuming nations will, however, increase as their economies have to meet unchanged payments for oil. At the other extreme, should production expand, financial effects would be of major magnitude. Production at present levels would, presumably, leave us in a mid-position. Like any monopoly pricer, however, OPEC must consider demand elasticities as well as substitution elasticities of supply. The former are undoubtedly low (see *Petroleum Economist*, May 1974, p. 164). The latter, by technological necessity, are very low in the short run buy may be significant in the medium run and very high in the long run. Once a certain threshold price of oil is reached and the political costs assessed, a process of research, development, and production of alternative sources of oil and, more generally, other energy will set in—a process that may well prove irreversible. It appears that the process has been initiated. For new resources to have significant impact, massive resources must be allocated for this purpose. Although new resources may be relatively expensive, they do provide the necessary and rational long-term solution. In addition, ". . . if past examples of major research efforts can be taken as a guide, there is every likelihood that accelerating technological progress would reduce the relative price of energy substitutes. . ." (OECD 1973). In the immediate foreseeable future, however, we must cope with the problems of high oil prices and supplies under monopoly control by the producing countries.

Leaving aside the generally inflationary effects of higher oil prices and the serious repercussions they have on fertilizer prices—and, therefore on food production and prices, particularly in the less-developed countries—there remain problems concerning the international flow of resources and, consequently, the international monetary system and balance-of-payments. There is little specific to be said about these problems. The main element in the picture is uncertainty. The only certainty is a massive upsurge in the income of producing countries (see Table 3.3). In 1974 oil consumers will pay an estimated $63 billion more than the year before. With total world exports valued at $510 billion in 1973, the increased cost of oil alone will account for some 12 percent of that trade.

Corresponding to these balance-of-payments surpluses, of course, are deficits in the consuming nations. It has been estimated that the OECD countries, instead of having a combined surplus of $10 billion, will incur a deficit of $30-35 billion, while the deficit for developing conntries will be around $10 billion (World Bank report quoted in *Petroleum Economist*, May 1974).

TABLE 4

Oil Revenues of Producing Nations, 1965-74
($million, assuming 1973 production levels)

Nation	1965	1970	1972	1973[a]	1974[a]
Saudi Arabia	655	1,200	3,107	4,900	19,400
Iran	522	1,136	2,380	3,900	14,900
Venezuela	1,135	1,406	1,948	2,800	10,000
Libya	371	1,295	1,598	2,200	8,000
Kuwait	671	895	1,657	2,100	7,900
Nigeria	n.a.	411	1,174	2,000	7,000
Iraq	375	521	575	1,500	5,900
Abu Dhabi	33	233	551	1,000	4,800
Algeria	n.a.	325	700	1,000	3,700
Indonesia	n.a.	239	555	800	2,100
Qatar	69	122	255	400	1,200
Others[b]	16	150	222	550	1,700
Total	3,847	7,933	14,722	23,150	86,600

[a]World Bank estimate.

[b]Excludes North American and Communist countries.

Note: Average dollar income per exported barrel of oil is $0.77 in 1965, $0.92 in 1970, $1.47 in 1972, $2.05 in 1973, and $7.69 in 1974.

Source: Petroleum Economist, May 1974.

The oil-exporting countries are not expected to be able to offset more than $10 billion of their combined surplus by means of expanded imports. Therefore, by the end of the 1970s these countries may have accumulated surpluses of some $350-400 billion, with consumers having corresponding deficits.

In general, this situation is a complete reversal of previous conditions. In the past the developed countries as a group tended to have a balance-of-payments surplus on current account sufficient to cover the outflows on capital account for purposes of aid and investment. Conversely, the combined current account of developing countries showed a deficit that was offset by inflows on capital account. This has changed. Developed oil-importing countries are now certain to incur deficits on current account; and for less-developed countries, the current account deficit will increase. Under these conditions it is open to question whether the traditional flow of funds from developed to less-developed countries will continue. Given that the producing nations cannot increase their own imports to absorb more than a fraction of their export earnings, the conclusion must be that all oil-consuming countries—both developed and less-developed—will face the prospect of deficits on current account for some time. To maintain balance-of-payments equilibrium, and to prevent adverse repercussions on the world economy, these deficits must be financed—through capital inflows.

As long as the oil-producing countries keep the surpluses in the form of financial claims—that is, they do not use the money to claim real resources in terms of goods and services— they in effect finance the deficits: their current account surplus generates a capital flow of equal magnitude to the oil-importing countries (see Pollack 1974; Heller 1974, Ch. 9). The crucial question, though, is whether the distribution of these flows will be such that each deficit country is assured of financing. The surpluses are more likely to flow into the developed countries, where economic stability and well-developed capital markets are assured, than into developing countries. Thus, to maintain an orderly world economy, arrangements must be made for channeling surpluses to those areas where they are most needed. The International Monetary Fund (IMF) is currently attempting to establish a special fund—oil facility—to grant additional credit facilities to countries with balance-of-payments difficulties due to high oil prices (*IMF Survey,* February 4, 1974).

The IMF initiative is a truly international effort to solve the immediate monetary problems, and so far has had the support of the oil-producing countries, primarily Iran and Saudi Arabia. However, there seems to be more interest among the Arab producers in more specifically directed projects, such as the Arab Fund for Economic and Social Development, the Islamic Development Bank, the Arab-African Bank, and the Kuwait Fund for Arab Economic Development. To the extent that funds are channeled through these and similar institutions, the likelihood increases that some countries will have difficulty financing their deficits, and that access to financing will be tied to political considerations. This is not surprising, nor should it be. What it heralds, of course, is the possible emergence of new political and economic relationships that reasonably could be expected to affect future events.

Most surpluses are expected to accumulate in short-term currency deposits, primarily in the Euro-currency market but also in the traditional money markets of New York, London, and Paris (*International Economic Report of the President* 1974, p. 50). As long as the money is held in short-term form, there is the risk of its being switched among currencies, adding an element of uncertainty to the ongoing efforts to reform the international monetary system. It is therefore desirable to convert these deposits into long-term assets. The question then arises as to the possibility of major markets absorbing the large amounts available, and whether any new institutions may be called for. No unequivocal answer can be given at this point. One can equally well foresee recession and global economic disintegration and some perfectly acceptable equilibrium condition permitting continued growth and prosperity.

Whatever may come, the long-awaited reform of the international monetary system will be postponed until the forces unleashed by the oil crisis have
worked themselves out and a definite pattern of financial relationships is
discernible.

SUMMARY AND CONCLUSIONS

International trade in oil is characterized by heavy dependence of most
consuming nations on a few major producing areas, the most important of
which is the Middle East. The major part of the world's supply of oil is produced, refined, transported, and marketed by eight highly integrated international oil companies. In the past these companies owned the oil they produced,
and controlled both prices and levels of production. The oil crisis of 1973
showed clearly that these controls had shifted to the host governments.

The crisis had two features: a reduction in oil supplies through decreased
production, and drastic increases in oil prices. Both were the culmination of a
process of change that, evolving throughout the post-World War II period,
changed the fundamental nature of the international oil industry.

In essence, the process entailed the entry of independent oil companies
into international operations and the discovery of large new oil reserves in the
established oil-producing areas, as well as in new regions outside the Middle
East. At the time of discovery, and for some years thereafter, new supplies
exceeded demand, resulting in downward pressure on world oil prices. An unexpected decrease in posted prices in 1960 had a severe impact on producer
countries' revenues and, to prevent a repetition, OPEC was formed. Its main
objectives—to raise the oil revenues of host governments and to gain control of
oil resources—were achieved.

In terms of revenues, the organization agreed with the oil companies in
1971 to raise prices substantially through 1975. The agreements were renegoti-
ated as a result of the dollar devaluations in 1971 and 1973. By the end of
1973 the procedure was to dispense with negotiation, and prices were set unilaterally by producing governments. The oil companies—majors as well as
independents—lost control of prices.

In terms of control of resources, undeveloped parts of old concessions
were returned to host countries. These, together with concessions for new
areas, were let on conditions that gave producer governments a partnership
role. As a result the governments' influence on production and pricing grew
substantially. At the end of 1972 this influence was also accepted in older concessions as arrangements were made for majority government participation by
1982. Despite the agreements, however, most producer nations showed intent

to take majority control at much earlier dates. Since part of the produced oil belongs to the governments under the participation agreements, the oil companies lost part of the supply under their control. To meet demand requirements, the companies buy back the participation oil at prices higher than those paid for owned oil. Consequently, the average cost has risen. In addition, producer governments have formed their own national oil companies, whose range of activities is growing. To the extent that national companies take participation oil, nondomestic companies may find supply difficulties rising.

While these developments were certain to occur sometime, OAPEC brought events to a climax. By reducing oil supplies in pursuit of a purely political objective—the war against Israel—OAPEC accentuated a sellers' market already in existence because of growing world demand and the emergence of the United States as a major oil importer. The ensuing high prices were a manifestation of OPEC's exploitation of its monopoly position.

Because the price increases were ad hoc, and not the result of carefully formulated policy, the world economy must cope with problems of new international financial relationships, as well as with the possibility of financial disturbances and major changes in trade flows.

It is not possible to speculate on what the future will bring, for the only basis of analysis is uncertainty. Barring acts of force, it is safe to say, though, that the fundamental changes in the nature of the international oil industry are irreversible, were foreseeable, and will have far-reaching effects.

ENERGY: ISRAELIS, ARABS, AND IRANIANS
Don Peretz

In the 1973 October war there was a spectacular convergence of international crises in the Middle East. These crises were not necessarily linked; each might have occurred independently. What was remarkable was the simultaneous flare-up of this series of events, which like a chain of exploding trip wires threatened to culminate in an international disaster of the first magnitude. Although the danger is not yet past, rational action rather than hysterical reaction seems to be the modus operandi.

Among the crises in October were the quarter-century dispute between Israel and its Arab neighbors; Soviet-American relations and the test of detente; U.S. relations with its European allies; relations between the radical and conservative Arab regimes; Israeli tensions within the Labor government and with the right-wing opposition; and the international energy crisis.

Since October intraregional relationships have been in greater flux than at any time after the Arab cold war between radical and conservative regimes during the 1960s. Great as were the changes wrought in 1967, when a new Middle East emerged, they have been dwarfed by events since October 1973. Arab oil was a major factor in both periods, on a scale exceeding that at any other time in recent history.

The petroleum weapon was not only effective against the United States and Western European countries considered too friendly to Israel; it was also an instrument in changing radical regimes into conservatives, and second- or third-level countries into regional powers. The absolute reliance by Egypt on Saudi oil not only intensified deradicalization of the republic, but finally led to its de-Nasserization. The new balance of power also diminished Israel's military

superiority. Until October, assistance received by Egypt and Syria from the
Soviet Union was counterbalanced, if not exceeded, by support Israel obtained
from the U.S. government and American Jewry. American policy in the region
had been based on maintaining Israel's military supremacy. Now it will be difficult, if not impossible, for Americans to compete with the oil largess from Arab
producing countries to the "front line" states.

OPEC

Since Middle East oil became a commodity of international importance a
little over half a century ago, there has been a cycle of surplus and shortage.
International demands for Middle East oil have fluctuated, as have the many
and conflicting estimates of world oil resources over the years.

In times of supposed petroleum surpluses, the often parsimonious attitudes of Western, mostly British and American, oil companies have created
hostile feelings in the Middle Eastern countries where these companies operate.
Only a dozen or so years ago there was a surplus era—1960 was a buyer's year
for oil. Soviet petroleum was flooding Europe, other newcomers were entering
the crude oil market, new reserves were being discovered, and production capacity began to exceed the market, with prices on the downgrade. This was only
four years after another Middle East crisis, the 1956 Suez War, which had
caused one of the coldest winters in postwar Europe. Because of the conflict
the Middle East oil flow had been curtailed for several months. But now the
crisis was past, and in 1960 Standard Oil of New Jersey decided to knock 14
cents off the posted price per barrel. This 7.5 percent decline, some Arabs suggested, was being used as a pressure on the revolutionary regime in Iraq to re-
tract some of its demands for a greater share in oil profits. The loss to Saudi
Arabia for 1960-61 was some $30 million, a drop of about 10 percent in its oil
revenue.

In the past Arab countries, and other so-called underdeveloped countries
that depended heavily on exports of a single commodity, had passively accepted
actions taken by Western industrial powers. The first major change occurred in
1950, when Saudi Arabia, following an example set by Venezuela during 1948,
reached an agreement with Aramco to share net profits from its oil on a 50-50
basis. This arrangement soon became the standard formula for determining payments to governments and producing companies.

In 1960 the situation suddenly changed. Saudi Arabia's Minister of
Petroleum Resources, Sheikh Abdullah Tariki, rushed to Baghdad to pledge
solidarity in the face of Anglo-American pressure. Other Middle Eastern and
non-Middle Eastern oil-producing countries joined the meeting. With the

encouragement of Venezuela's Minister of Mines and Hydrocarbons, Dr. Juan
Perez Alfonzo, they banded together, forming OPEC to restore and stabilize
the pre-1960 prices. The original membership—Iraq, Iran, Kuwait, Saudi Arabia,
and Venezuela— has since expanded to include Algeria, Qatar, United Arab
Emirates, Libya, Algeria, Nigeria, Ecuador, Gabon, and Indonesia. Nearly all
nations that depend heavily on export of this primary product have joined the
international producers' cartel.

Initially OPEC was regarded scornfully by many international observers,
including oil company officials. Even its own members were somewhat skeptical about the organization's capacity to survive. Rarely were Arab states able to
take concerted action, even for their own benefit, to say nothing of cooperating
with Persians, Africans, Latin Americans, and Asians. The newborn infant not
only survived but grew in strength, until it seems to have become almost as
strong as the international petroleum cartel. Continuation and flourishing of
OPEC for over a decade has undermined one of the prevailing stereotypes about
Middle Easterners: that they can never accomplish anything together.

OAPEC

For more than two decades the Arab states had recognized the potential
of oil as a political weapon. The Political Committee of the Arab League established a committee of oil experts in 1952 to discuss the political use of oil, including a refusal to supply Israel. To assist the committee, the League established a permanent Petroleum Bureau in 1954 (renamed Department of Oil
Affairs in 1959), supervised by the committee. In 1954 oil affairs were shifted
from the Political Committee to the Economic Committee, with the intent to
use petroleum income for Arab socioeconomic development. Since then the
Department of Oil Affairs has periodically sponsored Arab Oil Congresses to
discuss petroleum development and its political uses.

The first formal agreement between oil-exporting countries was signed in
1953 when pre-revolutionary Iraq and the Saudi monarchy agreed to exchange
information and to hold periodic consultations on petroleum policies. Initially
each country used the agreement to extract information about improved terms
in concessions obtained by the other signer.

In contrast with OPEC, which was formed primarily for economic purposes, several oil-producing and nonproducing states formed the Organization
of Arab Petroleum Exporting Countries (OAPEC). It developed from a meeting
of finance and oil ministers held in Baghdad during August 1967 to discuss the
aftermath of the Six Day War the previous June. The ministers agreed on the
necessity of a unique Arab organization that would utilize oil to develop their
collective power as an international political lever.

Although the Arab states had stopped their flow of oil during the Six Day War, and oil shipments to Europe had been cut off in the 1956 conflict, pumping was resumed soon after the cease-fire. Experience in the previous two months, according to the Saudi Arabian Oil Minister, Ahmed Zaki Yamani, showed that the embargo decision "hurt the Arabs themselves more than anyone else, and the only ones to gain any benefit from it were the non-Arab [oil] producers" (Mikdashi 1972, p. 85). In 1967 consumer countries began to substitute oil from the United States, Venezuela, and Iran. The United States, considered the principal target, was not hurt by the 1967 embargo because its imports from the Middle East were relatively small, only 300,000 barrels a day. At the Khartoum Summit Conference of Arab chiefs of state during August, it was decided to reject the oil boycott proposed at Baghdad. Instead the Arab states resumed pumping, "since oil is a positive Arab resource that can be used in the service of Arab goals. It can contribute to the efforts to enable those Arab states which are exposed to the aggression and thereby lost economic resources to stand firm and eliminate the effects of the aggression" (*Middle East Record,* 1967, p. 264).

OAPEC was formally established five months later, in January 1968 at Beirut, by Saudi Arabia, Kuwait, and Libya. The founders represented conservative Arab regimes that were attempting to extend their political influence by economic means. Although invited, radical Iraq was reluctant to join the three regimes that appeared to be using their leverage for conservative political purposes. None of the original OAPEC members had participated in the Six Day War, but the Arab defeat by Israel provided them with the opportunity to use their revenues to strengthen their positions relative to the defeated radicals, Syria and Egypt.

OAPEC's objectives were undisguisedly political: to increase the strength and unity of the Arab world through a massive organization combining all Arab oil companies. Through major commercial deals and involvement in large-scale downstream operations, OAPEC hoped to influence political behavior of consumer countries. It also aimed to coordinate the activities of its own members (Schurr and Homan 1971, pp. 139-40).

Saudi Arabia, Kuwait, and Libya originally wanted the organization's membership restricted to any Arab country in which oil "constitutes the basic source of its national income." When it was established in 1968, the only independent country other than the founders that could meet this requirement was Iraq (petroleum did not replace wine as Algeria's principal source of national income until 1970). Furthermore, membership was open only to those approved by three-quarters of the votes of founding members, which gave any of the three founders a veto.

The restrictive nature of OAPEC membership was undermined when the Libyan monarchy was replaced by a revolutionary regime in 1969. The organization lost its conservative hue with subsequent admission of Algeria, in May 1970. Abu Dhabi, Bahrain, Dubai, and Qatar also were admitted in 1970. With admission of the "progressive" governments of Egypt, Iraq, and Syria in March 1972, the conservatives were almost balanced by the radical regimes.*

During the period between the June war and the 1967 August Khartoum conference, the Arab states divided between conservative oil-producing regimes that opposed economic warfare, especially the use of oil, and radical non-oil-producers joined by Iraq, then the only "progressive" with a large oil income, advocating suspension of oil exports, closure of the Suez Canal, and withdrawal of Arab deposits from British banks—which they believed would create difficulties for the West. The radical regimes intended such sanctions as punishment for alleged intervention in support of Zionism and as a means to influence Western countries to pressure Israel. The economic measures failed because the Arab world as a whole, and the oil-producing countries in particular, lacked a coordinated policy. Each of the countries that had suspended oil shipments in June resumed production after the war without consulting its neighbors. Instead of imposing an embargo, the Khartoum participants decided to abandon economic warfare and to use their income to compensate the defeated nations for their losses.

The oil monarchies of Saudi Arabia, Kuwait, and Libya agreed to make annual payments of £135 million to Jordan and Egypt "until the effects of the aggression are eliminated. . . . In this way, the Arab nation ensures that it will be able to carry on this battle, without any weakening, till the effects of the aggression are eliminated" (*Middle East Report* 1967, p. 264). The end of the "effects of the aggression" meant, for Egypt, until the Suez Canal was reopened and, for Jordan, regaining the West Bank seized by Israel during the war.

THE ARAB COLD WAR

Use of oil revenues by the conservative regimes after the June 1967 debacle served to depolarize political alignments that had been forming before the war. During the previous decade Egypt, under Nasser, had been developing an Arab socialist ideology as the basis for both domestic and foreign policies. At home the revolution concentrated economic control and administration in government hands. Abroad, Nasser gave increasing support, both substantive

---

*Oman and Tunisia have applied for membership. Dubai withdrew at the end of 1972, after a dispute about Persian Gulf dry dock locations.

and ideological, to new revolutionary regimes in Iraq, Syria, and Yemen. With backing from Egyptian sources, revolutionary plots were unsuccessfully hatched in Lebanon, Jordan, Saudi Arabia, and the Maghreb. Egypt's deepest revolutionary commitment abroad was support of the revolutionaries in Yemen against the monarchy. Thousands of Egyptian troops and millions of pounds were expended in the protracted civil war that came to symbolize the struggle between the radical or "progressive" and the conservative or "reactionary" Arab regimes. The monarchy in Yemen, supported by Saudi Arabian military aid and the backing of other conservative Arab regimes, was able to hold out against the republican regime from 1962 until a cease-fire was negotiated in 1967.

Egypt's defeat by Israel in June 1967 and its subsequent dependence on income from conservative Arab oil regimes seemed to deradicalize Nasser's inter-Arab policies. In the months following the war, the Egyptian stance changed from leadership of the radical regimes to mediator between the radicals and the conservatives. This was clearly evident in the growing differences between Cairo, on the one hand, and Damascus and Baghdad, on the other. Although Syria had been among the three defeated Arab nations in the June war, it rejected UN Security Resolution 242 of November 1967 as the basis for a peace settlement. Both "progressive" Egypt and "reactionary" Jordan accepted the resolution, thereby agreeing conditionally to the existence of Israel. Since Syria had refused to attend the Khartoum Summit Conference, it was not a recipient of the petroleum largesse given to both Egypt and Jordan. Despite the similar outlook of Syria and Iraq on the Palestine problem and relations with Israel, Iraq did not volunteer to share its oil revenues with fellow revolutionaries in Damascus. Instead, Syria was isolated; and Nasser now played the role of intermediary rather than protagonist, frustrating unified action by the "radical" front.

Inter-Arab relations were further complicated between 1967 and 1973 by the rise of a new political phenomenon, the Palestinians. Before 1967 most politically active Palestinians were supporters of one or another of the Arab regimes; and the Palestinian guerrilla organizations were affiliated with, and trained and supplied by, armed forces of the various Arab governments.

Defeat of the Arab nations in 1967 radicalized many of the younger Palestinians, who had become totally disenchanted with all Arab leadership. After June a spate of new or reorganized groups emerged with a common purpose: establishment of a democratic, secular Palestinian nation. Although differing in tactics and sometimes in ideology, the Palestinian organizations agreed on dismemberment of the Zionist Jewish state. A major ideological difference was between those who focused primarily on "liberation of Palestine" and those who supported revolution throughout the Arab world. These differences soon brought some Palestinian organizations into conflict with various Arab governments, especially Jordan and Lebanon, which sought to curtail their guerrilla attacks into Israel. Although some of the commando organizations received extensive financial support from Kuwait and Saudi Arabia, others opposed what they considered the "reactionary" regimes in these countries.

The clash between moderates and radicals over settlement of the Palestine problem was brought to a head after Egypt and Jordan accepted the cease-fire and proposals for political settlement in the so-called Rogers plan during 1970. The Palestinian commandos refused to accept the American proposals and the cease-fire, and were supported in their militancy by Syria, Iraq, and Algeria. Opposition to a settlement short of their ideological goals was underscored by intensified guerrilla warfare, including hijacking of European commercial airliners, thereby precipitating direct confrontation with the monarchy in Jordan. Revolutionary Egypt again played the role of moderator and pacifier in negotiating a halt to the civil war between Palestinian radicals and the Jordanian king. Later Egypt was to mediate between the Palestinians and the Lebanese government when the latter attempted to prevent the commandos from using southern Lebanon as a base for attack on Israel. A fundamental question in this shifting of alliances and transformation of Egypt from "radicalism" to "moderator" is whether such changes would have occurred without financial backing from conservative Arab oil regimes.

OIL AND THE ARAB DISPUTE WITH ISRAEL

Events in the Middle East since OPEC was formed indicate that the Arab-Israeli conflict was not the cause of the international oil situation. Arab relations with Israel offered an occasion for intensifying policies restricting production that had already been initiated or discussed. Libya began to restrict production to half of what it was in 1970 long before the 1973 war for market rather than political reasons, and price hikes were requested by Iran although it maintained friendly relations with Israel. During the 1960s OPEC pressures on world markets increased to a point where the price of oil had more than doubled or tripled without any relationship to Israel.

Although factually correct, this is a somewhat misleading statement. Despite the upward escalation in price for each gallon of gasoline used by the American consumer, he still pays less to the producing country than for federal and local taxes. Profits of the American oil companies have not declined. They have increased in the last decade, although the companies argue that these profits are necessary for expansion of production facilities or development of new oil sources. Thus it is important to keep in mind that doubling the price of oil in the producing countries does not double the price paid by the consumer. Increases paid since 1960 have been collected by our own government and the oil companies. These price rises have had little to do with the state of Israel. Rather more significant is the accumulation of huge dollar surpluses by the Middle East oil-producing states.

Profits have increased so tremendously that some countries in the area now have more dollars than they can profitably spend or invest. Saudi Arabia was able to use only 60 percent of its oil revenue in 1973. The ministate of Kuwait had some $6 billion in investment. Abu Dhabi's income reached the ridiculously high sum of $50,000 per person annually, and is expected to reach $100,000 per person by 1980. With dollar devaluation and a surplus of Western investments, some Arab leaders decided that a barrel of oil in the ground was worth more than several barrels on the market. It has become increasingly difficult for Western countries to provide any convincing argument that expansion of output is worth their while. As one commentator observed, if the Arabs can't eat oil, they can't eat gold either. Once they have collected their first few billion dollars, the smaller Middle Eastern countries can cut production or stop it altogether for a lengthy period without suffering major harm.

The situation of Saudi Arabia, holder of the largest reserves and the major oil producer in the region, illustrates the dilemma. More than a year ago its officials began to discuss possibilities of investing in downstream facilities, that is, investing its dollar surplus in distribution of oil, gasoline and their by-products in the United States (Middle East Institute 1972, pp. 95-105). But the proposal was never taken very seriously at the consumer end of the line. The U.S. government has a program to attract foreign direct investment that focuses primarily on establishment of new manufacturing but not on such strategically important areas as energy. The oil companies have shown little enthusiasm about Arab interest in downstream activity. According to the U.S. Commerce Department, "There are reports . . . of small direct investments, through intermediaries, in such fields as real estate, banking and trading operations. The preponderance of Persian Gulf investments here are in securities (portfolio investments) and are made principally through third parties. While growing, such portfolio investments are not significant relative to the total U.S. capital market, to the best of our knowledge" (New Perspectives on the Persian Gulf 1973, p. 161). Nevertheless, the Saudi government has been under pressure from the United States to increase production because of growing energy needs in Europe, Japan, and in America itself.

THE OCTOBER 1973 WAR AND OIL

Before October 1973 few American observers thought that Saudi Arabia would cut off or even cut down its production of oil. The Saudis, and most

other Middle Easterners, seemed too dollar-hungry, despite the declining value
of American currency. Thus, when Saudi Arabia, Kuwait, and other Arab countries took concerted and relatively speedy action to cut back production to
stop the flow of oil to certain European countries after outbreak of the war,
eyebrows were raised among those who believed that the Arabs would never
get together. But again it should be emphasized that the war did not cause the
cutback. It merely presented an occasion for the Arab states to undertake an
action that seemed to have economic wisdom, that would have come sooner or
later, but that those who were friendly to the United States had been reluctant
to take. Iraq, no great friend of the West, never officially joined the embargo,
although it stopped exporting for a short time when it could not obtain a sufficiently high price. Libya also left loopholes, and its oil shipments continued on
a limited basis to some countries. U.S. Commerce Department figures disclosed
that Saudi shipments to America never completely stopped, even after four
months of the embargo. Other leaks showed in imports from countries that do
not normally export to the United States, such as Colombia, Italy, Chile,
Bolivia, and Peru. Despite the leaks, the embargo was an overall success, reducing American imports from 6 million barrels daily in September to 5 million
during the following months of 1973-74 (New York *Times,* April 10 and 13,
1974).

The Arab embargo on the United States, Holland, Portugal, South Africa,
and Rhodesia was declared for political purposes, because the countries mentioned were either too pro-Israel or colonialist-imperialist. In addition there
was a general cutback in Arab oil production that reached a height in December of 25 percent of September levels, or about 4 million barrels a day. The
cutback began after a decision by Arab oil ministers on October 17, more than
10 days after the war started, with across-the-board cuts of 5 percent per month
until Israel withdrew from occupied territories. Saudi Arabia blocked stronger
measures, refusing to follow Iraq's example of nationalizing American oil
interests. Only after announcement of Nixon's intent to supply Israel with $2.2
billion in military aid did Faisal consent to the embargo. On November 4 the
Arab oil ministers decreed a 25 percent cutback but waived an additional 5 percent cut in December as a "gesture" toward Japan and the European Economic
Community in response to their "balanced" statements. By January additional
cuts were terminated in response to the Kissinger peace efforts, and a decision
was taken to increase production by 10 percent, resulting in a 15 percent reduction from prewar levels. The embargo was finally ended, over the opposition of
Syria and Libya, with Algeria insisting that the "weapon" be kept in reserve
after the Kissinger disengagement talks.

The spiraling increase in Middle East oil production and rapid accumulation of dollars had a direct effect on the scale of warfare. Without this accumulation few of the countries would have been able to obtain the arms necessary

for fighting a first-class war. Although the Arab countries directly involved, Egypt and Syria, are not oil-producing nations, it is widely believed that a substantial amount of the costs for their expensive Russian weapons were paid by the Arab oil producers. According to David Binder in the New York *Times* of October 21, 1973: "The financial support for the Middle East war has pitted the oil billions of King Faisal of Saudi Arabia against the huge voluntary contributions of American Jews to Israel." While other financial factors were important, "the Saudi Arabian aid to Arab neighbors—principally Egypt—and the American Jewish donations are the decisive elements in the current conflict. According to the diplomats and intelligence operatives, King Faisal promised President Anwar el-Sadat of Egypt . . . that Saudi Arabia would not only subsidize the war, but also cover the Cairo Government's resulting debts. This was considered by Western diplomats to be crucial to President Sadat's decision to open the hostilities October 6. The Saudi commitment to the war against Israel was also a factor in King Faisal's decision to use his country's oil supply as an economic weapon against the United States and other countries that support Israel."

Egypt entered the war with a stagnating economy, a $250 million foreign-trade deficit, and a gross national product of only $6.7 billion, slightly lower than that of Israel, which has less than a tenth of Egypt's population. Yet Egypt was committing $1.5 billion, or nearly a quarter of its GNP, to military expenditures. Syria, with a GNP of about $2 billion, was also spending about a quarter of it on military supplies. There is little doubt that Egypt and Syria would have been unable to initiate the Yom Kippur war had President Sadat not received the financial backing of King Faisal.

Despite its poverty, in 1972 Egypt became the nation with the largest percent of GNP devoted to military expenditure—the figure reached 20.2 percent, according to the Institute of Strategic Studies in London. The Institute also reported that Jordan (17.4 percent) and Syria (11.5 percent) were among the five nations in the world with the highest percent of GNP devoted to military expenditures, matched only by Israel (18.2 percent and South Vietnam (17.4 percent) (*The Military Balance 1973*, pp. 74-75).

Oil revenues made it possible for these really third-level countries to fight a first-class war, consuming quantities of material that would have been prodigious for even first-class powers. The tank and air battles fought in Sinai and on the Golan Heights surpassed most of the battles fought by the major powers during World War II. The costs of the three-week war consumed not only annual outlays for military expenditures but, according to some estimates, surpassed the annual GNP of the combatants. They incurred losses in the billions of dollars, but within a few days were able to replenish their military hardware with fresh supplies from the Soviet Union—which, knowing of the Arab dollar reserves, demanded a quick payment—and from the United States, which initiated one of the largest airlifts in history from American debarkation points directly to the Sinai battlefields.

Arab capacity to pay quickly for a complete new arsenal also directly affected Israel, for now it too had to keep up its supply from the United States and to restock its very high but unanticipated losses. According to Israeli Finance Minister Pinhas Sapir, the war cost more than $2 billion during the first three weeks. Israeli government specialists have given a figure of 30 billion Israeli pounds, or roughly $7.1 billion, as the total cost. Beyond the military expenditures, the war cost Israel some $480 million in losses from reduced productivity in the national economy. These losses and expenditures have slowed the economic boom that began in 1967, bringing to an end the free-spending era in which Israelis were purchasing cars and television sets, and taking trips abroad.

Syria's economy was also greatly disrupted by the scale and intensity of the war. Israeli air attacks destroyed the country's two largest oil refineries, shut down power plants, causing blackouts and cuts in industry; and did extensive damage to the ports of Tartus and Latakia.

Arab oil also became a weapon in the great-power competition for influence in the region when polarization of the conflict between American and Soviet client states led to the convergence of the energy crisis and a test of detente. Ironically the oil weapon, which has been advantageous to the Soviet Union within the larger spectrum of international relations, was supplied by Arab countries that had long been considered aligned with Western interests, such as Saudi Arabia and Kuwait. Even at the height of the embargo, negotiations continued with these and other Persian Gulf countries for purchase of American weapons. On the other hand, Iraq, which had similar ties to the Soviet Union, continued to ship oil to the West.

The political and economic backing given by the oil-producing countries to the "front line" states increased both Syrian and Egyptian bargaining power in negotiations for a cease-fire and a peace agreement. Certainly the selective and planned use of the oil embargo against some countries, and the cutback in production and exports to others, strained relations between the United States and its Western European allies, which depend on Middle Eastern oil for up to three-quarters of their energy supplies. The oil situation caused a fundamental change in European policies toward the Arab-Israel conflict in which most countries called for Israeli withdrawal from territories occupied in 1967. During the war all members of NATO except Portugal refused to permit the United States to use their bases for transfer of arms to Israel. In June 1974, when nine members of the European Common Market called for a dialogue with twenty Arab states on matters of economic and scientific cooperation, Secretary of State Kissinger expressed U.S. concern.

At the inter-Arab level the conflict again showed the importance of oil

income as a major element in suspending the Arab cold war between conservatives on the Arabian peninsula and the "radical" regimes of Syria, Egypt, and
Iraq. While it is true that Arab rhetoric has always been unified against Israel,
never before have any two Arab armes been able not only to plan, but also to
carry out, an initially successful attack against their common enemy. The lack
of any concerted anti-Israel policy has characterized inter-Arab relations for
more than a quarter of a century, so it was indeed surprising to see not only
joint military planning but also the secrecy with which the October attack was
implemented in cooperation with Saudi Arabia, and the extent to which King
Faisal has gone along with President Sadat's military and political initiatives. In
the past it was more likely than not that the Egyptian would be castigated by
the Saudis for so much as suggesting a truce with Israel, to say nothing of
entering direct negotiations with the Jewish state. Even more surprising has
been the reported willingness of Syria and of Yassir Arafat, leader of the largest Palestinian commando organization, al-Fatah, to enter the impending peace
negotiations. Since Arafat too has been heavily financed by oil revenues, especially from Saudi Arabia, one could readily speculate that financial considerations were of some significance in his recent political turn-about.

IRAN

The energy crisis precipitated by the October war gave non-Arab members of OPEC an opportunity for greatly expanded profits. As a result of the
shortages, all international oil costs rose sharply; and even Indonesia, Venezuela,
and Canada exploited the occasion to extract higher prices for their exports.
(In 1973 Indonesia earned a gross of nearly $1.5 billion from oil exports, which
provided 53 percent of its foreign-exchange earnings. During 1974, with nearly
the same production, the country will earn at least $4 billion, according to the
New York *Times* of January 1 and 26, 1974.)

Iran has probably been the major beneficiary of the Arab war against
Israel. Although sympathy of most of the country's 32 million people is with
their fellow Muslims in the Arab world, the government has kept aloof from
the conflict. The Shah was hesitant to become too closely aligned with the
radical Arab regimes, and he desired to maintain his close ties with Israel. While
supporting the UN resolutions calling for evacuation from territories seized in
the 1967 war, Iran continued to ship oil not only to the West but also to Israel.
Exports to the United States leaped from 9.8 million barrels in December to
13.5 million in January 1974.

Israel figures large in the Shah's plans for the future of the Middle East.
The country's toughness and fast rate of economic development are admired,

and its regional goals are compatible with those of the Shah. Its existence, in his view, helps block the "bolshevik threat" and keeps Persia's traditional Arab competitors on guard. To maintain this balance Israeli and Iranian intelligence exchange information, and Israel provides technical, military, and security assistance.

The Shah's fear of encirclement through Soviet influence in Iraq and India has given Israel a very favorable image. "Without Israeli power in the Middle East," reported an observer in Teheran, "the Shah feels that the Arabs would be difficult to control and the Russians would very much gain an upper hand in the entire area" (New York *Times,* November 10 and December 30, 1974).

In a recent interview with a Lebanese journalist, the Shah stated that he saw "no contradiction" between Iran's support for the Arabs and continued economic ties with Israel. Why, he asked, should Iran be forced to accept the Arab lead in cutting ties with Israel when the Arabs refused to follow Teheran in its anti-Left crusade?

As a Muslim the Shah has supported Arab efforts to restore East Jerusalem to Jordan. The religious connection was emphasized during the October war, when the Iranian press repeatedly wrote about "Muslim" rather than "Arab" soldiers. However, student unrest and orthodox concern were kept under control with strict censorship, lest too much enthusiasm be worked up for a jihad in Palestine.

To counter the Communist threat Iran was also reported to have sent troops to help Sultan Qabus Ibn Said against Marxist "freedom fighters" in Oman's Dhofar district. The Popular Front for the Liberation of Oman and the Arab Gulf announced that some 3,000 Iranian troops—others asserted 30,000—were stationed in Dhofar, near the border of South Yemen. Supposedly three crack battalions from the Shah's Special Forces were spearheading a drive against rebel "liberated areas" (New York *Times,* December 31, 1973).

Persian-Arab relations have historically been strained for religious, as well as political and economic, reasons. In the centuries-old tensions between Shiite and Sunni Muslims, Persia, with its 90 cercent Shiite population, has naturally identified with the former. More recently Arab-Persian animosities were intensified by the Shah's suspicions of the radical Arab regimes. During the 1960s there were verbal battles between Radio Cairo and Teheran in which President Nasser accused the Shah of being a reactionary tool of imperialism, and was in turn accused of being a Soviet puppet. As Egyptian foreign policy mellowed, Iran's relations with neighboring Iraq worsened. Iraqi Baathist ties with the Soviet Union, establishment of at least five anti-Shah clandestine radio stations in Iraq, Baathist arms shipments to and training of Baluchi separatists in Pakistan and eastern Iran, and Iraqi encouragement of Arab separatist sentiments in Iran's Khuzistan region, which the Iraqis call Arabistan, led to deterioration of relations between the two countries. Following Iranian take-over of three tiny, nearly uninhabited but strategically important islands in the Strait of Hormuz, which were claimed by the United Arab Emirates, Iraq expelled several thousand Iranians. Some 300 of them were accused of being infiltrators and were threatened with execution by the Iranian government. Iran retaliated where Iraq was most vulnerable, by assisting the Kurdish rebellion against the Baghdad government.

The crisis came to a head early in 1974, when the two nations mobilized troops along their 630-mile border. After military clashes leaving 65 dead, the UN Security Council effected an agreement to negotiate a comprehensive peace. Secretary General Kurt Waldheim's special representative, Luis Weckmann-Munoz of Mexico, blamed the fighting at least in part on use of different maps marking a border that the British had administered for decades without precise identification.

Although agreement was reached on their mutual frontiers, the two countries have yet to settle differences over the Shatt el-Arab at the head of the Persian Gulf. Not only are major ports of the two countries dangerously close in this area, but the possibility of offshore oil deposits invites threats by each side to extend its territorial jurisdiction into waters claimed by the other.

Iran's political affinity with other conservative monarchies on the Persian Gulf would seem to make them natural allies against radical Iraq. Of the 14 Gulf states only Iraq is not royal, and it is ideologically in conflict with the region's kings, sheikhs, and sultan. However, since the British decision to leave the Gulf in 1968, the Shah has had pretensions to "fill" the resulting "power vacuum." His references to the Gulf as "his lake," and to his intentions to intervene militarily should there be any political changes detrimental to Iran's interests, have aroused many Arab suspicions. Seizure of the three Hormuz Strait islands was opposed not only by Iraq but also by the conservative Arab regimes.

Iran's naval buildup and outreach to the Indian Ocean, and its acquisition of 40 warships and purchase of additional modern destroyers and submarines from West Germany, have raised a spectre of Iranian imperialism among many of the smaller Arab states. The American effort to promote regional cooperation among the conservative regimes, with the Iranian-Saudi relationship as the key, is, according to Lee Hamilton, Chairman of the U.S. House of Representatives Near East Subcommittee:

> . . . fragile at present and is based on negative rather than positive considerations. It is based on a common political vision of kings surviving in a sea of ex-kingdoms, a common distrust of the Soviet Union and its political maneuverings, and a common dislike for the policies and actions of some neighbors. Such matters can create only lukewarm bonds especially against a background of deepseated religious,

tribal, cultural, and political legacies that fuel an undercurrent of tension and suspicion between Iran and Saudi Arabia. (*New Perspectives* 1973, p. vi)

The undercurrent of rivalry between the two political and economic "rival allies" in the Gulf was apparent in their disagreements within OPEC. Saudi Arabia, despite its support of the oil embargo, urged restraint in raising prices, Iran, although refusing to participate in OAPEC's embargo, has been the most avid supporter of escalating prices, which in the long run will have a more serious effect than the temporary cessation of petroleum production.

The Shah's grand design to counter "Bolshevism" had led him to view opposition leaders in the Pakistani province of Baluchistan as part of the Communist threat. The Soviet "pincer movement" against Iran has included support for Bangladesh as a way to weaken Pakistan, according to the Shah. Bengali secession would stimulate irredentism among the Baluchis in West Pakistan, who would then set a subversive example for the Iranian Baluchis. The new regime in Afghanistan is also under suspicion as a secret ally of the Soviets because it has greater sympathy for the Baluchis than did the previous rulers.

To support "stabilization" efforts the Shah has purchased 80 American Phantom jets costing $2.5 million each, with another 100 coming at a cost of $5 million each. This will give Iran a modern fighter-bomber force of about 355. Britain will supply 800 Chieftain tanks costing $480 million, which will be added to 400 M-47 tanks for a total force of 1,700. Additionally, 660 helicopters, including 200 gunships and 18 large Chinooks, have been ordered. Thus the Shah will be able to dispatch his "stabilization" force to any point on the Persian Gulf within hours, if it can bear up under the strain of maintenance pressures and can provide the training necessary to operate such an extensive military force (*Strategic Survey 1973* 1974, p. 42).

Although Iran spent only 6.2 percent of its GNP on the military during 1972, its large income from oil, which ranks second in the Middle East only to Saudi Arabia, has enabled Iran to purchase more weapons than any other country in the area. Its arms budget in 1973 was more than $2 billion, on the same order as such middle powers as Canada, the Netherlands, East Germany, and Sweden.

Oil income has enabled the Shah to cultivate his aspirations as the predominant power in the Persian Gulf region. Not only is Iran the most populous country, but it is making the most rapid advances in industrialization and economic reform, and has the consequent political clout. Iran has abandoned former irredentist goals of expanding territorially into any of the neighboring states. The Shah recently decided to forgo claim to Bahrein as an imperial province. Instead, he is concentrating on building the largest, best-equipped, and most powerful army in the region. His vision is to make Iran the arbiter and stabilizer of the status quo. If a revolutionary junta should succeed in overthrowing the Persian regime, it is likely that other conservative monarchies and sheikhdoms in the region would soon be toppled. Iran's position as chief bulwark of stability, defined in terms of the status quo, has not prevented accommodation with the Soviet Union, including trade and military agreements with its not-so-conservative northern neighbor.

Despite the Shah's fear of Bolshevism, he has taken the lead in urging OPEC to escalate its oil prices by 300 percent, 400 percent, or more within a year. While the United States and Europe were greatly disadvantaged by the price rise, it was developing countries most susceptible to radical ideologies that were grievously hurt. A study by the Overseas Development Council in Washington showed that some 30 of the world's poorer countries were being brought to the brink of "catastrophe" by price policies advocated by the Shah. To help mitigate the dangers to their economies, Iran proposed in February a new development fund backed by oil money, pledging more than $1 billion to help ease the problem for poorer countries. However, the question remained of whether such a fund would be large and timely enough to prevent the collapse of major development plans in countries such as the Central African Republic and India. Without credit assistance from Iran, India would have had to expend all of its income from exports (about $1.8 billion) for oil imports during 1974, of which Iran supplied about 65 percent (New York *Times,* February 23, 1974). According to Walter Levy (writing in the July 1974 *Foreign Affairs*), the cost of oil for developing countries will jump from $5 billion in 1973 to $15 billion in 1974. The increase of $10 billion will exceed all foreign aid these countries received during 1973.

BILATERALISM

The picture drawn so far shows the cards belonging to the Middle East players in this international oil game. But do they have all the cards?

Oil-producing countries need the West, not only as consumers for their major source of income but for other reasons as well. Too severe shortages could seriously harm Western economies, thus undermining their potential as future buyers of Middle Eastern oil. Japanese exports to the Middle East of textiles, iron, steel, electrical equipment, and vehicles totaled $1.2 billion in 1973. Could Japan keep up the pace of exports if faced with a fuel shortage?

Several Arab countries depend heavily on Western military hardware. In American aid legislation for 1973, Kuwait and Saudi Arabia were to become major importers of U.S. military equipment. According to Representative Lee Hamilton, during 1973 the U.S. Navy had a $600 million equipment and training program in Saudi Arabia and had agreed to sell an additional $1 billion in arms to the kingdom. Under a similar agreement Kuwait was to purchase $600 million worth of arms. The *Economist* (London) of May 4, 1974, reported an agreement between Saudi Arabia and the United States for another $1 billion in arms sales. An agreement signed with the United States in April 1974 provided for development and modernization of the Saudi national guard that would cost $335 million. The United States was to provide armored vehicles, antitank weapons, and artillery. Additional weapons were to be purchased from France and England by Saudi Arabia and several smaller sheikhdoms. In 1973 Britain negotiated a five-year contract of $600 million with Saudi Arabia for aeronautical equipment, and even tiny Kuwait and Abu Dhabi were purchasing dozens of fighter planes from France—although Abu Dhabi had no pilots (*Near East Report,* May 29, 1974; *Strategic Survey 1973,* 1974, pp. 42-45). Saudi Arabia and Kuwait are wary of the radical regime in Iraq, which received over $1 billion in arms supplies from the Soviet Union, and both are skeptical of the Soviet alternative. Egypt, for example, has a Soviet steel mill operating at a huge loss. After Russia recently built a canning factory for Iraq, an outbreak of botulism was blamed on some of its products.

Most countries of the Middle East import much of their food, especially wheat and rice. In 1973 Saudi Arabia imported 434,000 of its 554,000 tons of wheat and wheat flour; Kuwait was nearly 100 percent dependent on imported feed, and Iraq 38 percent dependent on imported wheat. Egypt, Lebanon, Jordan, and Syria also required imported foodstuffs. Because of recent poor crops in the area, the Middle East could become as large a market for U.S. grain as either China or India. The United States has thus become one of the region's biggest food suppliers. Some have suggested that the United States could use its "wheat weapon" if the Arabs persist in using their "oil weapon."

It is obvious that the West and the Middle East could injure each other in a trade war. Food energy could be used in retaliation against industrial energy. Both are vital, and neither side can do without the energy supplied by the other. However, the Arabs have the advantage. A report prepared for Congress by the Library of Congress showed that the United States never supplied more than 10.2 percent of the total wheat supply to the 16 countries in the region. Algeria and Saudi Arabia were most dependent, with American wheat supplying between 28 and 40 percent of the latter's needs. Two-thirds of American rice exports to the Middle East went to Saudi Arabia. Arab grain purchases are so decentralized, and their individual purchases so small in the world grain market, that they could easily buy from third countries without attracting attention. The report concluded that although U.S. imports of Arab oil reached 9.2 percent of American consumption in 1973, this shortfall could not be made up in the near future. Therefore:

The leverage available to the Arabs through their oil boycott far exceeds

any leverage that might be available to the United States through a
food embargo since the Arabs can meet their relatively small food
import needs from other sources in the world market, while the United
States cannot meet its relatively large petroleum needs from other
sources (*The United States Oil Shortage* 1973, pp. 61-64).

SHIFTING ALIGNMENTS

Deradicalization of the Middle East began after the 1967 war, when Saudi
oil income was essential to Egypt for its recovery from defeat. Old feuds between the Saudi monarchy and socialist Egypt were laid aside as the two nations increasingly found their policies converging. With the succession of Anwar
Sadat to the presidency in 1970, socialist ideology was played down, modest
steps were initiated toward decentralization of government economic controls,
and the pan-Arab theme was deemphasized. However, these changes did nothing
to break the military-political stalemate with Israel. Its apparent policy of con-
verting the status quo of the Six Day War into a permanent situation led to
increasing frustration in the Arab world and disillusionment with President
Sadat's leadership in Egypt. Frustration and disillusion finally culminated in
the October attack by Egypt and Syria, breaking the nearly seven-year-old
stalemate. Israel was forced, through disengagement negotiations, back from
the Suez Canal and into smaller areas on the Golan Heights. Indications were
that with American support, further Israeli withdrawals could be anticipated as
part of an overall peace settlement.

Now both Egypt and Syria, the two former leaders in the socialist van-
guard, had the United States and Saudi Arabia to thank. The urgency given to
the American search for peace through negotiations of Secretary of State Henry
Kissinger was reinforced by the oil weapon. No American Secretary of State
had devoted so much concentrated time and energy to the Middle East, or to
any other peace effort—nor would that have been the case had it not been for
Arab oil and its political use by OAPEC. Neither would Egypt and Syria have
been able to conduct their October military campaigns without the arms purchased with Saudi and Kuwaiti oil income.

President Sadat announced that he wanted to end more than 18 years of
dependence on Soviet arms supplies and that he would seek weapons from
other, including Western, sources. He openly criticized the Soviet Union for
insufficient attention to Egypt's military needs and even hinted at diplomatic
deception by Moscow in an attempt to force a truce before Egyptian gains were
realized in the October war. As relations with Moscow cooled, warm ties developed with the United States. The Egyptian President poured encomiums on
Secretary of State Kissinger, calling him "my friend and brother."

In his 1974-75 aid request to Congress, President Nixon asked $250 million for economic assistance to Egypt, including help in reopening the Suez Canal. Symbolic of the new relationships were visits to Cairo by West German Chancellor Willy Brandt and by President Nixon, the first visit by an American President to Egypt since World War II. In Cairo, Presidents Nixon and Sadat established far-reaching agreements on political, social, economic, and cultural exchanges. A high-level commission including the American Secretary of State and Egyptian Foreign Minister would work out arrangements to develop and to encourage American investment for Egypt in petrochemicals, transportation, food and agricultural machinery, land development, power, tourism, and "a host of other economic sectors," at an estimated value of over $2 billion. Most startling was agreement by the United States to sell nuclear reactors and fuel to Egypt for peaceful development. The Presidents' joint statement reemphasized UN Resolution 242 as a basis for "a just and desirable peace" and underscored the first official U.S. recognition of "the legitimate interest . . . of the Palestinian people" (New York *Times,* June 15, 1974). Fearing too sudden an Egyptian tilt toward the West, Yugoslavia's President Tito warned Sadat against overdependence on any Great Power.

Within Egypt, de-Nasserization was signaled by open attacks on the policies and personality of the republic's first President. The new trend was marked by dismissal of Nasser's former confidant, Mohammed Hassanein Haykal, from his post as editor of the country's leading daily, *al-Ahram,* and Haykal's replacement by Ali Amin, an editor who had been ousted by Nasser for being too pro-Western. More substantive measures included return of property formerly confiscated from "reactionary capitalists," denationalization of cinemas taken over from private owners 13 years earlier, encouragement of private investment and initiatives in construction and transportation, greater freedom for private merchants in import and export business, discussion of plans to reactivate the stock market, and promises of a "more open" society with emphasis on individual rights and free enterprise.

Emergence of Saudi Arabia as a regional power by virtue of its petroleum resources—the largest in the Middle East, with daily production approaching that of the United States—was emphasized by Sheikh Ahmed Zaki al-Yamani, Minister of Oil and Minerals. (Saudi daily production was about 8.5 million barrels in 1973-74, approaching the 9 million barrels a day in the United States.) Sheikh Yamani took the lead in both OPEC and OAPEC as spokesman for the Arab countries. At OAPEC conferences during 1974, he supported President Sadat against other producers by urging that the oil embargo against the United States be lifted. In OPEC he openly opposed the Shah of Iran's efforts to continue the upward spiral of oil prices. Saudi Arabia's new importance was dramtized by Secretary of State Kissinger's several trips there during the disengagement negotiations and by the country's inclusion in President Nixon's Middle East itinerary during June 1974.

Although Saudi Arabia forced Aramco into a new agreement in which it took over 60 percent of the company's concessions and assets at least 10 years in advance of the terms of a previous negotiation, a "milestone" pact was signed almost simultaneously with the United States during June 1974. The pact established two joint commissions on economic and military cooperation, with four joint working groups to consider plans for the country's economic growth; to develop technical and educational skills; to negotiate technological cooperation in such fields as solar energy and desalination; and to develop desert agriculture. A new military commission would assist in training programs already under way for modernization of Saudi armed forces. According to American officials, the series of agreements would serve as a model for cooperations between the United States and other Arab countries.

The agreements between the United States and Egypt and Saudi Arabia strengthened Western ties with the most politically significant and economically important Arab countries. Following Kissinger's successful efforts in negotiating a disengagement between Syria and Israel, and President Nixon's June visit to Damascus (previously known as the Hanoi of the Middle East), a new relationship was established with what had been considered the most militant Arab country. Full diplomatic relations were reestablished for the first time since 1967, and President Nixon announced that the Syrian President would soon visit the United States. The Damascus talks were also believed to have included promises to obtain American economic aid for Syria totaling some $100 million.

Defection of Syria and Egypt from the radical position of "no negotiations" with Israel, from a break-off of diplomatic relations with the United States, and toward overt discussion of a peace settlement left Iraq and Libya in isolation. Iraq continued its dependence on the Soviet Union for economic, military, and technical assistance. Surprising was the *volta face* of Libya from a policy of Islamic-motivated anti-Sovietism toward alliance with Russia. After being rebuffed by Cairo in his demand for a Libyan–Egyptian union, Libya's President Qaddafi attempted to replace Egypt as one of Russia's main allies in Arab North Africa. In summary, the disengagement negotiations, peace talks, and oil and trade agreements following the October war realigned the most important Arab states in mutually friendly relationships with the United States. The remaining radical regimes, such as Iraq, Libya, and the People's Republic of South Yemen, had neither the economic nor the military power to counterbalance this new alignment.

Throughout this era of newly developing political patterns, OAPEC had played an important role as distinct from OPEC. Within the Middle East the most significant difference between the two organizations was omission of Iran from the Arab group. OAPEC was more tightly organized, although deliberate efforts were made to avoid rivalry between the two. OAPEC's charter decrees that its policies and actions avoid conflict with OPEC, and that decisions of the larger group are binding in all members of OAPEC. According to the Saudi Oil Minister, "OPEC is the mother and our Arab Organization the child" (Mikdashi 1972, p. 105).

The Saudi government has sought to expand the functions of OAPEC to include establishment of joint business ventures and international marketing projects, including an Arab tanker fleet. Although there has been no outright clash between the two oil organizations, Iran has regarded OAPEC with natural misgivings, since it is the only major Middle East producer not included. Furthermore, OAPEC could become the basis for a unified economic policy that would challenge the Shah's pretensions to dominate "his lake." Potential rivalries between Iran and Saudi Arabia are probably inevitable as the Arab kingdom seeks to use its oil revenues to catch up to Iran in modernization, development of industry, and acquisition of sophisticated military technology.

If the conservative Arab regimes on the Persian Gulf continue to coordinate their oil policies, they could become a countervailing force to the economic pressures being exerted by the Shah on world markets. On the other hand, the Shah's political independence and his refusal to become embroiled in the Arab-Israel dispute will be a counter pressure in the event OAPEC again considers using the oil weapon against the West. In the meantime Saudi Arabia and Iran, each with its own aspirations to dominate the Gulf, have worked out a modus vivendi that maintains the conservative status quo. With political backing of Egypt and the neutralization of Syria, a new Muslim tripartite bloc may be emerging in the Middle East.

6

THE ENERGY CRISIS AND U.S. POLICY IN THE MIDDLE EAST
John C. Campbell

The Middle East war speeded up the tempo of all the predictions on the energy crisis that were being made before it erupted. We were then talking about the gradual squeeze in which the United States would find itself as the 1970s went on: Arab oil countries might slow down the rate of increase in their production as our own domestic production declined and the demand curve went up by 4 or 5 percent each year. We knew we would have some short-age of fuel oil in the coming winter, but that was because of our own inadequate refinery capacity, not an expected sharp drop in the availability of crude oil. For crude we counted on filling the gap with imports: from Venezuela, from Canada, and increasingly from the Persian Gulf. Central to the future supply for Europe and Japan, as well as for the United States, was increased production from Saudi Arabia.

King Faisal, since April of 1973, had been making remarks to the effect that maybe oil and politics did mix after all—a reversal of his former position—and that his American friends should realize that he could not ignore the total American partiality for Israel against the Arabs. But the question as we saw it was whether, instead of expanding Saudi production to an eventual 20 million barrels per day, he might stop at 15 million, or maybe 12 or even 10. Then, when war came, we had to face the fact that after the Arab governments' deci-sions of October 17, 1973, the Saudi level dropped from 8 to 6 million barrels per day in a couple of months, comparable declines took place in other Arab states, and the United States was cut off entirely by a special embargo. That embargo was later lifted, and the policy of production cuts was not carried to its logical mathematical conclusions; but the producing countries have demon-strated very clearly that they can use their control of production to punish or reward as political reasons impel them.

The Arab states have shown, moreover, a remarkable solidarity that history had not led us to expect. Some of them learned from their experience in OPEC negotiations with the international oil companies how high were the financial rewards of sticking together. They had only to apply the same bargaining power to political ends. The "oil weapon" has proved its potency and its usefulness in spite of some nonparticipation on the Arab Side (notably Iraq), the difficulty of controlling the destination of oil shipments, and the fact that the squeeze hurt the Europeans and the Japanese, who are relatively more favorable to the Arab cause, more than it did the Americans, who have more oil of their own.

The President's message of November 7, 1973, described some of the ways of providing alternative sources of energy. But these measures take time to produce results; and even if all are adopted and pushed vigorously, we know we will still need Arab oil over the next 10 years. Whether we get it or do not get it makes a tremendous difference and highlights the great importance of future American policy toward the Middle East.

The fourth round of Arab-Israeli war is now history. Violently fought with many of the latest and most sophisticated weapons, it ended with the two sides facing each other across cease-fire lines not so distant from the old lines, though it was significant that these were not the same positions as before. The two main protagonists, Israel and Egypt, with a substantial assist from the whirlwind diplomacy of Henry Kissinger, have agreed on a relocation and separation of forces along lines drawn east of the Suez Canal, which is now in Egyptian control and can be repaired and reopened to traffic. Israel and Syria, in a more difficult negotiation that also required American mediation to succeed, reached a similar agreement in June 1974. If American diplomacy can go on from there to help achieve the miracle of a political settlement, the parties and the world will have reason to be grateful.

The Middle East has had its miracles in the past, although most of them happened some 2,000 years ago. The history of the past 25 years counsels skepticism. Even if a political settlement may be attainable between Israel and Egypt, the other borders of Israel may remain in dispute; and the question of the future of the Arabs of Palestine will not yield easily even to the most brilliant diplomatic efforts. And Egypt cannot afford to become isolated from the rest of the Arab world by going too far ahead in dealing with Israel.

Should we conclude, then, that the war of October 1973 brought no great change? On the contrary, it has had the most significant consequences and contains some remarkable lessons.

LESSONS OF THE OCTOBER WAR

Arab Victory

First, the Arabs won the war. Perhaps that conclusion needs some explanation. They wound up losing more territory. They did not defeat Israel's armed forces. If there had been no cease-fire, the Israelis probably would have gone on to inflict a crushing defeat on the Egyptians. But the salient fact, from the political point of view, is that the Arabs took the decision to fight in order to break the stalemate; they fought and fought rather well; they seized and held territory; they showed that they could handle modern weapons, taking a heavy toll of Israeli lives and equipment; and they did in fact break the stalemate, forcing the outside world to take new positions and new initiatives. Furthermore, compared with the war of 1967, the circle of Arab participants had widened: Iraq, Kuwait, Saudi Arabia, Libya, Algeria, and Morocco joined in with men, planes, money, or oil measures.

The psychological effects for the Arabs were electric. Sadat became a hero; he had accomplished what Nasser could not. No matter how close they came at the end to another resounding defeat, the Egyptians and other Arabs were bound to see the prospect of an eventual victory—if not next time or the next, then the next one after that. They will conclude that what they have always said about numbers and persistence telling in the end has been proved by what happened in October. For better or worse, for peace or more war, the Arabs have gained a confidence they did not have before.

Israeli Invincibility

Second, for the Israelis the myth of their invincibility and the wisdom of their strategy were shaken, if not shattered. They had counted on their ability to go on defeating the Arabs in short, sharp, and not very costly actions whenever the latter might choose the test of battle. When this did not happen, critics appeared to question the conduct of their leadership; and the leaders themselves had to reflect on the price of overconfidence. Would they go further, to rethink their standard assumptions about the country's position and its policies? Such rethinking was not often perceptible in the early postwar pronouncements of the government, and still less in those of most of its critics within Israel. The gains made by the right-wing Likud in the election of

December 1973 seemed to show a popular current of discontent with the Meir-Dayan policies as not being firm enough. That critique was directed chiefly at Israel's lack of preparedness for the Arab attack and at the way the war was waged. The emphasis was on carrying on the old policies, only more effectively, with more determination and vigor: there must be more arms from the United States, but also a bigger arms industry at home and greater independence of decision; continued possession of the strategic territory needed for security, more Israeli settlements there, and no political concessions to the Arabs living there; total preparation for war when it comes again; and a clear superiority over the Arab states in effective military power. But a policy of inflexibility was not possible unless Israel was willing to risk the loss of American support. The new Rabin government, which took office in early 1974, made the concessions necessary to reach the agreement with Syria on a cease-fire and separation of forces, but had anything but a free hand to go further.

Many Israelis will be asking themselves whether existing policies will hold for the indefinite future. Can this community of 2.5 million Jews keep itself armed to the teeth, spending so mucy of its substance on defense, mobilizing its peoples whenever the Arabs take a threatening posture? Perhaps more important, can it afford to ignore and defy the views of the world on the issue of the retention of conquered territories, counting on the United States as the only ally it needs? The next question is whether it can count totally and indefinitely on the United States, which may assert other interests of its own. It was, significantly, an American as well as a Soviet decision to bring about a cease-fire at a time when Israel had not yet won the war militarily.

For the Israelis the question of security and how to get it is one of survival. As they debate it in the heat of their internal political struggles, they will have to face questions more difficult to answer than in the confident atmosphere of 1967-73. Can they wait confidently for the Arabs eventually to make peace on Israel's terms, or must they think about making concessions for peace now? Will they look more seriously at proposals for demilitarization of border areas, UN peacekeeping forces, and international guarantees, which up to now they have tended to shrug off as useless? Can they continue to put off the question of the status of the Arabs in the West Bank and the Gaza Strip? The few leaders like Ariyeh Eliav, who had urged such rethinking before the October war, might find a more sympathetic hearing.

The Soviet-American Relationship

Third, we have had a testing of the Soviet-American relationship. Frankly, it was a frightening experiment. The two powers did not act promptly to restrain or stop the belligerents. They got involved with massive arms aid. At one moment they came, or appeared to come, to the brink of war.

Just what happened on the Soviet side is open to a variety of interpretations. One is that the detente in fact proved itself. Official Soviet statements have said that without detente, it could have come to war. According to this theory, the Soviets showed that they put the connection with the United States above the policy of all-out support of the Arabs to make strategic gains for themselves. They chose to argue Sadat into accepting a cease-fire, and they worked with the United States to get it adopted by the United Nations on October 22.

But there is another interpretation: that detente did not really work in the Middle East at all, and nearly failed in its most elementary and limited aim, the avoidance of nuclear war. According to this view, the Soviets probably knew that the Arab attack was coming, did nothing to stop it, and initially gave the Arabs heavy arms support. Only when it became clear that Israel had gained the upper hand did they push for a cease-fire. And then, when things became more difficult for Egypt, they were ready to risk sending Soviet troops to the Middle East, and were only dissuaded when the United States reacted strongly to warn them off..

Many of the points of this latter interpretation are well taken—although the question of the U.S. worldwide alert on October 25 is still wrapped in some mystery and much controversy—but there is also much to be said for the proposition that the top Soviet priority before, during, and after the Middle East war was to keep a constructive relationship with the United States in bilateral ties, in Europe, and to some degree elsewhere. For that reason they did not want to take great risks in the Middle East that might destroy the relationship; and while they were ready to squeeze what they could out of the unexpected Arab success, they wanted no part of a military confrontation or showdown. There may have been some differences in the Soviet leadership on how to handle the crisis, but the Brezhnev seal was definitely on the agreement with Kissinger for cease-fire and negotiated settlement. The question of who was bluffing whom in the exchanges of October 25 is not easily clarified. Brezhnev was under great pressure to enforce the cease-fire, for the Soviet position with the Arabs was at stake; but we may be allowed to doubt his intention to send masses of troops to Egypt to engage in war with the Israelis and probably the Americans.

Do the Soviets really want a settlement? That is an old question, to which we may perhaps give a new answer, though hardly a definitive one. After this last round of war, they seem to feel that movement toward a settlement is better for them than the risks of failure to move at all. But it must be a settlement that will keep their position with the Arabs strong. Hence the repeated insistence on Israel's evacuation of occupied Arab territories. And they do not want to see the conflict ended solely through the diplomacy of the United States, although they refrained from sabotaging Henry Kissinger's efforts to bring Egypt and Israel together in an agreement on disengagement of forces and also joined the United States in sponsoring the peace talks at Geneva. They did not go all-out to block the Israeli-Syrian agreement, but they did not help either. The main purpose of Andrei Gromyko's visits to Damascus and talks with Kissinger appeared to be to involve the Soviets shomehow, in order to protect their own interests and to make good their claim to a Great Power role in the region.

Effectiveness of the Oil Weapon

The fourth lesson of recent events is that we have seen the oil weapon used effectively. We have also seen the reaction of Europe and of Japan. The nine members of the European Economic Community, on November 6, 1973, adopted a resolution in which they said that a peace agreement should be brought about between the Arab states and Israel in accordance with UN resolutions and that it should include a number of points, among them the necessity of putting an end to Israel's occupation of territories held since 1967, and recognition that a just and lasting peace would have to take account of the legitimate rights of the Palestinian Arabs. It so happened that the phrasing of those two points went beyond UN Resolution 242 and coincided with specific interpretations and demands made by the Arabs and rejected by Israel.

Japan has issued no formal statement of this kind, but official Japanese spokesmen have made it clear that the Japanese are leaning to the Arab side in their interpretation of Resolution 242, and they are in fact making all kinds of diplomatic efforts to show the Arabs that Japan is sympathetic to them.

Were these moves simply appeasement or giving in to Arab blackmail? Such charges have been made in the United States and in Europe. Or are the Europeans and Japanese so vulnerable with respect to oil that they have no real alternative to giving in to Arab political demands, in the hope of avoiding a cut-off or reduction of vital fuel supply? Let us note, incidentally, that they did not save themselves from the effects of the announced cuts in Arab production, and of the deeper cut that by December 1973 reached 25 percent of the September level. The Arabs seemed to believe that by penalizing the Europeans and Japanese, they could force them to put pressure on America to put pressure on Israel. If this was the purpose, it did not achieve that result, although it certainly succeeded in stimulating differences between the United States and its allies. The Arab oil-producing states later reduced the production cuts and stated their desire to favor countries sympathetic to their cause; but the overall decline in the availability of Arab oil, along with the sharp rise in prices, continued to hurt both Europe and Japan.

The way in which the Middle East crisis rent the Western alliance provided a series of lessons that Europeans and Americans have only begun to absorb. The former were shocked by Washington's apparent disregard of their interests and failure to consult on moves taken in a moment of crisis that President Nixon later described as the most difficult for world peace since the affair of the Soviet missiles in Cuba in 1962. Americans, however, felt deserted in time of need and resentful that European countries not only failed to help in a contest with the Soviet Union but denied facilities useful for the American effort to supply arms to Israel and thus counterbalance massive Soviet shipments to the Arab states.

Actually, the differences on Middle East questions had existed long before October 1973. The sudden revelation of the much greater vulnerability of Europe to the shortage of oil deliberately created by the Arabs brought them clearly to the fore. The Europeans hoped they could insulate themselves from the Arab-Israel conflict by taking a symbolic pro-Arab position, and they did not see the alliance relationship as obliging them to support what the United States was doing. The United States, as Secretary Kissinger said publicly, saw it quite differently.

CONTINUITY AND CHANGE IN U.S. POLICY

The United States made it quite clear that its foreign policy would not be changed because of pressure from Arab countries exploiting their monopolistic position on oil. Nevertheless, there was no longer any doubt that the energy crisis was taken seriously in Washington and that it was not unrelated to relations with the Arab states. The chosen strategy was to convince the moderate Arab governments—and this was the burden of Kissinger's discussions with Egyptian and Saudi Arabian leaders in the weeks following the war—that the United States is not committed to 100 percent support of Israel.

The spectacular exercise in diplomacy by which the American Secretary of State brought Egypt and Israel, and then Syria and Israel, together on practical terms for observance of the cease-fire and on a relocation and separation of forces was in one sense a personal tour de force by Dr. Kissinger; in another, it was the application in new circumstances of a long-established American policy. His predecessor, William Rogers, had attempted to promote just such an "interim settlement" in the Suez-Sinai area, and so had others before him. The obstacles—some inherent in the conflict and the attitudes of the antagonists, some in the varying strands of American policy itself—were too great to be overcome. Then the war brought changes in the outlook of both sides and, significantly, in the influence of the United States.

The effectiveness of a mediator is not necessarily determined by his total neutrality and disinterestedness. Ambassador Gunnar Jarring had both qualities, but could not bring the parties together. The United States could be effective because it *was* interested, and because it had some clout with both sides. The genius of America's handling of the war crisis lay in a paradox: massive support of Israel to enable it to keep fighting, and, by the insistence on a cease-fire before either side had won a decisive victory, creation of a situation in which it was possible to promote talks leading to disengagement on the Israeli-Egyptian front and to negotiations for peace. The United States thus demonstrated to Israel that it was committed to that nation's existence, and to the Arabs that it was not committed to an Israeli victory comparable with that of 1967. The key was the demonstration that the lines would be kept open between Cairo and the Egyptian Third Army on the east bank of the Suez Canal. It was not Moscow's declarations, but Washington's pressure on Israel, that saved that Egyptian army from isolation and destruction. Consequently, Kissinger had the chance to establish a position of confidence with Sadat that made possible his mediatory role. In these circumstances he could accomplish what Rogers could not: an agreement encompassing Israeli withdrawal to the passes in Sinai east of the Suez Canal. He was able to do it without promising Sadat eventual support for regaining all of Sinai and without assuring Israel that it was this far and no farther. Similarly, in the Israeli-Syrian agreement, the return of Kuneitra was essential to the conclusion of an accord; but the parties held to their established positions so far as the main Golan Heights area was concerned. Those questions were left for discussion at Geneva, where each side would be called upon to carry the negotiation to the next stage.

The United States and Israel

Where does the United States go from here? First of all, the obvious course is to push for political settlements, with the momentum of the agreements already attained. But in this endeavor there should be no false optimism. Can we expect the Israeli government to accept a withdrawal from most or all of the occupied Arab territory? For those Israelis who can countenance the idea at all, it depends on how far they are expected to pull back and on what the terms and compensations may be. The question, unfortunately, may be dedetermined by the vagaries of domestic Israeli politics; and the gains of Likud, plus the differences within the ruling Labor "alignment" and its need to bargain with smaller parties for votes in the Knesset, raise many doubts. To negotiate on matters vital to the nation's future requires strong leadership with wide public support, which is not in evidence. But the process of negotiation and accommodation has to start, and America's relationship to Israel is crucial.

From the time of Israel's birth the United States had an obligation, unspecified in any formal document, not to permit its independence to be destroyed. Israel has realized the importance of American support but inevitably has had questions about what it meant in practice as the nation faced the task of protecting its own security in the day-to-day, year-to-year struggle with the Arabs. Specifically, the Israeli leaders were more interested in American arms and in secure borders, strongly held by their own forces, than in treaty guarantees. After they gave up Sinai and the Gaza Strip under pressure from Washington in 1956-57, in return for American pledges on the maintenance of freedom of navigation through the Strait of Tiran, they found those pledges not worth very much 10 years later when Nasser declared his blockade. This lesson, which the Israelis never forgot, had a great deal to do with their intransigence in holding the territory they conquered in 1967.

Finally, there has been a fundamental difference of interest and approach between Israel and the United States. The former quite naturally looks at everything that happens in the region through the prism of its own fears and hopes for continued security, seeking the best possible position in terms both of the local military balance and of the international diplomatic alignment. The United States has global interests involving other powers as well as specific interests in the Arab world that run counter to its interest in Israel. Through the years the U.S. policy of simultaneously pursuing the security of Israel and an Arab-Israel settlement went its ambiguous way without gaining either end—indeed, it could not do so, given the prevailing dispositions in Jerusalem, in the Arab capitals, and in Washington itself. The October war, in its revelation of vulnerabilities on all sides, brought about some change in those respective dispositions and, accordingly, new prospects in the relations of the United States and Israel.

Yet if the atmosphere is new, the elements of the problem are familiar. It may come down to the question of pressure and guarantees: U.S. pressure to induce Israel to give up all or most of the occupied territories in order to reach a settlement, and U.S. guarantees to provide in different form the security thereby lost. Israelis may be skeptical of what a paper guarantee may be worth if the Arabs attack by surprise, as they did in October 1973, but this time from within close range of Israel's centers of population. Yet skepticism about the old policies, which plainly did not guarantee security, is also growing. Hence American pressure for a negotiated settlement with the Arabs may not meet total opposition in Israel. There are dangers in whichever course is taken and, if the choice is for settlement, at least a hope that they will not be permanent. America cannot intervene in internal Israeli politics; but its policies on arms aid, guarantees, and other matters will be taken into account. Of course, American pressure might undermine a Labor government, especially if its supporters or partners were inclined to break ranks. But adoption of a hard-line policy, whether the ruling party is Labor or Likud, would have no substance without American material support. What it might do is transfer the controversy to the internal politics of the United States.

The United States and the Soviet Union

A second essential task for American diplomacy is to strengthen and build on the Soviet interest in a settlement. It is a task that presupposes, of course—and the supposition must be constantly tested—that such an interest exists. The Soviet Union profited from the existence of the dispute in the past. Indeed, that was its admission card to the club of Middle East powers. It still is wholly on the Arab side and has no diplomatic relations with Israel. Soviet propaganda has for years condemned Israel as an aggressor, even in the October war, which, no matter who fired first, is pictured as the natural consequence of Israel's aggression and conquests of 1967. For better or worse, the Soviets see their whole position in the Middle East as dependent on maintaining close ties with the Arab states, unreliable as they may be. They are not going to push for a settlement that will require them to force terms on their Arab friends or lose the influence and prestige they now have. But they can see, as we can, the instability of the present cease-fire arrangements, the inevitability of another round of war if nothing further is done, the risks of a continued unlimited arms race in more and newer weapons, possibly even nuclear weapons, and the more dangerous involvement of both the USSR and the United States.

Brezhnev seems to have agreed with Kissinger, as the UN Resolution of October 22 says, on moving together for a settlement based on Resolution 242 "in all of its parts." The United States cannot do it alone. We may be tempted to try, since at this stage the United States is the only possible middleman, and Kissinger's success thus far is rather heady wine. Yet the interim agreements on the separation of forces and acceptance of buffer zones are only the prelude to the far more complex and difficult negotiations on peace terms. If Egypt and Saudi Arabia, the two pivotal Arab states, can be persuaded to work with the United States toward peace with Israel, well and good. But one should not underestimate the strain that such a course will put on their relations with other Arab states and political movements, especially if the Soviet Union chooses to play on those strains to its own advantage. In the last analysis the Soviets can probably veto a settlement if they are left out. We have to test them by trying to work with them. If detente can be extended to the Middle East—and it has not been, except in the most primitive sense—that may help to save and strengthen it elsewhere. If it cannot, the chances of an Arab-Israeli settlement will surely be much reduced.

THE UNCERTAIN FUTURE

More hopeful as the prospects may be as a result of the fourth round of war, the world must be as prepared for failure as for success. How can the United States deal with a situation of prolonged nonsettlement? Can we meet it in the fashion of the period 1967-73, arming Israel to keep the balance and waiting for the parties to negotiate? The answer is "no," because there is no stable balance in the present situation on the ground, although the disengagement agreements have reduced the immediate dangers, nor in an arms race with both sides piling up tanks and planes and missiles, and perhaps atomic bombs. We saw how great quantities of weapons and equipment were consumed in the two weeks of fighting. That means that in the future both sides will try to pile up bigger stocks than ever, to be able to cope with surprise attack.

The interval before another round of war, moreover, may be shorter than the last time. President Sadat has taken risks in agreeing to the new cease-fire and disengagement lines east of the Suez Canal without getting a commitment from Israel, or from the United States, that the Israelis will later withdraw to the old Palestinian-Egyptian frontier. If time passes without progress at Geneva or elsewhere, Sadat will be under increasing pressure to try another tack: to reduce his reliance on American diplomacy, to play the Soviet card, or to resort once more to the test of war.

For the United States it is no longer possible to have two separate policies for the Arab-Israel area and the Persian Gulf area, keeping the balance in the first, through arms aid to Israel, while also arming and maintaining the best of relations with the oil-producing Arab states in the Gulf. When King Faisal decided in the spring of 1973 to relate the rise in Saudi oil production desired by the Americans to America's consideration for Arab interests in the conflict with Israel, and to use oil money to help Egypt pay for Soviet arms, the effect was to merge the two areas into one. The King's decision signaled a fundamental change in the situation. For twenty-five years the rulers of Saudi Arabia, however much they resented America's support of Israel, had maintained friendly and cooperative relations with the United States and with the Arabian-American Oil Company (Aramco), which produced and exported oil at the rate deemed best for its business interests while the Saudi government took its agreed share of the profits. The Israeli occupation in 1967 of East Jerusalem and its Muslim holy places, about which Faisal had strong feelings, put a strain on Saudi-American relations. What really changed matters was the combination of increased Saudi wealth and confidence, following a series of successful negotiations with the international oil companies that resulted in higher income and participation in Aramco, a more active Saudi role in inter-Arab affairs, and the desire of Aramco for a rapid expansion of production that Saudi Arabia itself did not need.

The King appeared to have at his disposal a means of greater influence on American policy than any Arab state had previously possessed. He did not use the oil weapon before the October war, waiting to see whether his American friends would get the message. When the war came, and with it large-scale U.S. aid to Israel, he hesitated no longer and cut off all oil deliveries to the United States, as did the other Arab producing countries. President Nixon and Secretary Kissinger have made clear that this country's foreign policy would respond to its own interests and not bend to economic pressure from outside. But the central point of the Saudi message got through. The United States was on notice that the supply of Arab oil badly needed in the industrial nations, and increasingly in the United States itself, was not unrelated to the two main Arab claims against Israel: withdrawal from the territories occupied in 1967 and a just settlement for the Arabs of Palestine.

Does Iran, a non-Arab state and the Persian Gulf's second largest producer, provide an alternative to Saudi Arabia and the possible freedom from dependence on Arab oil? The Shah has followed a policy of pushing up Iran's production, with the purpose of getting the highest possible income in order to develop the country, although if he can get increased prices for producing less, he may well do so. At best, Iranian production will level off at 8 or 9 million barrels per day; and although that oil would meet a large part of our import needs, the United States would have no exclusive claim on it. If U.S. Arab relations deteriorated to zero, Iran's oil would indeed be a lifesaver; but Iran has no interest in being drawn into a position more antagonistic to Arab states than it already is in by virtue of the natural rivalries of the Gulf region, and America is right in following its present course of maintaining good relations with both Saudi Arabia and Iran and trying to encourage friendship and collaboration between them. The idea, which makes its appearance from time to time, that the United States can protect its Middle East interests by relying on Israel and Iran, letting the Arabs stew in their own oil, rests on false assumptions about Middle East oil and Middle East politics.

Its own interests in the Arab world and concern for those of its allies in Europe and the Far East counsel the United States to avoid the position of isolation, alone with Israel, in which it has increasingly found itself in recent years. The question is whether it can find its way to that often-talked-about even-handed position in which it can retain ties and influence with the Arabs—or rather, with enough key Arab leaders and governments—without abandoning Israel. Henry Kissinger, like his predecessors, has been in search of that position; and his experience in the months following the October war has provided some ground for optimism.

Over the longer run there are two essential conditions to be met. One—

and this requires an assist from the Russians—is to disentangle the Arab-Israel question from the military balance between the superpowers, so that it can find its level as essentially a local dispute. Second, the policy of support that American administrations have given to Israel—which has been virtually automatic, whether for reasons of public opinion or Congressional politics or admiration or attachment to an idea—has to become more discriminating, for there are important considerations on the other side. To be more specific, while the United States should continue to support Israel's secure existence and be prepared to guarantee it through a binding bilateral treaty, that does not mean it should uncritically accept Israel's definitions of the requirements of its own security, any more than it should accept the Arabs' definition of their inalienable rights. The guarantee would not be forthcoming, of course, until the parties agreed on a territorial settlement.

The United States has to have the flexibility of a non-polarized position. Both Israel and Russia, each for its own good reasons, have been for polarization in the Middle East. There is a school of thought in this country that is for it also, believing the Arabs and Russians are working together against us and that only full American support to Israel can hold them off. The theory ignores differences between the Arabs and the Soviet Union and among the Arabs themselves, and, by assuming their solidarity in anti-Americanism, tends to create and reinforce it.

Even if the two conditions mentioned above are met, there is still the basic question of how much anything the United States can legitimately do in its relationship with Israel—and here crude pressures and any change in the commitment to Israel's survival are excluded—will affect the policies of the Arab states, particularly those whose oil is needed here and especially in Europe and Japan. Will appeasement work? Will the Arabs simply gobble up any concessions made and demand more, counting on their oil power to see them through?

Israelis, remembering many extreme threats from Arab leaders and fearful for their survival as an independent nation, ask questions about Arab aims. If the Arab states regain the borders of 1967, will they then press for the borders of 1947, those that were drawn by the UN resolution in November of that year but never came into existence because of the subsequent war? Will the ultimate demand be for an end to the state of Israel, which is a declared goal of the Palestinian resistance groups? Those are questions that governments urging Israel to go back to the 1967 lines must also ask themselves. Yet responsible Arab leaders have stated that if and when they get back the territories lost in 1967, they will recognize and coexist with Israel. Those statements have to be tested in practice, not rejected out of hand as calculated or unconscious deception. After the negotiation of borders, which might include certain modifications of the 1967 lines in such places as Jerusalem, the Israel-Jordan border, or the Golan Heights, both Israel and the Arab states would have treaty obligations to respect them; and outside powers, including the United States and the Soviet Union, would have treaty commitments to prevent their violation. Israel, before signing peace settlements, has a good case to insist on such commitments and on assurances, particularly from the United States, on precisely how they would be fulfilled in case of war.

Similarly with the question of the oft-mentioned "legitimate" rights of the Palestine Arabs, how far do their rights go? This could be an open door to impossible demands and renewed war. The demand of resistance groups for a new secular state comprising all of Palestine can be dismissed. It would mean the liquidation of Israel, which would resist by force. But the right of the Arabs of the West Bank and of Gaza to be free of Israeli occupation and domination, and the need to reach some acceptable compromise on Jerusalem, are a different matter. How the Palestinian Arabs are to exercise self-determination is a complex question. But they cannot be denied it merely on the grounds that they might want more. Again, Israel would be entitled to the most effective guarantees.

It may be assumed that the oil weapon, having proved its worth, will be used, or held in readiness for use, as long as significant negotiations are in progress or in prospect. Even if the present objectives are limited to Israeli withdrawal from the occupied territories and self-government in some form for the Palestinians in Gaza and the West Bank, it may be a long time before those ends can be attained. But this is not a matter in which all the pressure is on one side. For the oil-producing countries there is a point at which the loss of revenues will cut into national development programs. It is perhaps unlucky for the consumers that the countries that will reach that point first or are already there—Iraq, for example, did not cut production or curtail exports to Europe and Japan after October 1973—are not now among the big producers, and that Saudi Arabia, the biggest producer, has more modest needs and large cash reserves. Even without the Israel question Saudi Arabia will have economic reasons for not producing as much oil as the consuming countries will want. Those Arab countries with small populations and plenty of money are interested in the conservation and appreciation of their oil in the ground. For them playing politics with oil is relatively painless. Even they, however, wish to develop their economies rapidly and to make their weight felt beyond their own frontiers, and for both purposes large oil revenues will be needed.

Other factors also should induce some restraint. One is the danger of overplaying the hand. King Faisal and the other Gulf rulers do not want a total break with the United States and the West. They do not want to provoke an economic war to the death or possible military moves if the situation gets desperate enough. They do not want to have to turn to the Soviet Union. Another unknown factor is whether the solidarity of the Arab states on oil will persist indefinitely, as each government is faced with different pressures and different opportunities, and as rivalries for leadership and disputes over policy on Palestine and other questions inevitably arise. The conservative rulers of the Gulf states are also concerned with the security of their dynasties and their political regimes. They fear revolutionary currents, of both the Arab and the Soviet variety. They can hardly be comfortable in a situation in which their countries become the center of tremendous international pressures and contentions, which in turn will stimulate internal unrest.

The other side of the coin is what the United States and other consuming countries can do to protect their own interests. Consumer solidarity should be useful in meeting shortages and in bargaining with the producing countries, but the simple idea of a consumers' cartel to counteract the producers' cartel is no real answer to the problem when the bargaining power is so heavily on the latter's side. More positively, they should look to what they can do to cooperate in the economic and social development in individual oil-producing states and in the Arab world as a whole—not just to provide swimming pools and Cadillacs for sheikhs in Saudi Arabia or Abu Dhabi, but food and jobs and education in Egypt, which despite the greater wealth of others, is still in most respects the key country in the Arab world. Since the Arab world has shown an unexpected unity, even if in opposition to the West, it may be in the West's interest to accept and cultivate that unity in offers and acts of economic and cultural collaboration, rather than to try to weaken it and play upon the Arabs' divisions. If Arab unity is a myth, let the Arabs themselves expose and destroy it.

Most important of all, to help meet pressing needs and to get out from under the dangers of dependence on the decisions of a few rulers, this country and others have to discover, explore, and exploit other sources of energy, as they are now setting out to do. This is the most promising way to acquire bargaining power on matters of supply and price. The United States will not have real leverage for some years, because it has started so late; and Western Europe and Japan are in a much less favorable position. But the fact of seriously setting out on that course could itself have an effect on the calculations and the conduct of the oil-producing states in the Middle East.

We will never get back to the old days of free-wheeling foreign-owned oil concessions in the Middle East and plenty of cheap oil. We may in time, if the right decisions are taken, reach a situation where we are getting expensive oil and other expensive forms of energy from a number of sources, including the Middle East and perhaps the Soviet Union, without the vulnerability to critical shortages we will be experiencing in the next few years. But the Middle Eastern part of that more optimistic outlook still rests on an assumption: that somehow the world and the peoples of the Middle East will be relieved of the awful burden of the Arab-Israel conflict in its present destructive form.

THE POLITICAL-
MILITARY BALANCE IN
THE PERSIAN GULF REGION

Alvin J. Cottrell

Ever since the Labor Government led by Harold Wilson announced, in January 1968, that it would withdraw all British forces east of Suez by the end of 1971, there has been much speculation about the future security and stability of the Indian Ocean in general and the Persian Gulf in particular. This speculation has stemmed from the fact that Britain had dominated the Indian Ocean and the route to India for over 150 years. This paramountcy was achieved largely with maritime forces and was done at a time when no other nation's navy could rival that of England. Interest and concern about this area has sharpened precipitately following the October 1973 Arab-Israeli war, when U.S. oil interests in the Persian Gulf were threatened immediately by what could have been critical damage had the embargo not been lifted. The danger of the reapplication of the embargo or slowdown in production still remains.

The number of British forces from all services present in the area from Aden to Singapore in 1968, at the time of the Wilson government's decision to withdraw, was 130,000—21,500 in Aden, 8,400 in the Persian Gulf, and the remainder in the region east of the Gulf (Martin 1972). Thus Britain's hegemony in the Persian Gulf rested no so much on the size of the British forces—which, incidentally, were not much larger than the present United Arab Emirates Defense Force (Abu Dhabi)—but on their symbolic significance as the projection of British power in a region where no other Great Power was located. It is important to note that of the three great oceans of the world—the Pacific, the Atlantic, and the Indian—the Indian is the smallest (17 million square miles when measured to 45 degrees south latitude) and, unlike the other two, is the only one where no Great Power is a littoral state. Hence it is inevitable that

Britain's withdrawal would lead to efforts of both local and external origin to fill the vacuum. Such developments have been under way from the moment the British announced the intention to withdraw their military presence in January 1968.

THE SOVIET AND AMERICAN PRESENCES

The first evidence of efforts to fill the vacuum was the Soviet Union's deployment of a naval force in the Indian Ocean on a 25,000-mile round trip from Vladivostok in March 1968. This force "showed the Soviet flag" in southern Asia, the Persian Gulf, and in the area of the Gulf of Aden (for instance, in the Somali port of Berbera, which has since become one of the principal Soviet ports of call in the northwestern Indian Ocean). Since that time, the Soviet naval presence has been concentrated primarily in that part of the Indian Ocean. The Soviet naval force has been maintained there at a consistently high level of approximately 3 to 10 combatants since 1968. The total of Soviet vessels, including at least 9 combat ships, reached approximately 20 ships during the Arab-Israeli October war, and has increased since then. Because of their enormous naval building program, the Soviets were able to deploy a force of this size, as well as about 95 ships in the Mediterranean simultaneously.

There should no longer be any doubt that the Soviets are very serious about their naval presence, and hence are exerting their influence on the balance of power throughout the Persian Gulf-Gulf of Aden-Arabian Sea region. Many commentators have tended to play down the Soviet Union's obvious· intent to fill the vacuum Britain left in this region; many attempted in the same way to discount Soviet efforts to replace the Sixth Fleet's hegemony in the Mediterranean when Soviet ship-days rose sharply there in 1964. All doubt should surely have been removed when the Soviet naval deployment outnumbered that of the United States during the Arab-Israeli war of 1967. Any suggestion that the Soviets did not mean business was shattered by their naval deployment in the October 1973 war, which surpassed the United States, if not in firepower, then certainly in the modernity and number of vessels deployed—98-70.

There is much skepticism in some quarters as to the political value of naval power in general and Soviet naval power in the Indian Ocean in particular; but there can be little doubt that there is much concern with the Soviet naval presence among such littoral states as Saudi Arabia, Oman, the Union of Arab Emirates, Bahrain, Qatar, Kuwait, Iran, and Pakistan. These countries fear that the Soviets will emerge as the dominant naval power in the area and that they encourage, merely by their presence, forces seeking to overthrow the current traditional regimes in the Gulf or that they would support local states or elements hostile to them should conflict ensue. This is why most states in the northwestern Indian Ocean, the sole large exceptions being India and Ceylon, privately prefer a U.S. naval presence in the Indian Ocean, if not in the Persian Gulf itself. Many would feel a necessity to accommodate the Soviet Union in local disputes if the Soviet presence were not countered by a U.S. one.

The U.S. naval force in the Indian Ocean has been limited to two destroyers and a command ship "home-ported" on the island sheikhdom of Bahrain in the Persian Gulf. This force was established in 1949, just after the British had moved their political headquarters from Bushire in Iran to Bahrain. The force, until the British withdrawal in November 1971, existed under arrangement made with the United Kingdom, which controlled the external and defense policy of Bahrain as well as the other Gulf sheikhdoms. The force was a rather antiquated one, which consisted usually of two rather old destroyers (25-year vintage) and an 1,800-ton converted seaplane tender that served the Admiral Commanding Middle East Force as his command ship.

Following the British departure, the United States negotiated a separate leasing arrangement with Sheikh Isa, the ruler of Bahrain, under which the United States took over approximately one-third of Britain's facilities at Jufair to support the continuance of Middle East force "home-porting" arrangements on the island. Many warned that the agreement was unwise because the United States would never have the wide acceptance the British had achieved over a century and a half. Indeed, the Shah of Iran publicly took a position against it (Cottrell 1971). In fact, however, most of the sheikhs, including the ruler of Bahrain, wanted U.S. forces to remain in the area, although their fear of radical Arab States and subversive elements made them understandably reluctant to be publicly vocal in their support of the U.S. decision to stay.

The United States has also, since the energy crisis began, begun to develop, in cooperation with the British, what has been termed a modest communications facility at Diego Garcia. Agreement was reached on establishing such a facility in 1965, but it was not until 1972 that Congress passed an appropriations bill allotting $20 million to its development. Diego Garcia is located 1,200 miles slightly southwest of the tip of the Indian subcontinent in the Chagos Archipelago, which forms a part of the Indian Ocean territory. It is 2,000 miles from the entrance to the Strait of Hormuz. The $20 million appropriation is far from adequate to make this anything but what has been described—a modest communications facility—because storage for fuel tanks, ammunition, and other requirements for maintaining a naval presence in the Indian Ocean would be needed to make it worthwhile as a facility to support a naval presence in the Indian Ocean. An airstrip of about 10,000 feet would be an additional requirement for its use as a maritime-air facility. A further $29 million has been requested for that purpose. But even if the money is made

available by Congress—and an opposition to it is developing, on the grounds
that the United States is provoking a naval armaments race in the area—it still
is a good distance from the Persian Gulf. Thus it is conceivable that even with
Diego Garcia, the United States would still require some littoral facility much
closer to the Persian Gulf.

What the development of Diego Garcia as a naval base will permit the
United States to do, however, is to maintain the necessary storage facilities for
its naval presence in the Indian Ocean without the extremely difficult logistics
problems and high costs of replenishing the present task force of about six combat ships all the way from Subic Bay in the Philippines. It will also provide an
excellent anchorage for naval vessels, since a natural anchorage already exists
and need only be deepened to handle ships with drafts of as much as 36 feet.
In fact, the cost of providing such improved facilities will be "amortized" within four years by reducing the cost of replenishing the naval task force from the
Pacific, a distance of 4,000 miles. The base at Diego Garcia will enable the
United States to be prepared to enlarge its naval presence in the Indian Ocean
in crisis situations much more rapidly if the need arises, just as similar facilities
in the Mediterranean now enable the United States to reinforce to almost
double its normal presence in conflicts such as the October 1973 war.

Recently, and for the first time, the Arab oil-producing states of the
Persian Gulf region have united to enforce, under Saudi Arabia's leadership, an
oil embargo aimed at the United States and Western Europe. Another significant manifestation of the close linkage between the Gulf and the Arab-Israeli
conflict that could affect the balance of power in the area and shift it decisively
toward the socialist or radical Arab forces and their Soviet supporters has been
the damage recently done to the continued presence of the Middle East force.

During the conflict, the Sheikh of Bahrain announced that he was giving
the United States the one-year warning required for terminating the agreement
because of U.S. support for Israel. He clearly would like to see enough progress
in the peace negotiations at Geneva to enable him to revoke the termination
notice because, despite his Arab ties, the Bahrain ruler is still fundamentally
pro-Western in his outlook. However, he cannot ignore the attitudes and policies of other Arab states in the area, especially Saudi Arabia. This action typi-
fies the position of the sheikhs who rule the Persian Gulf ministates. The
stronger the nonmonarchical—and, indeed, antiroyal—rulers throughout the
Arabian Peninsula and elsewhere in the Arab world become, the more threatened the Arab sheikhs and emirs feel.

Thus, without denying obvious and quite understandable political and
religious affinities for the Arab cause, it is clear that the moderate and pro-
Western Arab rulers in the Persian Gulf are compelled to adopt more radical
orientation that is, in many respects, contrary to their fundamental interests
and essential aims. Ironically, the Sheikh of Bahrain, largely because of the

success of nonroyal Arab forces—Egypt and Syria—in the October war, has been compelled to threaten the expulsion of the U.S. presence that he presumably had viewed as a deterrent to radical elements in Bahrain and elsewhere in the Gulf.

The U.S. force still remains on Bahrain, and it has been upgraded in quality if not in quantity since the 1971 agreement. It now consists of two more modern combatant ships (of 1960 vintage), destroyer escorts or whatever is available in Norfolk or other naval bases in the eastern United States. The seaplane tender *Valcour* (1,800 tons) has been replaced by a 14,000-ton transport, the *La Salle,* as the command ship for the Middle East Force commander. Still, it is questionable whether this force, while playing an important role, is an adequate symbol of the great stakes the United States now has in the Persian Gulf. It certainly is not adequate to protect against potential threats to the sea lines of communication leading to and from the Gulf. There is now some indication that the United States is trying to increase its naval presence in the area from three ships to a small carrier task force, which would be more commensurate with the growing stakes the United States now has as a result of the developing energy crisis. The crisis is likely to be prolonged into the 1980s and, because of the long lead time involved in its own national efforts to create substitutes for Middle East oil, the United States will remain vulnerable to a cut or slowdown in oil imports from the Persian Gulf, especially from Saudi Arabia, for perhaps as much as 10-15 years.

In the last days of October, the United States did move a small carrier task force of approximately six combatants and one or two supporting vessels into the Indian Ocean, presumably to emphasize U.S. concern for its interests in the Persian Gulf and perhaps to represent an alternative to the expulsion notice by Bahrain (New York *Times,* October 30, 1973). The carrier was the *Hancock* which, although it is in the improved *Essex* class, is quite old and is only 45,000 tons. The *Hancock* was then replaced by a carrier of the same vintage and size of the *Oriskany,* and it has since been replaced by the super attack carrier, the *Kitty Hawk* (80,000 tons). This size carrier and a small combatant force will remain in the Indian Ocean for as long as the incumbent command authority deems necessary. The force includes an oiler and five other combatant ships. While the purpose of the deployment was announced in a somewhat vague way, it is possible, whether intended or not, that the carrier force could help to offset some of the psychological ill effects that may have followed from the Sheikh of Bahrain's expulsion notice. In short, the United States is making clear that it will maintain a force in the area even if the termination notice is final.

It may be prudent to maintain such a force in the area, at least until the future of the Middle East Force becomes clear; and this may be what Washington intended. No matter what happens in regard to the agreement with Bahrain,

however, it seems that the United States is likely to maintain a relatively permanent carrier task force—it would probably spend 8-10 months of the year there—
of this size in the Indian Ocean, if only to serve notice on potential foes that
the United States has upgraded its naval presence to a level more commensurate
with its vital stakes in the region.

Even prior to the war, the Soviets had been supplying very sophisticated
weaponry to Iraq, the only nonroyal Arab government in the Persian Gulf, and
in April 1972 concluded a 15-year treaty of cooperation and friendship with
Baghdad that contains two clauses involving close military cooperation. In return for its aid, the Soviets have been developing the Iraqi naval base at Umm
Qasr. It seems possible that they will obtain something resembling U.S. "home-
port" facilities, but perhaps without dependents, in the Gulf just at the time
that the United States may be expelled from the area, thus leaving the Soviets
with the only external naval presence in the Persian Gulf.

The 15-year treaty contains two articles that deal with mutual defense
assistance.

Article 8

In the event of the development of situations endangering the peace
of either Party or creating a threat to peace or a violation of peace,
the High Contracting Parties shall contact each other without delay
in order to agree their positions with a view to removing the threat
that has arisen or reestablishing peace.

Article 9

In the interests of the security of both countries, the High Contracting Parties will continue to develop cooperation in strengthening
their defence capacity. (*New Times* [Moscow] , April 1972)

Article 9 specifically relates to the strengthening of Soviet and Iraqi defense forces. It is under this clause that the Soviets seem now to be modernizing
the Iraqi naval port of Umm Qasr. Since the Iraqi navy consists of relatively
small craft, we may assume that the Soviets are modernizing it with an eye to
using it frequently themselves.

There can be little doubt that the Soviets have made significant gains in
what we must assume is their maximum aim: to become the paramount external power in the vital northwestern area of the Indian Ocean. Since their first
"flag showing" visit in March 1968, following the British announcement in January of the same year, there has been only one period of approximately 10 days—
in the spring of 1969—when the Soviets had no surface combatant ship deployed
in the Indian Ocean. From a total average of over 1,500 ship-days in 1968 to
nearly 8,000 ship-days in 1974, the current number of Soviet ship-days in the
area now surpasses that of the United States by about 4-1 (Jackson, March

1974), although this could change somewhat if the U.S. naval force remains in the Indian Ocean and the current Soviet presence of over 20 naval ships is reduced. The latter seems unlikely, especially if and when the Suez Canal is reopened (Washington *Post,* March 7, 1974). The margin over the United States has been of the same magnitude in terms of in-port time, and this includes U.S. time spent in Bahrain. If Bahrain is not included, the Soviet advantage in in-port time would be closer to 7-1. For the Soviets these represent very recent deployments, which emphasizes the very sharp increase in Soviet naval power in the region since Britain announced its intention to leave.

THE LOCAL BALANCE OF POWER

The balance of external forces is closely related to the local balance, since much of U.S. and British policy is based on the political and military effectiveness of the local powers, particularly Iran—and, in the case of the United States, to a lesser extent on Saudi Arabia. The United States and Britain have both sold enormous quantities of arms to the Iranians, thus in effect establishing Iran as the paramount local military power in the Persian Gulf (Furlong 1973), with about 300 of the most sophisticated modern aircraft: about 165 F4s and over 100 of the most advances F5s scheduled for delivery. Further orders include the very powerful and highly sophisticated F14. Also on order is the P3, for purposes of air-maritime surveillance of the Persian Gulf and the Gulf of Oman. The Iranians, as is true of all the Muslim, but non-Arab, peoples of the region—Pakistan, Iran, and Turkey—are very good pilots. It is curious that these countries of the Middle East appear to be far more effective in the air than are the Arab Muslim states. It is interesting to note that Pakistan has been much sought-after by the Arab states for air training missions. The Pakistanis have provided such training for Iraq, Saudi Arabia, Jordan, Kuwait, and Libya; and there are reports they will now fly the several squadrons of Mirages that France is selling to Abu Dhabi—28-32 planes is the figure mentioned. They have also been hired by Malta to assist in the training program for Maltese civil aviation. Thus, while the Pakistani air force does not have the more sophisticated aircraft in their own inventory, they have been flying both Soviet and Western aircraft of the more modern types.

The Iranian advantage in the critical area of air power would appear to be not only quantitative but also qualitative. The Iranians are, of course, demographically superior, with a population of nearly 32 million. Their principal enemy on the Persian Gulf is neighboring Iraq, which has only about one-third the population. It does, however, have some very modern Soviet military aircraft, according to recent reports. Saudi Arabia, the largest Gulf state territorially,

is weak militarily and has a population of no more than 5 million. King Faisal
has been negotiating with the United States since before the October war for
about 25 F4s, and he will receive several squadrons of F5Es. Following the October conflict the Saudi government let it be known that they were negotiating
with the French for several squadrons of Mirage IIIs, and are said to be discussing the purchase of the Anglo-French Jaguar fighter (*Christian Science Monitor,* January 4, 1974).

The United States has moved much closer to the Saudis again; and while
the details are still somewhat vague, it would appear that an agreement for substantial and comprehensive military support and assistance of Saudi Arabia has
been reached between the United States and King Faisal. Presumably the Saudis
objected to a U.S. provision that the aircraft could not be transferred to any
other country, such as Egypt, in the case of another Arab-Israeli conflict. The
Saudis, however, in the past have had to hire foreign pilots to fly the aircraft,
such as the British-made Lightning interceptors, that they possess, paying them
as much as $2,500 per month (*Christian Science Monitor,* January 4, 1974).

The Shah, with a total of seven principal combatant ships, also has the
most powerful navy in the Persian Gulf. This force now numbers three destroyers (one from Britain and two recently received from the United States) and
four very modern British missile frigates built especially for Iran. The frigates
already have been delivered, and two more will be turned over soon. The
Iranians also have the largest army in the Persian Gulf: 170,000 troops armed
with modern weapons, including about 800 British Chieftain tanks. In short,
it is quite clear that Iran is the premier military power of the Persian Gulf, but
this will remain true only so long as the present balance prevails in the area. If a
change in the kind of royal or quasi-royal rule that now prevails throughout the
Persian Gulf-Arabian Sea area were to take place and the Soviets intervened on
the side of revolutionary forces of the kind we now see in Iraq, then Iran's
forces, however impressive in quality and quantity, may become inadequate.

The Shah's force is designed to defend his own country's territorial integrity and to assist in the defense of like-minded (royal or quasi-royal) rulers
throughout the Gulf. In his eyes, the two purposes are intimately related, for if
the Arabian side of the Persian Gulf were to fall to revolutionary socialist Arab
forces, or perhaps even nontraditional leaders, then Iran could be confronted by
a unified Arab bloc that had removed the common bond of royalty as a continuing force for stability in the Gulf (Hawley 1970, p. 266). It is not inconceivable that one day the Arab states may unite against the Shah as they did
against Israel in the October war.

It is, of course, possible that moderate nonroyal forces could come to
power in some states on the Arabian side of the Gulf; but it does seem likely
that, even if not as extreme as Qaddafi, they will not be as pro-Western or as

cooperative with Iran as has been true of the sheikhdoms and Oman and, to a lesser extent, with Saudi Arabia. Such new forces would not have the common bond of traditional or royal rule to counsel at least a modicum of cordiality and cooperation in local affairs. In the case of Iraq, the one nontraditionally ruled state on the Gulf, it seems highly doubtful that any change in the leadership will bring a more moderate government to power. A resumption of diplomatic relations between Iraq and the United States is a possibility. Such a development could bring some change in Iraqi policy; but Iraq would still be the one country in the Persian Gulf region that is not ruled by royalty, and it is difficult to see it as willing to accept anything resembling the status quo.

The October war turned even the conservative and pro-Western rulers of the Persian Gulf more in the direction of revolutionary Arabism, if only to protect themselves from the threats of coups and intervention in their affairs. For a while, at least, it also damaged one of the twin supports of U.S. policy in the area: the emphasis placed on relying on the two largest states in the Gulf—the monarchies of Iran and Saudi Arabia. However, provided continued success can be achieved in the Middle East by U.S. diplomacy, such as resulted in Egypt, Saudi Arabia may remain close to the United States. Saudi Arabia is the world's oil superpower, and Iran possesses the most powerful military force of the Gulf. Indeed, the principal reason why the Shah sought such a large arsenal of sophisticated weapons was his view, as stated twice to the author, that he had decided during the 1965 Indo-Pakistani war that he must be prepared to defend his own interests locally because U.S. policy in that war made it clear that he could expect no assistance from Washington if he became involved in local hostilities. The United States at that time, it will be recalled, cut off military assistance to Pakistan and also told the Shah that assistance provided to Iran under the Military Assistance Program could not be used to aid Pakistan in its conflict with India.

The military balance in this region has also been affected adversely for the United States and its allies by the dismemberment of Pakistan in the war of 1971. Pakistan was badly weakened by its defeat, and this has left Iran with a two-front threat. The balance of military power in the subcontinent is about 8-1 in favor of an India, under strong Soviet influence, that has a treaty similar to the one signed by Iraq and is now supplied with the most sophisticated Soviet weaponry. India also has about 30 military ordnance factories built with Soviet assistance, compared with one in Pakistan. The Indian factories are producing an estimated 100 tanks per year (Beirut *Daily Star,* January 8, 1974). It is also reported that the Indian air force is receiving about 100 MIGs per year from Russia.

Further complicating Pakistan's position is the overthrow of the King of Afghanistan by elements friendly to Russia. Again the common monarchical bond between the Shah and the Afghan King was an additional factor helping to moderate the Afghan-Pakistan border dispute over the Pathans in the Northwest Frontier Province or in the adjacent Baluchistan area of Pakistan, where Iraq and other radical elements are supporting a separate Baluchi state. This new state, as envisioned by its promoters, would include not only the 1.5 million Baluchis in the Pakistan territory of Baluchistan but also the equal number just across the border of Iran. Still, the Shah has some leverage over India because of the serious deterioration of India's economy as oil prices have risen. India obtains about three-fourths of its total oil supply from Iran. This led to a visit to Iran by Indira Gandhi, the first in many years by an Indian Prime Minister, to discuss her economy with the Shah. The Shah has agreed to help. Thus he will be in a position to counsel caution on India vis-a-vis Pakistan.

The Soviets and their allies have now encircled Iran and Pakistan with much influence in India and a fairly firm foothold in Iraq, as well as considerable influence in Afghanistan, especially among the young Soviet-trained and Soviet-equipped military elements who brought Prince Sardar Daud to power. Iran is arming primarily to defend its territorial integrity by buying huge quantities of very sophisticated weaponry from the West—about $3.5 billion to date.

Having said all this concerning Iran's preponderance of military power in the Persian Gulf region, it is still important to bear in mind that a close relationship exists between the local balance of power and the balance of superpower forces in the region. The Iranian military forces are undoubtedly powerful enough to deal with local threats to the security and stability in the Persian Gulf as long as the Soviet Union does not openly support Iran's enemies. Iraq and Iran have just resumed diplomatic relations, which had been severed since Iran seized the three islets near the entrance to the Strait of Hormuz—Greater and Lesser Tumb and Abu Musa—one day before the British system of protection in the Gulf was terminated on November 30, 1971. This "detente" between the two principal antagonists in the Gulf is not likely to endure for long, since it was Iran's only gesture of support for the Arab cause in the October war. The Iraqi government approached the Iranian government for a resumption of diplomatic relations so that Baghdad could shift its forces from the border with Iran to help the Arab cause, and the Shah agreed.

But these differences, both in kinds of rule and in political aims and ambitions, are too great for any lasting peace between the two states. Indeed, since the end of Arab-Israeli hostilities, sharp military engagements have taken place on the Iran-Iraq border in which many men have been wounded and perhaps 100 have died on both sides (New York *Times,* March 7, 1974). The Iranians see the Soviets possibly playing the same role in Iraq as they have played in Egypt and Syria, where they have been so effective in blunting Israeli air superiority by the introduction of very sophisticated missiles and where their navy has been deployed as a counter to the U.S. Sixth Fleet. Iranian military superiority could be similarly diminished by Soviet intervention of this sort in Iraq, where the Soviets have already spent over $1 billion in military assistance and have over 500 military advisers.

Thus the role that countries like Iran, the smaller sheikhdoms or mini-states, and Pakistan would like to see the United States play in the area would be that of projecting its military presence in a manner strong enough for the Soviets to be very wary of intervening in behalf of those states that seek to change the status quo.

Therefore, to maintain the balance so that Washington's diplomacy in the area will be effective, those who believe that naval power influences littoral states feel that the United States must have a presence of sufficient size to ensure that pro-Western countries in the area will feel free to continue friendly relations and policies. This would call for continuing military assistance and arms sales to U.S. friends and allies in the area, equipping them with adequate modern weaponry to meet potential threats to their security, and for a rela-tively permanent U.S. naval presence in the Indian Ocean. It might be prudent, no matter what the future of the Middle East Force, for the United States to retain the small carrier task force that entered the Indian Ocean in October 1973 and thus begin to meet the political and military challenge now posed by the larger Soviet naval presence in that region. Such a policy also calls for the improvement of the Diego Garcia facility as a precautionary measures against the possible implications of reopening the Suez Canal.

THE USE OF MILITARY FORCE TO SECURE OIL RESOURCES

Military intervention has from time to time been suggested if the energy shortage should become so critical as to cause economic chaos in the United States. A military intervention would probably not be beyond the physical capa-bility of the United States; but the dangers posed by such an action could be tremendous. The aim of the exercise would presumably be to seize adequate oil sources to enable the U.S. economy to function at a tolerable level. This means that the target of such an operation would have to be Saudi Arabia, since none of the other Middle East countries has oil in sufficient quantity to satisfy U.S. demands by itself.

The oil fields of Saudi Arabia are clustered on the Persian Gulf side of the country and are very close to the tanker-loading terminals. But oil fields are very vulnerable to sabotage. The prime targets would be the wellheads them-selves (the points at which lines from several wells come together) and the port facilities. The pipelines running between these areas would be an attractive but low-value target, for breaches in a line are easily repaired. Wellhead fires, how-ever, are a very different matter. Some of these, started by accident, have burned for over a month; and the difficulties of extinguishing such fires would be much greater in a war situation. The danger with oil-well fires is that they may cause the release of subterranean gas that would otherwise be carefully controlled, and thus change the conditions in the oil reservoirs to such an extent that the oil will no longer flow up the well pipes. The possibility of subsurface water flooding during a fire is also considerable; and this, too, could knock a full oil field out of production for many months.

Sabotage of the loading facilities and of the huge tankers is also a relatively easy task. If one or two of these supertankers were to be sunk or set afire, either in the Gulf port or on the narrow—three miles wide—shipping channel of the 26-mile-wide Strait of Hormuz where the Persian Gulf enters the Gulf of Oman, the clearing up of such obstacles could take a very long time. The idea of a quick, clean military excision must therefore be considered extremely questionable, if not impossible, for sabotage could easily turn any gains into catastrophic losses in terms of oil production and the ability to transport the oil. Both Sheikh Yamani of Saudi Arabia and President Boumedienne of Algeria have said that sabotage will be the inevitable result of any military moves by the West—and we would do well to heed their words. Kuwait and Abu Dhabi have already announced that they are wiring their wells for demolition. Such a move has also been suggested by Saudi Arabia. Still, a military intervention contingency plan will be necessary, since it is always possible that public pressure, should a future energy crisis worsen precipitately, could force some such action.

The oil supply areas present a wide range of attractive targets to both a potential global adversary and to small-scale dissident guerrilla groups. What has been written here relates specifically to the Persian Gulf region and the conditions prevailing therein, but it should be noted that some of the considerations have similar implications for other areas as well. There are only a few targets, but the damage that can be done in these few small areas is utterly disproportionate both to their size and to the nature and strength of the forces needed to cause critical damage. The current regimes of the Persian Gulf littoral have a long-term interest in making oil supplies available, but there are many groups or elements in this part of the world that do not hold—or reject—this aim. They constitute a continuing threat to the interests of a great part of the world.

The conclusion must therefore be somewhat pessimistic—the oil supply chain has many links; many are weak from a defensive standpoint; and an attack against any one link, or an integrated and coordinated series of lower-level attacks against several, could easily disrupt, if not totally sever, the oil lifeline of the world. All of this could take place even before the oil reaches the vital sea-lanes: the Cape Route, through the Straits of Malacca, and the Suez Canal (when reopened). The sea-lanes constitute the second part of the security problem, which may in future depend on the naval balance of power.

SUMMARY

The strategic complexion of the Persian Gulf-Indian Ocean region has changed dramatically since January 1968, when the British Labor government decided to withdraw from the area and thus end 150 years of British hegemony. The permanent U.S. token naval presence at Bahrain, which outlived Britain's withdrawal in November 1971 and which as a result of the October 1973 war is now in doubt, has already been outnumbered by the permanent average Soviet presence in the area. In the short time since Britain's withdrawal, the vital significance of Persian Gulf oil for Western energy requirements has become manifest. Britain's decision to evacuate the area east of Suez had been based upon both economic and ideological considerations rather than future fuel requirements, a circumstance that demonstrates the myopia and inability to link economics with strategy that too often blurs cogent policy projections.

The portents in the Indian Ocean for United States and, more generally, Western interests are blatantly unfavorable. Thus, for example, U.S. expectations based on 100 percent ownership of the world's greatest oil reserves in Saudi Arabia have already been shattered by partnership arrangements that will lead inexorably to Saudi Arabian control. This trend has been or is being emulated or surpassed in all principal oil-producing Persian Gulf states: Kuwait, Abu Dhabi, Iraq, and Iran.

Along with the changes in the control of oil production has come increasing political ferment within the Arabian side of the Gulf. Movements led by Palestinians and other radical or socialist Arab elements or states are already targeting the sheikhs, kings, and sultans who, except for Arab Socialist Iraq, rule the oil-rich states of the Arabian side of the Gulf. Looking ahead to the 1980-1990 time frame, a critical period in terms of energy resources, the question of the transnational context of political rule in the area becomes a crucial one. As stated above, the Persian Gulf is unique in that it is the only area of the world still under the sway of royal or quasi-royal rule. Only revolutionary Iraq constitutes a break in this otherwise solid chain of traditional rule and, significantly, it is Iraq that supports elements seeking to overthrow royal domination in the Persian Gulf.

Any projection of the future trends in this area must consider the near certainty that the chain of traditional leadership will be broken in other countries. Absolute kingships and other forms of hereditary rule are anachronisms in the modern world, especially where they fail to emphasize progressiveness—as is true particularly on the Arab side of the Gulf—and it is difficult to believe that such regimes can survive the last quarter of this century. It has been said that Saudi Arabia's King Faisal fears modernization precisely because he believes it will lead to the end of kingship, whereas the Shah of Iran believes that the only way to save the monarchy is to spend his oil revenues to improve the lot of his people, as he is now doing by providing the funds for 250,000 new jobs each year. Perhaps the only way royal rule can be saved as an institution in the area is by providing for constitutional monarchies. At present it is doubtful whether the present revolutionary forces in the area would find such a solution ideologically acceptable.

Indeed, there is reason to anticipate that the overthrow of any one traditional regime could trigger a chain reaction that might finally engulf the entire Arab side of the Gulf. Particularly, should an antimonarchical coup succeed in Saudi Arabia, we would most likely see all the lesser states bordering Saudi Arabia dominated to varying degrees by radical or socialist Arab leadership similar to that in Iraq or possibly even along the Colonel Qaddafi model. The political nature of a coup in Saudi Arabia is critical, since the smaller states would surely follow the Saudi lead.

There is only one country in the area that at this writing can escape such a chain reaction. Muslim but non-Arab Iran today controls the entire eastern side of the Gulf and is militarily more powerful and politically more stable than any of the states on the Arab side. Thus one might credibly project a situation in the Persian Gulf within the next two decades that would feature the disappearance of the only bond of relative stability in the area—the common cause of kingship and other forms of traditional rule—and the emergence of a potentially grave confrontation between radical Arab leadership on one side of the Gulf and Muslim non-Arab kingship on the other side. There is already a potential legacy of distrust between the two sides, particularly between the two principal Gulf states, Saudi Arabia and Iran. The collapse of monarchical rule in Saudi Arabia could foreclose any hope of the cooperative arrangements among the local states. This scenario is rendered all the more credible by the disappearance of the protective moats (principally Britain's hegemony) that in the past stressed the area's relative isolation from the world at large. The precipitate increase in the importance of Persian Gulf oil opens the way for the ambitions of external forces that are likely to hasten destabilization and potential conflict.

To summarize the prospects in the Middle East generally: Soviet-American confrontation in the area seems likely—whatever partial settlements are reached in the area as a result of U.S. diplomacy—in contrast with detente in other regions. At most we might expect the superpowers to exercise some restraints in regard to choice and manipulation of allies in the region. The Soviets will almost certainly continue to challenge and to attempt to establish paramountcy of influence in the remaining Western positions in the Mediterranean-Persian Gulf area. Hence, while the U.S.-Soviet political-military competition may be constrained by an overall climate of detente between the superpowers, the continuing clash of U.S. and Soviet interests and objectives in the Middle East will continue to prevent the total consummation of this detente.

8

IS THE ATLANTIC
ALLIANCE SOLUBLE
IN OIL?
Uzi B. Arad

Nineteen seventy-three was a crisis year for the Atlantic Alliance. Two latent problem areas exploded simultaneously with such force that they almost irreparably fractured it. One cannot but have serious doubts about the cohesion of a group of nations that shows signs of disintegrating under external pressures rather than uniting as one front. The simultaneous occurrence of a security and an energy crisis constituted as severe a challenge as the Alliance has weathered since its formation a quarter of a century earlier. Although these crises affected the economic viability of Alliance members and their international freedom of action, the Alliance appeared more divided than ever. Betraying at least a trace of *schadenfreude,* political commentators did not fail to note that 1973 was to have been celebrated as "the Year of Europe." Nevertheless, in a rather pathetic way, 1973 *was* the Year of Europe. It was then that America's relative economic and political decline began taking its toll—at the European periphery of the Alliance. In a way the real battlegrounds of the 1973 crises were not in the Middle East, but in Japan and Western Europe. For while the United States seemed eager to gain some friendship in the Middle East, it obviously had lost a great deal of influence in what should have been its strategic and economic backyard—Europe and Japan. Thus, the crises brought home the message that the Western front was not quiet at all; in fact, it was on the verge of collapse (Laqueur 1974b, pp. 196-221). The Alliance's members found that very significant differences exist among them, not only in the usual areas of trade and money, but also in energy and security, areas that were supposed to bring them together.

While Soviet-American detente did little to prevent the confrontation over the Middle East, it certainly had an effect on Western solidarity. If the perception of a Soviet military-diplomatic challenge underlay the formation of the Alliance, it was equally true that intra-Alliance disputes surfaced as the climate relaxed. Moreover, with the United States suffering the consequences of the Indochinese experience and the Soviet Union gaining the strategic upper hand, it was only natural that an economically resurgent Japan and Western Europe assert more vigorously than ever their distinct and often contradictory interests. But if security tended to unite the Alliance and economics to divide it, energy seemed to occupy a middle ground. Thus, just as 1973 was a year of truth for the Alliance, so energy could be seen the litmus test for the Alliance's strength and cohesion. The question that remains, then, is the role of energy and energy policies within the Alliance.

An understanding of the role of energy as a catalyst of integration or disintegration within the Alliance hinges upon a grasp of the entire energy area as broadly defined in space and in time. It is useful, therefore, to employ systemic conceptualizations while describing the Alliance and the Organization for Economic Cooperation and Development (OECD) as its most immediate environment. Similarly, the OECD energy system should be considered as it existed before the crisis if any sense of historical direction is to be given to the analysis.

For more than 20 years following the end of World War II, the transnational energy network operated as an intricately complex but highly efficient distribution system. Composed of companies, nations, international organizations, and other actors on the world scene, the system did not exist in a political vacuum. Instead, it was an important component of a liberalized world economic order institutionalized by the United States after World War II. Although the rules under which the system operated were not formalized explicitly, its vision and procedures followed the pattern established under the General Agreement on Tariffs and Trade (GATT). Thus, this group of highly modernized capitalist nations was soon integrated with the rest of the non-Communist world into a worldwide supply and distribution system that permitted little interference by opposing economic or political forces.

The energy system thus became virtually multinational—or multilateral—in structure. It also acquired a high degree of flexibility that produced an enduring stability. Serious energy troubles, to be sure, occurred from time to time; but none of them was sufficient to transform the system in more than a marginal and transitory way. Indeed, the ease with which the system survived these exigencies only illustrated its adaptability. Considering the salience of energy resources as strategic commodities and the immense geographical, physical, and economic proportions involved, this record was most impressive. The system weathered all difficulties, survived complications of all sorts, and continued its smooth and efficient operation.

Two fundamental factors accounted for such stability. First, despite high

high degrees of mutual dependence among member nations, the net disruptive effect of these situations was minimal throughout the period of stable multilateralism. Although delicate situations of interdependence are known to cause new forms of interpenetration and mutual sensitivities (Cooper 1968), the particular patterns of such relationships as they crystallized in the energy area seemed to negate one another, thus canceling out the inherent disruptive potential. The patterns of energy interdependence in the pre-crisis period can therefore be termed as symmetrical. That symmetry maintained the balance.

Second, just as it was the dominant actor in the system, the oil industry was also the main source of the system's flexibility. The existence of a mature multinational oil industry translated the reciprocal dependence patterns into a continuous and dynamic relationship. This industry, true to its geocentric orientation, spread across, rather than along, political boundaries. Moreover, the industry was not only the main protagonist in the system but also the guardian of multilateralism. Clearly, its growth and prosperity depended upon the existence of a market with minimum political constraint. It took care, therefore, to cushion and protect the system from disruptive forces. The industry served as a buffer to absorb many political blows that would otherwise have destroyed the system.

But even at the high point of its existence, the multilateral energy system was extremely fragile. Its continued stability was contingent upon the system's working along carefully balanced multinational patterns. Such internal symmetry enabled the system to withstand the vicissitudes of power politics that plagued it, just as they did other areas of interaction and exchange. Still, circumstances change, and the myriad balances could not last forever. As the 1960s drew to an end, it became painfully clear that not only was the energy system undergoing a significant transformation, but the entire OECD and the liberal economic order supported by the United States were showing signs of severe strain. The energy system was disintegrating rapidly into its subcomponents, mainly because its balance was being disrupted.

The forces that were causing the breakdown were both exogenous and endogenous to the system. Energy interdependence proved that, like other areas of functional interdependence, it was intrinsically unstable. Moreover, it was observed that relationships among interdependencies only increase their respective weaknesses. Thus, as the world monetary system deteriorated, so did the energy system—not without some causal connection between the two.

As far as the energy system is concerned, two types of pressures can be shown to have "rocked the boat." First, the multinational oil industry was losing its grip over international trade, thus allowing a virtual revolution in that area to occur. Second, the symmatry in producer-consumer dependence patterns gradually gave way to a more lopsided interdependence that increased producers' power and decreased consumers' leverage. This crisis exploded in 1973, but the conditions that brought it about began taking shape much earlier.

The history of energy systems, like that of specific energy resources, is cyclical rather than continuous. Systems are often transformed by dialectical processes. While the eruption of crises is symptomatic of such changes, it should be borne in mind that crises are transitory. Sooner or later new stable points are attained and a new system emerges. We are still in the age of oil and fossil fuel, and simultaneously at the height of the crisis of multilateralism as an international modality of trade. It is far from certain how different the new system will be; but an analysis of the old system, its disintegration, and the forces that seem to be shaping the emerging system can be undertaken.

THE ERA OF MULTILATERAL ENERGY INTERDEPENDENCE

The system of interdependence that characterized the 1950s and 1960s was the culmination of a long-term trend of expansion, with respect to both volume and geographical spread of interregional energy trade. The dominant force in that expansion was clearly petroleum. In 1925 liquid fuels accounted for under one-third of world energy exports; in 1968 they reached 90 percent (Darmstadter 1971). Furthermore, liquid fuels incrementally accounted for virtually the entire increase in energy trade. By interdependence, therefore, more than spatial aspects are meant; it is a state of consumers' dependence on an increasingly omnipotent energy source—oil.

The shift of world energy trade from coal to oil radically transformed the geographical structure of energy trade. Having almost no indigenous crude oil, both Western Europe and Japan drifted into a condition of high dependence on oil imports. The United States, on the other hand, lost its prewar prominence as an oil-exporting nation and moved toward a posture of restrained, low import-dependence. All the advanced industrialized countries have become dependent on liquid fuels; but dependence on oil is related to dependence on international trade, so that, almost without exception, nations of the non-Communist world exhibit a relatively higher degree of dependence on oil than the closed economies. The post-World War II period, characterized by significant liberalization of world trade, therefore witnessed a growing import-dependence as North America turned from a position of being a net exporter to that of a net importer of energy, and an expansion of the proportionate size of the energy trade. From 7.5 percent of total world trade in 1937, energy's share grew to 9.0 percent in 1953 and 9.6 percent in 1965 (Darmstadter 1971, p. 126). Clearly, the growth of trade in energy and the liberalization of international trade formed the necessary basis for the kind of interdependence that emerged in the 1950s and matured in the 1960s.

Throughout the 1960s Europe sustained an extremely high degree of dependence that gradually increased—from 92.1 percent in 1960 to 96.3 percent by the end of the decade. The geographic pattern of sources, however, changed considerably as the share of supplies from the Middle East decreased from 72.9 percent to 50.1 percent in the same period. Despite this decrease in dependence on Middle Eastern sources, no significant change occurred in Western Europe's general dependence on imports, for that decrease was paralleled by an upsurge of imports from North Africa. In 1960 only 8 million tons, or 4.4 percent of total supply, came from North Africa. By 1970 it reached 194 million tons, or 31.4 percent. The period, though dynamic in terms of sources, was stable in terms of very great dependence (OECD 1973).

The same is true for Japan's supply—only more so. Clearly, there could not be a much greater degree of dependence than Japan's. The meagerness of its indigenous oil production leaves no alternative to meeting increases in demand by increases in imports. Thus, whereas the amount of crude oil imported by Japan increased from 26.9 million tons in 1960 to 169.5 million tons in 1970, a change by a factor of six, the level of dependence remained as high as it was at the beginning of the decade, with a slight increase from 98.2 percent to 99.5 percent of total supplies (OECD 1973).

This trend of energy-deficient blocs is completed with inclusion of the North American continent, where trends of dependence over the 10-year period appear to show similar stability. But if no change in dependence patterns for Japan and Western Europe implied, in effect, extreme levels of dependence, the converse is true for North America. Clearly, with roughly four-fifths of its oil demand being satisfied from indigenous sources, the North American continent enjoyed a more favorable position than Japan or Western Europe throughout the 1960s. Although consumption rose from 512.8 million tons to 755.8 million tons in the ten years, the increase in degree of dependence was 2.2 percent and the general level remained around 20 percent of total supply (OECD 1973).

There is, of course, a form of dependence that offsets import dependence: the exporter's dependence on oil revenues. Clearly, the normal procedures of economic exchange inevitably involve such mutuality of advantage. The fact that that oil was produced and marketed throughout the era of multilateralism implies ipso facto the existence of a common interest among producers and consumers alike in maintaining the system. What is unique, however, is the almost total absence of attempts on either side to capitalize on the vulnerabilities that result from such dependence. The reason is that exporters were as highly dependent upon their oil revenues as consumers were upon imports.

The extreme degrees of dependence can be seen not only as quantitative levels but also as a qualitative situation that presented few alternatives or substitutes to the commodity. There was no readily available substitute for oil for Japan and Western Europe, and neither was there a readily available alternative source of foreign exchange or revenues for the oil-exporting countries. The capital deficiency of the oil-exporting countries balanced and mitigated the otherwise dangerous effects of Western energy deficiency. In a sense, the symmetry in interests stemmed from the asymmetry of the economic situation. Thus, precisely because all major oil-importing countries were developed and modernized societies, while all major oil-exporting countries were developing and modernizing societies, there could exist a unique moment of balanced interdependence.

In 1955 Venezuela was the main exporter; in 1972 it was Saudi Arabia. This stable north-south relationship, however, could be maintained only so long as the underdeveloped producing countries concerned needed all the earnings they could derive from their resources. That condition was satisfied through the era of precrisis multilateralism—not necessarily because oil earnings constituted the sole source of governmental revenues for most exporting countries, but because the payments to exporters per unit of production were low enough to maintain their interest in increased output for increased revenue. In 1955 the Middle Eastern countries earned $0.811 per barrel; in 1960, $0.775; in 1965, $0.800; in 1970, $0.917; and in 1972, $1.472 (Petroleum Information Foundation 1973). Hence the corresponding flow of payments did not bring any accumulation of capital to the exporting countries. Most of them absorbed the revenues as quickly as they received the money, often in building development plants that were expected to catapult them into a stage of economic development that would lessen their excessive reliance on oil as a source of revenue. Paradoxically, then, the way to reduced dependence was through increased dependence, since ambitious development plans required extensive investment and, hence, increased production.

The oil-exporting countries were thus responsive to increased Western demands because the resulting higher income could be absorbed, a situation that resulted from low and stable "government takes." The low government takes were in fact determined by the oil industry, which maintained firm control over the market during the period of multilateralism. As noted earlier, the industry operated both as the guardian of the system and as the most active participant in it. The industry was exploring for, producing, and marketing oil throughout the world, and doing so very efficiently. More than anything else, it endowed the system with its distinct multinational character, for the multinational oil firms were an integral part of the multilateral system. The order and stability that characterized that system has had much to do with the role and position that the oil industry came to occupy.

Oil companies were among the first to develop multinational operations. The tendency of corporations dealing in raw materials to integrate backward and establish a structure typified by vertical integration brought them to a global scale of operation. In fact, the oil industry is not merely a group of multinational companies. It is, in essence, the multinational industry par excellence. The seven largest oil companies, often described as the "seven sisters," appear among the top fifteen multinational firms. Moreover, five of these companies operate in more countries than the group's median. But it is not size and scope alone that account for the importance of the industry; it is the position of oil as a singularly strategic commodity. Its importance enhanced the political awareness and activity of these companies, and symbiotic relationships between companies and their home and host governments were typical of the energy system (Tanzer 1969). The major oil companies controlled the market, determined prices, decided on amounts to be produced or to be paid to governments. Their very existence and modes of operation constitute the core of the system. Consequently, the system acquired the multinational character of the companies.

THE ENERGY SYSTEM IN DISEQUILIBRIUM

The late 1960s and early 1970s saw numerous indications that the liberal economic order erected and dominated by the United States since World War II was breaking down. American involvement in Vietnam, with the ensuing decline from its past position of hegemony, and growing economic tensions within OECD reduced America's ability to sustain an economic order contrary to the nationalistic tendencies of most other nations. The energy system, until then effectively cushioned against such effects, became more exposed to governmental intervention, mostly at the production stage. Then the economic-strategic environment further aggravated these processes of disintegration from within. The 1967 Arab-Israeli conflict, paralleled by growing Western dependence on Arab oil, created a dangerous proximity of issue-areas, later to be linked by the Arabs as diplomatic leverage in the form of the oil weapon. Inflation in the Western world did nothing to alleviate the concerns of oil-exporting countries, for it affected their import expenditures; nor did the sorry state of the international monetary system help exporters to find safe savings outlets. In short, the multilateral system had to cope with a far less hospitable world environment than before.

The system had survived past periods of external pressure. What made the early 1970s different was that this time the system also began crumbling from within. The delicate balances that characterized its internal structure were alerted; as the system seemed less and less stable, the greater the strains that its presumed interdependence were called upon to withstand. Essentially, what happened was that as the environment of the energy system deteriorated and the patterns of internal dependence lost their stabilizing symmetry, excessive expectations were placed on the flexibility of the system. These strains may not have destroyed the system, but they certainly threw it into a "tailspin" disequilibrium whose overt manifestations were revealed with the great energy crisis of 1973-74.

The single most important disequilibrating force on the energy scene was the emergence of the Organization of the Petroleum Exporting Countries (OPEC) as a cartel strong enough to revolutionize the price-determination process. Spiraling prices became the catalyst for a series of developments that avalanched into a state of acute crisis. OPEC was formed in 1960 with the declared objective of arresting a successive lowering of prices by the oil companies. Its original members were Iran, Venezuela, Saudi Arabia, Kuwait, and Iraq; since then almost all exporting countries have been admitted. Although it originally had varied aims, OPEC evolved into a negotiating forum of producers versus companies, and finally into a body determining prices unilaterally. What started as an attempt on the part of exporters to improve their bargaining power versus the oil companies culminated in OPEC's becoming a supranational organization with direct influence over the world oil market.

In its early years OPEC was ignored by the companies and its effectiveness was minimal. Only 10 years after its foundation could OPEC claim to have fulfilled its main aim of extracting the power over price determination from the companies. The Teheran and Tripoli agreements of 1971 marked a revolutionary change in the system. The market had never actually turned from a buyers' into a sellers' market in real terms; but 1971 was the year when sellers exercised their full power of negotiation with the oil companies, while the latter were exposed as lacking both interest and leverage to offset the effects of such a reversal in the balance of power. A combination of circumstances occurring in 1970 surely facilitated this outcome: the unexpectedly rapid increase in European demand, the closure of Tapline by a Syrian bulldozer, and enforced production cutbacks used as a lever for higher prices on the vulnerable independent oil companies operating in Libya. All these events had the effect OPEC desired: that of a cartel in a tight-supply situation. Demands for higher prices were consequently made, first by Libya, then by all exporters. In the Teheran meeting, in which a company delegation led by British Petroleum met representatives of the Persian Gulf countries, an agreement was signed that gave producers a $0.33 rise in posted prices, plus provisions for future price increases. In return, the companies were guaranteed that no further claims would be made. Later, at a meeting in Tripoli, even better terms were concluded for Mediterranean producers. The two 1971 agreements sent oil prices skyrocketing at a rate unprecedented in the history of international trade. This watershed was to grow into a crisis of global proportions.

The attitude of oil-importing countries, as reflected in the position held by the companies, changed from attempting to preserve the multilateral system, possibly through a line of resistance to OPEC's demands, to seeking to appease its members. There is a fundamental difference between the two attitudes. The former risks confrontation for the sake of long-term stability; the latter appears incrementally cheaper because it defers a confrontation, but in effect could prove even more destabilizing in the long run as demands are escalated. This is precisely what happened following the Teheran and Tripoli agreements, both typical outcomes of appeasement. The agreements, which were to run until 1976, were greeted in many quarters with a sigh of relief, as heralding a long period of stability (Yaari 1973). Clearly, the reverse has happened, as is usually the case following the adoption of appeasement postures. Appeasement signaled the end of a Western commitment to the multilateral system as it existed. Thus, if the market did not necessarily change from a buyers' to a sellers' market, significant change occurred in the behavior of companies and home governments alike. From a conservative stance to preserve the status quo and resist the OPEC challenge, they shifted to a submissive position in an attempt to accommodate the revolutionary force that OPEC essentially represented.

Needless to say, even when negotiating on behalf of their home governments and with their tacit approval, the oil companies were in a totally different position from OPEC. OPEC, after all, was an international organization representing sovereign states; the oil companies, on the other hand, were commercial enterprises basically following their self-interests. Furthermore, by virtue of their middle—or buffer—position, the companies could spread the increased costs and pass them on to consumers. The very confrontation between oil firms and political entities was biased against the companies, and ultimately against the consuming countries. The acceptance by consuming countries, especially by the United States, of such a situation was a major blunder. Such avoidance of direct negotiation was, however, only one aspect of the new line of appeasement.

Typically, within weeks following the agreements the OPEC countries began reneging on their commitments and imposing a series of endless "supplementary agreements" on the consuming countries. Each was presented as a "last demand," but companies acquiesced, passing the costs along, and the prices have been spiraling ever since. In 1971 the posted price for Iranian light crude stood at $2.27, in 1972 at $2.47, in August 1973 at $3.05, in mid-October 1973 at $5.09, and in January 1974 at $11.65 (Issawi 1972; Petroleum Press Service, 1972-74). The price increases, however, had a secondary and no less disruptive effect on the system. They radically altered the delicate balance in dependencies between importing countries and exporting countries by making at least some of the latter less dependent on their oil revenues, and, more importantly, by making more consuming countries dependent to a greater degree on a smaller number of oil-exporting countries. In other words, there has been an erosion of the balance on both the demand and the supply sides.

By the early 1970s, it thus became clear to the United States that its oil import quota was no longer tenable and that a drift into high import-dependency was almost unavoidable. The growth rate of energy demand did not strain the system; it was, rather, the drastic increase in importers' dependence that modified the precrisis patterns of mutual dependence. In retrospect, then, one could observe that as the United States moved from a national policy of low dependence into one of increasing dependence, a significantly greater burder was placed on the multilateral system, which had been designed to handle only Japanese and European dependencies. In 1970 the United States was satisfying 23 percent of its domestic demand by importing oil; in 1971 imports grew to 26 percent; in 1972, 29 percent; and the share of imports in pre-embargo 1973 was a staggering 37 percent of demand. Most laissez-faire projections for the rest of the decade showed a steeply increasing curve.

For the system to remain in equilibrium following such increased importers' dependence, a similar increase should have taken place for exporters—their need for or reliance on their revenues should have increased correspondingly. In fact the contrary happened. First, the increase in prices following the Teheran and Tripoli agreements had the effect of reducing exporters' dependence on their revenues in direct proportion to the price hikes. Clearly, the higher the posted prices, the higher the government take. To the extent that producers' dependence on oil revenues is determined by their absorptive capacity for such revenues, the trends that could be extrapolated following the 1971 revolution in posted prices all show a decrease in producers' dependence and, hence, greater reluctance to meet Western demands for their exports. Whether one makes high or low price assumptions, extrapolations show that the second half of 1970s would present maximum tensions between supply and unsatisfied demand as revenue surpluses begin accumulating in OPEC countries. Such projections may never materialize, but they are symptomatic of a growing awareness of the emerging asymmetries.

In addition, the decrease in exporters' dependence was further accentuated by the concrete geographical form it acquired. Western demand for oil could be more and more satisfied by Middle Eastern and North African supplies. If in 1971 those regions supplied about 53 percent of the Free World production, that share was expected to grow to 56 percent by 1975 and 58 percent by 1980 (Middle East Information Series 1973). The concentration of Western reliance on this volatile region was particularly problematic, for the major Middle Eastern producers were the least dependent of all exporters on a continuous flow of oil revenues.

As Western thirst for oil grew, Saudi Arabia seemed to be most responsive, increasing its production at a rate commensurate with Western demands. Saudi Arabia had reasons to consider production freezes. At 1971 production levels it clearly had enough revenues flowing in to maintain its growing economy. Increased production, all with high government takes, could only present Saudi Arabia, the "swing state" in the oil business, with an "embarrassment of riches."

The kingdom lost money twice in dollar devaluation and lacked adequate investment channels; it therefore could not respond favorably to Aramco's ambitious production expansion plan—up to 20 million barrels daily by 1980 (Yaari
1973).

Thus in 1973 the energy system entered a period of acute disequilibrium,
a situation of increasing Western dependence on Arab oil caused by a great reduction in export-dependence on the part of producers. That export dependence
decreased following the embargo and price hikes of October 1973-January
1974 can be seen as the flow of revenues going to producers is compared with
precrisis flows: an estimated $95 billion in 1974, as compared with an esti-
mated $27 billion a year earlier. The Arab states alone were expected to receive
$51 billion in 1974, as compared with $15 billion in 1973. It was under such
circumstances that the multilateral system was strained by an unprecedented
level of import-dependence.

Restriction of supply, whether for political reasons or as a cartel policy,
is only likely to aggravate the state of disequilibrium by creating conditions for
even higher oil prices in a tight supply situation. The question that confronts
the West, then, is to find the most promising way out of the vicious circle. So
far there have been no serious attempts to break the disequilibrating processes;
there have been, however, signs of Western efforts to restore stability. One
thing is clear to all: the crisis resulted from an overly strained system of fragile
patterns of interdependence. A constructive way to restore stability would be
to reduce the strains on the system and to restore a modicum of balance to it.

TWO APPROACHES TO RESTORING STABILITY

To the extent that a crisis is a situation of change, the world is still undergoing a period that can be termed an energy crisis. The period is characterized
by perennial smaller crises, often in the form of shortages, and rapid and sometimes violent changes in the many factors that make up an energy system. Still,
there are numerous signs indicating the possible ingredients of the new system
that is likely to take shape as a new equilibrium stage is reached. The basic elements that concern this study, however, are the new patterns of dependence
and cooperation that will replace or augment those of the system now under
pressure. There are two distinguishable approaches to future world cooperation
on energy. Both combine what is essentially an acceptance that the old system
of multilateralism has been discarded with certain corrective actions. Also,
neither approach is reactionary, in the sense of trying to reverse the course of
events that led to the current disequilibrium. For example, actions to bring
about a collapse of OPEC, an inherently weak group, are no longer explicitly

discussed at policy-making levels, although such a line could have been effective. Both approaches also seek to compensate for the disintegration of multilateral interdependence by concentrating on intensifying inderdependence along certain lines. The approaches differ, however, regarding along which lines dependence ought to be strengthened. In reality, they represent diametrically opposed schools of thought with respect to the issues of maintenance and management of interdependence. If each were to be implemented in its pure form, totally different situations would be created.

The first school of thought, shared by many American energy planners, views the horizontal axis of cooperation among consumers as most likely to restore stability, expecting consumers' cooperation to be paralleled by producers' cooperation, already institutionalized through OPEC. The solution recommended by proponents of this course, therefore, is to channel producers'-consumers' interdependence into a single pattern, thus restricting the scope of interdependence. At the same time, however, increased interdependence would occur among consumers as they form a united bargaining front vis-a-vis the producers' front. The dialogue that is likely to ensue would be one of increased vertical competitiveness and decreased vertical cooperation. Conversely, the horizontal axis would manifest decreased competitiveness and increased cooperation.

The second school of thought, typified by French and Japanese energy policy-makers, seeks to reverse the order of priorities delineated above. The advocates of this school also wish to reduce the excessive strains of interdependence; but for them the desired axis of cooperation is vertical—between consumers and producers. Clearly, the effect of such a course of action would be to reduce multilateralism to bilateral arrangements on a country-to-country basis. The vertical approach rejects horizontal cooperation because it is suspicious of any such interdependent relationships and would prefer clear national policy courses. Second, the potentially disruptive element is apparent in the horizontal approach; it is more latent in the vertical one. In the longer term it is worth bearing these differences in mind, for they may signal an attitude toward cooperation in general. Such a signal could give us the clue for the future of interdependencies.

Horizontal Cooperation

It is hardly surprising that among all protagonists in the world oil game, the United States should be most consistent in its advocacy of free trade and multilateralism. As noted before, such a policy was not only in line with the liberal outlook that dominated American planning after World War II, but was closely linked to the fact that such a multilateral system represented American hegemony and control. In the old multilateral system the five major American companies were dominant, and the norms governing world trade clearly benefited the United States. This is the spirit that is reflected in Undersecretary of State William Casey's remarks: "We believe that the long-term interests of both consumer and producer nations will be served best by an open system in which all those capable of finding, developing, and marketing oil resources can have an opportunity to do so" (*Department of State Bulletin* 1973). So long as such an open system implied American-British domination of the system through their companies, no additional international organization was necessary. The creation of OPEC, however, turned everything upside down, with power shifting from the companies to OPEC. Inevitably the American position, as Casey put it, "requires that consumer countries intensify consultation among themselves and with producer nations on their policies and avoid misunderstandings of each other's positions which could lead to a competitive struggle for exclusive arrangements." This is a diplomatic formula for what amounts to the suggestion that the only reply to OPEC's notion of producers' collective bargaining can be a consumers' organization that will bargain collectively on behalf of its members. The rationale is simple enough: if the system was destabilized by unilateral cooperation among exporters, stability could be restored by similar cooperation on the part of the importers.

An alternative option is to attempt to break the exporters' cartel. To economists who favor free trade and who realize that cartel dynamics are essentially unstable, this option looks both attractive and feasible (Adelman 1972-73). Such an option, however, does not appeal to several interested parties. The oil industry feared the implication that it would have to withdraw from the production stage. Government officials disliked the conflictual nature of such a policy, even though it was only economic. Advocates of horizontal cooperation believed that their line would result in negation of OPEC's power without necessitating tactics that smack of trust-busting. But to critics of a concerted policy by consumers, even horizontal cooperation appeared to be a prescription for confrontation with OPEC. OPEC members and some oil executives see things this way. To them, OPEC's existence is neither ephemeral nor illegal, and should be accepted. Still, horizontal interdependence transcends the mere formation of a counter-OPEC organization. The moderate approach along these lines emphasizes a multitude of actions that need be taken by consumers in concert. An example of such a platform is Walter Levy's proposal for an Atlantic-Japanese energy policy. Ten broad categories are developed according to Levy's conception (Levy 1973):

1. Develop a program for optimum diversification of supplies, based on a study and review of energy demand and supply, including

tanker, pipeline, and refining availabilities.

2. Develop new energy sources, especially atomic energy and energy from unconventional sources, through a joint research program.

3. Create national and multinational incentive, investment, and guarantee programs for the development of new energy sources.

4. Establish broad terms of reference and parameters acceptable to oil-importing countries for oil supplies from producing countries, which cover purchases, service contracts, concessions, and so on.

5. Set up a contingency system for stockpiling, rationing, and equitable sharing of imports between all members to be put into effect in case of an over-all or specific country emergency.

6. Set up a joint and coordinated research program that looks into all methods of conservation of energy, including research on battery-powered cars, nuclear-fueled shipping, savings in motor car transportation, and so on.

7. Review and coordinate programs of economic development and technical assistance for producing countries.

8. Review prices, costs, and the balance-of-payments effects of oil imports of member countries and of developing countries, and set up a program for support and adjustment if necessary.

9. Review the government revenues of major oil-producing countries and their impact on world trade, world capital flows and short-term money markets, and set up a program of financial cooperation if necessary.

10. Review the dependency of Middle East producing countries on the exports from the free world's oil-importing countries of industrial and agricultural goods and military equipment, and technical know-how, shipping and services. Assess in light of this the mutal interdependence and the means that might be available to cope with an oil or financial emergency.

Although Levy's program is couched in highly general and moderate terms, it represents an ambitious form of horizontal interdependence. Its ambitiousness lies in the fact that it assumes that the condition importers share in common is sufficient to bring them together for comprehensive planning of the sort Levy envisions. This program also suggests, of course, the establishment of a central organization with authority vis-a-vis importers not unlike that of OPEC vis-a-vis exporters. This International Energy Council, however, would still be predominantly a consumers' organization, for the policy of horizontal interdependency Levy recommends is aimed at preventing two kinds of situations: a disequilibrated system with weakened companies and OPEC hegemony over oil and money markets, and—and more alarming to Levy—a system in which

OPEC divides and conquers by picking off one importing country after another. In other words, Levy's argument for consumers' cooperation rests on his rejection of the antithetical approach—that of vertical interdependence.

Vertical Cooperation

Clearly, the position of those who prefer vertical interdependence stems from their differing assumptions. The fundamental premise underlying this approach is its disillusionment with international—or transnational, for that matter—cooperation. The nationalistic-mercantilistic outlook typical of this approach is even more pronounced, since it identifies notions of multilateral interdependence and free trade with American hegemony or attempts at preserving American systems. This is why the United States favors horizontal cooperation, while countries such as France and Japan, possessing longstanding nationalistic attitudes, combine a preference for vertical interdependence with their resentment of American economic hegemony. In all fairness, however, there is more to vertical interdependence than mere anti-Americanism. There is the realistic observation that, despite the generic common interest in being net importers of energy, OECD members are far from sharing similar positions on and interests in energy.

In fact, there are quite a few inherent differences among OECD countries, aside from the differences in orientation. First, while both the United States and Japan are geographically remote from the Middle East and North Africa, Europe is adjacent to these regions. The European proximity is a geoeconomic and political parameter that cannot be ignored. Second, even the worst dependence projections for the United States do not place it in the category of extreme import-dependence to which Europe and Japan belong. Third, in absolute terms, Europe is by far the largest buyer of North African and Middle Eastern oil: even high American dependence would still amount to less than half the quantities Europe will be importing from that area. Fourth, as noted above, the system that brought about a crisis is identified with the United States. In effect, many Europeans and Japanese believe that American need for Middle Eastern oil has done much to drive up prices—and not without tacit American agreement. Fifth, the fact that five of the seven major oil companies are American is viewed as a distinct inequality; the companies are assumed by Europeans and Japanese to be American instruments at worst, and self-serving entities at best—and certainly not protective of each consuming nation's interests. Furthermore, countries such as France, which have national companies of their own, are competing with the United States, Britain, and their multinational oil companies. Sixth, and perhaps most important in terms of the options available to them, not all oil importers can avoid either form of inter-dependence by falling back onto an autarkical policy of self-sufficiency. This is a crucial point to observe, because those with high autarkical potential are also producers of energy despite their net deficit, while countries with little autarkical potential are probably not even producers on a domestic scale. Consequently, the interests of large-scale producers such as the United States can hardly be similar to those of Japan, say, when it comes to such crucial parameters as the price of energy. North America enjoys a far more advantageous position than Europe or Japan:

| | Oil-Saving Capacity | Degree of Self-Sufficiency in | |
| | | Oil | Total Energy |
		(percent)	
Japan	0.6	0	11
Italy	0.7	6	15
Belgium	0.8	1	18
France	0.8	5	22
United Kingdom	0.9	2	53
Germany	1.0	7	51
Netherlands	1.1	7	64
Canada	1.1	98	110
United States	1.4	74	89

Notes: It should be stressed that oil-saving capacity (the proportion of industrial to non-industrial use of energy) is a very rough relative indicator of how countries rank in this particular aspect, but it can in no way be interpreted as an absolute measure.

The degree of self-sufficiency is the indigenous supply as a percentage of total primary energy requirements. Figures apply to 1971, and have changed somewhat since then.

Source: OECD 1973.

A policy of North American self-sufficiency is clearly feasible; it does not escape Europe and Japan that if mercantilism is the name of the game, autarky is its supreme manifestation. This advantage enjoyed by the United States and Canada (Britain, Norway, and the Netherlands to a lesser degree) can manifest itself to their favor both in a context of vertical interdependence, with the United States being in a better position to strike its own bilateral deals if it so chooses, and in a context of horizontal interdependence, with the United States bargaining from a superior stance within the consumers' group.

Finally, not all importing countries share the same position or policies in general world affairs, the United States least of all. In an age of interdependence, where linkage strategies are part and parcel of international behavior, it is not enough for mutuality of interests to be present in only one or a few functional areas, since cross-functional linkages are likely to disrupt any cooperative arrangement made along strict functional lines. Thus, the fact that the United States is a world power with global responsibilities and commitments is irreconcilable with European and Japanese regional orientation. In American thinking, energy is not a prime determinant of foreign policy, while freedom of action in foreign affairs is assumed to be of paramount importance. On the other hand, Japan and Europe can place energy and the safeguarding of its supply higher on their order of priorities, thus subjugating foreign policy to energy policies.

The implications of this for a country like France are simple: in spite of denunciations of such policy as a "beggar my neighbor" type of activity, vertical interdependence seeks to strengthen importer-exporter ties. This is achieved by the following procedures: First, outflanking the oil multinationals and establishing direct government-to-government contact, leading to the bilateral pattern. Second, an agreement for a guaranteed supply of oil (or gas) at certain prices for a predetermined period is attained. Third, a higher-than-usual price for such "safe" supply is negotiated, but the payment is often made in other than pecuniary forms. Arms, credit, and technological assistance are common substitutes for money. This barter aspect of vertical interdependence is not necessarily indicative of the foreign-exchange difficulties that could otherwise arise; rather it is typical of the spillover of interdependence from the energy area into others. This is done deliberately to offset the increased import-dependence of the consumer. Fourth, the pinnacle of vertical interdependence is the recycling of money into the importing country as a form of investment. Ideally, then, proponents of vertical interdependence would like to see heavy exports of goods and services into the producing countries, paralleled by heavy investments by producers in the economies of the importing countries. Presumably such intensification of producer-consumer interdependence will restore stability to the market as each finds a suitable partner and each develops a stake in the prosperity of the other, thus reducing the incentive for such punitive exercises or arm-twisting tactics as that of brandishing the oil weapon.

CONCLUSION

This analysis demonstrates that the multilateral energy system as it existed for more than 20 years after world War II was a very fragile construct. Its basic stability hinged on the continuation of a series of delicate internal balances. Most important of these balances was that between the patterns of export- and import-dependence, the latter referring to the consuming countries' need for revenues accruing from the exporting of oil. As a result of the multinational oil industry's keeping the price of oil well below the monopoly level, the system evolved symmetrically in the two crucial dependence areas and multilaterally with respect to its mode of operation. It lasted for two decades because, when balanced, energy interdependence proved to be quite flexible and efficient.

The system came under pressure in the 1960s, when counter-multilateralism forces, mainly in the exporting countries, began undercutting the oil industry. Some importing countries formed their own national companies. The principal event, however, was the coalition of the oil-exporting countries to form OPEC. That organization failed in its declared purpose as long as the industry and home governments of the major firms were committed to the multilateral system—in effect, an American-British hegemony system. The watershed came in 1971, when, under somewhat disadvantageous circumstances—principally an American drift toward increasing import-dependence—the consuming nations changed their position from resisting OPEC to appeasing it. Then, with Pandora's box wide open, prices skyrocketed, the industry lost almost all influence over producers, and supply stopped being responsive to demand as curtailment of production occurred, be it for explicit economic reasons or economic-diplomatic linkages. The entire system collapsed into acute crisis in late 1973.

In reaction to the limits to multilateral international cooperation and in an effort to reduce the burdens placed on the patterns of energy interdependence, two alternative courses of action have emerged. The rationale dominating the first, a proposal for joint Atlantic-Japanese cooperation in energy, is that disunity among importers and solidarity by exporters have been the principal causes of the crisis. It is therefore asserted that only by forging a concerted program of action by consumers can a semblance of balance be restored to the disequilibrated system. Its critics point out that the weaknesses of such a plan lie in the fact that the United States, which purports to lead the new energy alliance, is in a totally different position from most European nations and Japan. Thus, neither America's energy status nor its overall global policies are reconcilable with the organization or programs advocated by proponents of such increased horizontal interdependence.

Critics of horizontalism recommend verticalism, the establishment of closer and more extensive ties between consumers and producers, usually on direct government-to-government levels. The differences between the two approaches are clear. One suggests restrictions on interdependence via multilateralism within two blocs—one of importers, the other of exporters. The other approach advocates the elimination of multilateralism in favor of bilateralism. Moreover, the former necessarily implies a policy of resistance to the oil exporters' demands; the latter, their appeasement. Insofar as multilateralism is represented by Americans and bilateralism by its European and Japanese allies, the question arises of the effects of such divergence in opinion on the cohesion of the alliances, principally the Atlantic Alliance.

Clearly, the United States will not seek to impose its vision on its European allies. Still, there seems to be a compromise policy that would be compatible with American-European and, by implication, Japanese interests. First, a policy of capacity for or actual achievement of relative self-sufficiency for the United States may be advantageous to all concerned parties. The United States would minimize the dangers and vulnerabilities connoted by dependence, thus maintaining the international freedom of action it desires. Europe and Japan would not have to compete with the United States for world oil, thus lessening the stresses that were taxing the energy system before the crisis exploded.

Finally, even the oil exporters would not necessarily resent a low American energy profile, which would exert less pressure on them to expand production beyond the point that is optimal from their standpoint. In other words, an American avoidance of a dangerous drift into dependency would simultaneously alleviate strains on the system and remove one of the causes of the crisis. Second, the group of oil importers who have little or no autarkical potential of their own, except for the long run, could form a mini-import organization and also cultivate a producers-consumers relationship in a concerted fashion. It is, in short, a mixture of vertical and horizontal interdependence. Policies followed in accordance with these principles stand a good chance of re-creating a viable energy system.

The conclusion drawn above implies, however, that North America should divorce its energy policies from those of Europe and Japan. Paradoxically, this course of action is also necessary for the maintenance of the alliance. As noted in the introductory remarks to this analysis, economic affairs seldom offer an opportunity for full international cooperation. Thus the pillar of the Atlantic Alliance is the common defense it provides. Trade, money, and energy are all areas of intense rivalry within the Alliance, as they are even within the European community itself. The Alliance should, therefore, not be expected to be united in areas where its members are in natural competition. So long as security concerns predominate, the Alliance will last. If energy continues to occupy the top priority, the Alliance will probably collapse. The future of the Alliance, then, is certainly not a function of its being soluble in oil.

It is quite difficult to see how the two schools of thought on energy cooperation could be reconciled. The least dangerous solution would be for the United States to seek energy independence, at least relative to the politically and economically problematic Arab oil. Japan and most European nations would simultaneously find their own mixture of vertical and horizontal interdependence, a combination much more feasible once the United States embarks on its own program. But cooperation has often fallen short of what was required to maintain tranquillity and prosperity. A cooperative solution on the part of the West is needed if the oil challenge is to be blunted. Otherwise, the crisis will be prolonged and future solutions will inevitably be less cooperative on all counts.

9

SOVIET-AMERICAN RELATIONS AFTER THE ENERGY CRISIS
Abraham S. Becker

It may seem churlish to begin this chapter by discounting the centrality to its discussion of the present volume's focus. But, to this observer at least, it does not appear that the energy crisis is a central fact of the evolving relations between the United States and the USSR. This is not to deny the reality of some connection. The energy crisis links directly with the growth of U.S.-Soviet trade and thereby to the progress of detente. Because it impinges on U.S. relations with its allies and with the developing countries, the energy crisis indirectly affects U.S.-Soviet relations as well. However, it is not likely to be one of the major determinants of the course of Soviet-American relations, for it will probably not radically alter either the internal or the external conditions of these relations—neither the domestic structures and mutual perceptions of the protagonists, nor the elements of the international balance of power. Thus, whether China and the USSR remain hostile to each other or achieve rapprochement, whether the mutual security treaty continues in force and as the basic cement of U.S.-Japanese relations, whether southern Asia runs a nuclear arms race, whether Western Europe falls gradually under Soviet sway—none of these major external conditioning factors seems likely to be determined by energy developments. The one region in which energy seems most closely connected to the confrontation of Soviet and American power is the Middle East. But while oil is evidently a key factor there, it is not the only one.

In brief: from a present vantage point—which may, of course, turn out to furnish a distorted perspective—the energy crisis does not seem to promise a fundamental impact on Soviet-American relations, because it is only marginally linked to the fundamental issues. This paper discusses the two sets of issues in which the energy crisis does seem to play a relatively significant role: U.S.-Soviet trade and superpower interaction in the Middle East. However, to understand the direction in which Soviet-American relations in these areas are headed, it seems necessary first to try to understand the general context.

THE STATE OF DETENTE

In mid-1974 U.S.-Soviet relations seem to be in a state of uneasy suspension. Many believe that there has been a deterioration since the heyday of 1972 and the first part of 1973; certainly there has been no substantial progress on major unsettled issues since then. Ahead lie the uncertainties of the continuing Middle Eastern crisis and governmental instability in Western Europe. Is the present halt in the progress of the Soviet-American detente merely a temporary interruption of a process that will soon resume its previous course, or does it portend approach to a watershed in the relations of the superpowers?

Two years have passed since President Nixon first journeyed into Moscow, there to sign a series of path-breaking agreements, including the two on strategic arms limitation and the Declaration of Basic Principles of Mutual Relations. A number of other agreements were concluded then and afterward, ranging from the specifics of trade, cultural, and scientific exchanges to the General Accord on Prevention of Nuclear War signed at San Clemente on June 22, 1973. Both sides considered the network of agreements to be of enormous significance. Georgii Arbatov (1973), the influential director of the Institute on the USA of the Soviet Academy of Sciences, declared that "a shift of historic significance has been outlined in relations between the USSR and the United States. The essence of this shift is the transition from cold war to relations of genuine peaceful coexistence. . . . " For the United States, the accords seemed to signal the end of the race for unilateral advantage. President Nixon (1973) believed they placed U.S. efforts "on a broader foundation . . . [of] new attitudes and aspirations."

Both sides expected that further steps would be taken to hasten and strengthen their rapprochement. Arbatov was confident: "There is no doubt that major positive advances in Soviet-U.S. relations are at hand." President Nixon was scheduled to pay a second visit to the USSR in 1974, at which time Washington hoped SALT II would be ready for celebration at the summit. An article in the October 1973 issue of the prestigious journal of Arbatov's institute hailed the "unprecedented turn in American public opinion": attitudes to the USSR were found to be more favorable than at any time since World War II (Petrovskaia 1973).

Now, on the eve of the President's departure for Moscow, the prospects for U.S.-Soviet cooperation have faded considerably. SALT II appears to have encountered substantial difficulties; the Congress still seems unwilling to grant the USSR most-favored-nation status; and in the Middle East, the Soviet desire for a major role in the process of reaching a settlement often seems to assert itself in the support of militancy and obstructionism. Perhaps the situation manifests a loss of energy in the forward thrust of U.S. foreign policy, which may be associated with the deepening domestic political crisis. In any case, there is evidently considerable disillusionment with the magic of detente. Many Americans ruefully agree with Senator Henry Jackson (1974a) that "the detente has gone from a dream to an incantation without acquiring a definition along the way."

The souring of American attitudes on detente has a number of causes. A cooling of the original ardor for rapprochement was doubtless to be expected. When the ice was thick, as Stephen Rosenfeld (1974, pp. 264-65) reminds us, it seemed important only to break through; and the nature of the means employed was considered secondary. With the breakthrough completed and the pressure for action reduced, there was an opportunity for second thoughts.* One example of a turnaround in American views was the wheat deal, which looked like a boon for the balance of payments in 1972 but like an inflationary giveaway in 1973. More significant in substance was the ebbing enthusiasm for the SALT I accords, particularly the limitations on offensive weapons. As the Soviet missile program developed, the Interim Agreement seemed less and less like a judicious balancing of Soviet numbers against American technological know-how. Two years later it is not just inveterate hawks who are concerned about the prospect of the Soviets' MIRVing their substantial edge in megatonnage.

Another major influence in the same direction was Soviet behavior in the October 1973 Arab-Israeli war (Becker 1974). Breshnev and Nixon had pledged at San Clemente just a few months before to "act in such a manner as to prevent the development of situations capable of causing a dangerous exacerbation of their relations." Moscow violated that pledge before, during, and possibly even after the war. The Kremlin did nothing to prevent the Egyptian-Syrian attack or to warn Washington. After the fighting started, Moscow urged other Arab states to join the battle, turned a deaf ear to pleas for a cease-fire, and massively reinforced the Egyptian and Syrian forces. When the tide of battle turned and the USSR ardently supported a cease-fire, the threat of an Israeli victory elicited a Soviet warning of readiness to intervene unilaterally to freeze

---

*Rosenfeld also believes that increasing limitation of U.S. power abroad "domesticates" U.S. foreign policy, forcing it "to go over the same political hurdles and to submit to the same political processes that are par for the domestic course. Less and less does foreign policy evolve from a professed and coherent world view. More and more does it reflect a test of strength among competing domestic forces. This is the nature of the politics of detente."

the battle lines. (But see Sadat's charge that Moscow in effect tried to trick him into a cease-fire, in the New York *Times* of March 30, 1974). After the war, Moscow enthusiastically supported the Arab embargo on oil shipments to the United States and the Netherlands. "To a Western eye," a New York *Times* editorial (March 16, 1974) complained, the Soviet attempt to conduct economic warfare against the United States with one hand, while simultaneously promoting American investment in Siberia, "looks strangely contradictory." The editorial's conclusion was sober: "There is no certainty that Moscow shares the American goal, emphasized again last week by Secretary Kissinger, of achieving 'a stable international order.' Events in the Middle East make it increasingly clear that, in Moscow's view, detente has very narrow limits."

Thus, Moscow's role in the October war and in the embargo aftermath, as well as the awakening consciousness of the continued Soviet military build-up, have been major factors in the partial disillusion with detente in the United States. When the Nixon administration cautioned that the United States and the USSR were simultaneously adversaries and partners, the U.S. public nodded assent; but in fact it expected to see more of the partner roles and less of the adversary roles. The hope that Soviet-American relations were changing in fundamental ways had led to an emphasis on the partnership and comparative neglect of the adversary relations.

Nevertheless, the exercise of assigning weights to the two components and attempting to measure the net outcome is an idle game, for it fails to come to grips with the central issue of Soviet perceptions and motivations. It will not do to approach the subject of Soviet-American relations as if Soviet perceptions of detente were a relatively faithful reflection of our own. Soviet views of the bilateral relation have a rationale of their own, for which simplistic notions of detente, whether passionately pro or equally fervently con, are totally inadequate.

The Russian word corresponding to detente, the favored Western term characterizing recent U.S.-Soviet relations, is *razriadka.* As the Soviets remind us (Trofimenko 1974), the etymology of both terms refers to basic disarmament measures. In French *detente* means "slackening of the string of a crossbow"; in Russian *razriadka* literally means "removing the charge from a weapon." Thus, both cultures implicitly note that the critical beginning of a warming of the atmosphere lies in the removal of physical danger to oneself and to one's opponent. Had detente been understood in that manner in the West, considerable disillusionment would have been avoided. But in part because secondary detente impulses—cultural and trade agreements, scientific exchange missions, and the like—have developed more rapidly than the primary one of military-political defusing, expectations have been aroused that were excessive in relation to the stage of the U.S.-Soviet rapprochement. Such expectations were bound to be disappointed, and the result was another swing of the pendulum in public appreciation of the issues of U.S.-Soviet mutual involvement.

It may appear that the Soviets adopt the same perspective. *Izvestiia*'s noted political commentator, V. Matveev (1974, p. 57), said: "It is quite clear that cooperation in the economic, scientific, technical, and other spheres can best develop in the absence of crisis situations in the world, in the absence of any danger of armed conflicts between states, above all of a world thermonuclear conflict." Soviet statements have emphasized the necessity of solidifying the "political detente" with "military detente." But here, too, a simple projection of our own perspective into the Soviet framework would be an error.

Although Moscow and Washington have subscribed to a number of agreements in the arms control field, their approaches differ in major respects. The classical Western proposal aims for a set of self-contained measures that provide for a balancing of the security interests of the two sides within a framework that assumes noncompliance to be inevitable unless verification mechanisms are inextricably attached. Successful conclusion and operation of such agreements is seen as building confidence and trust, thereby enabling the participants to move to higher stages of the process.

The Soviet reaction does not explicitly reject the balanced-security approach to building international trust but puts major emphasis on direct confidence-building measures. (In fact, "equal security" is a mainstay of Soviet discussions on arms control.) Balance of power, the core of the Western conception, is viewed as deficient because it perpetuates the arms race, mutual suspicions, and, therefore, the danger of war. With its complex definition of symmetry and its paraphernalia of verification, the Western approach, a prominent Soviet arms-controller stated at a limited U.S. meeting, yields at best "a different level of the balance of power and military confrontation but not the elimination of the latter." Soviet preference was for an approach that, looking to the achievement of "equal security," made possible the use of

> . . . more flexible solutions that take into account the interests of
> the states participating in the negotiations. . . . "Equal security" can
> be achieved on the basis of international legal recognition and possible
> legal agreements between the interested states on the principles of
> inviolability of frontiers, renunciation of the use of force, and peace-
> ful coexistence. It can also be achieved on the basis of reduction of
> both foreign and national armed forces and armaments undertaken
> with consideration of the interests of all those participating in the
> security system.

The Soviet analyst stressed the panoply of measures subsumed under the heading of peaceful coexistence—agreements on economic, scientific, and

cultural cooperation, on the joint communication of principles of peaceful relations, on declarations of adherence to principles of noninterference in internal
affairs, and the like. As an example, in Europe, "the most essential prerequisite
for the international security system . . . is the recognition and strict exercise
of the principle of territorial integrity and of inviolability of the existing
frontiers."

But does not the other side appreciate the delicacy of the nuclear balance
of terror? How can we then explain the gross difference in approach to reinforcing the structure of peace? Unpalatable though it may be, it must be recognized
that the Soviet leadership operates with a perception of the trend of world affairs that is substantially different from that held by most Americans.

One cannot read authoritative Soviet statements of the pre-October days
without being struck by the recurring theme of fundamental change in international affairs. At Alma-Ata in the summer of 1973, Brezhnev (1973) voiced
the "hope that the present detente is not a temporary phenomenon but the beginning of a fundamental restructuring of international relations." Arbatov
(1973), who saw the outline of a "shift of historic significance" in U.S.-Soviet
relations, hailed the results of Brezhnev's visit to the United States in June
1973 as a "major step on the path of implementing the April 1973 plans of the
Soviet Communist Party's (CPSU) Central Committee, which set Soviet foreign
policy a target of historic significance—making irreversible the positive changes
now taking place in the world situation." The vision that excited Soviet imagi-
nations was the prospect of finally exorcising the specter of a U.S. military attack, of setting in concrete the postwar order in Europe, of guaranteeing the
irreversibility of major gains of Soviet policy.*

What made the Soviet leadership so confident of the future? First and
foremost in all Soviet discussions is the "change in the correlation of forces in
favor of socialism." As weakness historically invited attack, so the increasing
military might of the USSR promises inviolability of its frontiers. Soviet security is not altogether guaranteed; the danger of war has not been completely
eliminated, and unyielding Chinese hostility is a matter of possibly increasing
concern. But the U.S. military threat may seem a generally manageable area of
Soviet politicomilitary policy, requiring a combination of military buildup with
appropriate foreign policy mechanisms: the arms control forums of SALT and
MBFR (Mutual and Balanced Force Reductions), efforts to legitimize the European status quo as in CESC (Conference on European Security and Cooperation), and the network of international trade and cooperation agreements.

---

*The fact that the Soviet view couples detente with a perception of historical trends
promising the erosion of American power is a major reason, according to some students of
Soviet affairs, why detente is a Politburo, and not just a Brezhnev, policy.

The 1969 International Conference of Communist and Workers' Parties believed that peaceful coexistence between states with different social systems had to be imposed on the imperialists. Soviet commentators, taking the pulse of U.S. opinion, assert their belief that the "realists" in the United States are becoming convinced that "Cold War" approaches are at a dead end: massive retaliation and flexible response have failed, smashed on the rock of Soviet resolution and growing military might. However, it was not just the achievement of military parity between the Soviet Union and the United States that deflected the latter from its Cold War cause. In the 1960s, "The overall correlation of economic, political and moral forces in the world shifted still further to the detriment of the United States. . . . It was then and only then that a real turnabout occurred in U.S. thinking, and it was then and only then that the U.S. ruling class approached an understanding of the need to find another basis for relations with the USSR and the other socialist countries . . ." (Trofimenko 1974, p. 11). The United States was undergoing a crisis in which foreign economic and domestic problems were intermixed. The Cold War, with its culmination in the cul de sac of Vietnam, had overstrained American resources, which were not inexhaustible. Thus, the United States had reached a crisis of priorities. These were the objective factors that made the U.S. ruling class, heretofore the foundation of the Cold War, increasingly appreciate the new realities. Meeting with David Rockefeller and Pepsico's President Donald Kendall convinced the political commentator V. Matveev (1973) that most influential Am American business "circles" were very interested in the removal of obstacles to the extensive development of U.S.-Soviet economic ties.

The new environment made possible a new approach to the task of securing peace, one that surmounted the limited possibilities inherent in a simple avoidance of military conflict. In his analysis of U.S.-Soviet relations, Arbatov (1973) notes that the Agreement on Basic Principles of Mutual Relations in May 1972 and the June 1973 Agreement on Prevention of Nuclear War indicate that neither power is content with "the mere declaration of its desire to prevent such a war." Both recognize "that the creation of truly reliable guarantees for preventing nuclear war demands the improvement of relations between the two countries, the growth of their mutual understanding and trust, and also a considerable normalization of the international situation." At the same time Arbatov, like almost all Soviet spokesmen or commentators, insists that this "does not erase fundamental class differences." There can be no ideological convergence of the two systems; the (class) struggle between the two must continue. But, as Brezhnev declared on several occasions, the "historically inevitable struggle" would be channeled to avoid the threat of nuclear conflict between the superpowers.

To a considerable extent, Soviet defensiveness about the ideological implications of peaceful coexistence must reflect an attempt to ward off attacks from the Left—not just Maoism, but especially the radical movements of the Third World. Moscow seeks to consolidate the status quo in Eastern Europe, but the Left charges that peaceful coexistence threatens to consolidate all parts of the status quo, including that of reaction and imperialism. The formal Soviet response is to affirm an "objective basis" for a close connection between peaceful coexistence and class struggle: "The more deeply the principles of peaceful coexistence are implemented, the more confidently the people fighting for a . . . radical change of the sociopolitical conditions in the world can act" (Bovin 1973).

But the analysts of Soviet policy also seem to be asserting that peaceful coexistence and class struggle are reconcilable because the struggle is increasingly being conducted on Moscow's terms:

> From a class, social, and political standpoint, the implementation
> of the principles of peaceful coexistence means: ensuring conditions
> of peaceful development for the socialist countries; curbing the im-
> perialist policy of aggression and the seizure and annexation of other
> people's territory; preventing interference by imperialism in the
> internal affairs of other countries, in particular, in suppressing the
> liberation struggle of the peoples, i.e., checking the imperialist "ex-
> port of counterrevolution"; and the banning of the use of force to
> settle conflicts between states. . . . The CPSU and the Soviet state
> organically combine a peaceloving foreign policy with support for
> the peoples' struggle against the aggressive policy of imperialism and
> with the implementation of the ideas of proletarian, socialist inter-
> nationalism. (Ryzhenko 1973)

There is not much here of "mutual understanding and trust." Instead, the rules of the game of peaceful coexistence make the class struggle an integral part. In the nuclear era, superpower military conflict may be inconceivable;* but certainly this is not true of civil wars, wars of national liberation, and other

---

*Some exponents of a military viewpoint do not appear to accept that dictum. To those who cry that nuclear war would mean the destruction of civilization, a rear admiral (who is also the holder of a doctorate in philosophical sciences) cited the CPSU program that if the imperialists unleashed a new world war, the peoples "will sweep imperialism away and bury it." After all, at least half the world's nuclear potential was controlled by the USSR, "and consequently is directed not against mankind but serves as a means of defending mankind. If the imperialists nevertheless unleashed a war against us, the modern weapons in the hands of Soviet fighting men would be a means of routing the aggressor and consequently a means of defending civilization" (Sheliag 1974).

revolutionary movements. The export of counterrevolution must be prevented and prohibited.* As to the export of revolution, "When a people has arisen against its oppressors or when the forces of progress are fighting against the forces of reaction, then helping this struggle is the sacred right and duty of those who take seriously words about democracy and progress, social justice and national freedom" (Bovin 1973).

From the Soviet point of view, the cardinal issue of encounters between Moscow and the West is still contained in the classical question of *kto kogo,* who-whom—who wins out over whom? The Kremlin's current perspective supplies the equally classical Soviet answer, although in considerably more sophisticated form than earlier versions. For the West, detente means increasing partnership in a framework of an ever widening set of common goals. To the Soviet Union, mutuality in that sense is unpalatable and impossible. The clash of these discordant views of the concept that is supposed to describe the policies of both sides suggests the judiciousness of the observation that the "West gains more from the reality of detente. . . . The East gains more from the mere appearance of it" (Stanley and Whitt 1970, p. 96).

SOVIET-AMERICAN TRADE

The question of "who over whom" has an American answer that is substantially different from the Soviet forecast of the outcome of peaceful coexistence. In the Nixon administration's view, the Kremlin is deluding itself. By entering into increasingly comprehensive agreements for economic, scientific, cultural, and political cooperation, the Soviet giant is, in the (London) *Economist's* phrase (December 29, 1973), being "Gulliverized." Peter Peterson, the former Secretary of Commerce, put it more diplomatically (1972):

Our purpose is to build in both countries a vested economic interest in the maintenance of a harmonious and enduring relationship. A nation's security is affected not only by its adversary's military capabilities, but by the price which attends the use of these capabilities. If we can create a situation in which the use of military force would jeopardize a mutually profitable relationship, I think it can be argued that our security will have been enhanced.

---

*"The Soviet Union has regarded, and continues to regard as inadmissible—more than that, as criminal—any attempts at 'exporting counterrevolution,' any outside interference aimed at suppressing the sovereign will of a revolutionary people" (Brezhnev 1974).

This is the "web of interdependency" that the two countries are supposed to be consciously weaving. In that web the strands that are intended to bind the most effectively are the ties of international trade.

Periodically, U.S. business is caught up in a wave of fascination with the potential "size" of the Communist-area market. Such was the case in the early 1930s, again immediately after World War II, and a third time with the detente in Soviet-American and Sino-American relations. "Size" often seems to mean little more than population and area, particularly with regard to prospects for the China trade. However, there has been an extraordinary increase in negotiating activity, and the press is full of announcements of unprecedented agreements for Soviet-American exchanges. Department of Commerce figures indicate that in 1973, Soviet-American trade more than doubled over the previous year's level, with imports increasing marginally faster than exports. Trade with China grew still more rapidly: U.S. exports to China in 1973 were 11 times, and imports were twice, as great as in the year before. Nevertheless, it is important to keep these changes in perspective. U.S. exports to all "socialist" countries, including China and Eastern Europe, accounted for 0.9 percent of total U.S. exports in 1969, rose to 2.1 percent in 1972, and in 1973 to 3.8 percent. The share of imports from these countries in the U.S. total rose from 0.8 percent in 1969 to 1.0 percent in 1973. Despite the spectacular growth of the last two years—and much of it was due to one-time grain deals—trade with all Communist countries accounts for barely 2.5 percent of total U.S. foreign trade; the Soviet portion alone, only 1 percent. Impressive percentage growth in U.S. trade with the Communist world in part reflects a low initial base. Communist countries are still far from being significant U.S. trade partners.

But what of the future? The 1972 Soviet-American trade agreement, the establishment of a U.S. government apparatus to encourage trade expansion, the announcement of a few trade spectaculars (such as Occidental's $2 billion fertilizer-chemical-gas deal—*Petroleum Intelligence Weekly*, September 4, 1972, and May 27, 1974) have whetted U.S. business' appetite and have held out the promise of vast potential for Soviet-American trade exchanges. Among the largest and most prominent deals under current discussion are those involving the development of energy reserves in the eastern USSR.

The lure of Soviet natural gas and crude oil resources has dazzled Western promoters for a number of years. Soviet oil has been marketed abroad since the Revolution, with interruptions for civil or world wars, in fluctuating volumes. Natural gas has been sent by pipeline to Eastern and Western Europe since the mid-1960s. In 1973 exports of crude oil and petroleum products came to 118 million tons, of which 68 million tons were sent to the "socialist" countries (including Yugoslavia) and 50 million to the rest of the world; almost 7 billion cubic meters of gas were exported (MVT 1973).

Although crude and product exports have been a classical feature of Soviet trade, it was not until the discovery and the initial development of the

Siberian fields in the 1960s that the USSR's oil and gas trade began to generate
bonanza fever in Western markets. Three major projects have been bobbing up
and down on a sea of economic and political uncertainty. The oldest was initially a purely Japanese affair: to secure a 25-year supply of 40-45 million tons
of Tiumen crude oil, transmitted 4,000 miles by pipeline via Irkutsk to
Nakhodka on the Sea of Japan and then by tanker to Japan. The other two involved natural gas, one projecting a pipeline from Tiumen to Murmansk, where
the gas was to be liquefied and transported to the U.S. east coast at the rate of
2 billion cubic feet per day (about 20 billion cubic meters a year), dubbed the
"North Star" project, and a similar project of somewhat smaller magnitude that
would have brought Yakutsk gas to both Japan and the U.S. west coast, again
via Nakhodka. What captured the Western imagination in these deals was not
so much the volume of oil and gas involved—the planned gas imports would
have added less than 10 percent of U.S. consumption in 1972—but the dollar
size of the deals, an element skillfully underscored by the U.S. promoters. A
figure of $45 billion was featured in press reports, now ascribed to North Star
alone and including the Yakutsk-U.S. west coast project.

Japan and the USSR have been discussing joint development of Siberian
resources off and on since 1966. Broad general agreement on development
plans or agreement "in principle" seems to have been reached a number of
times, and the general outline of the scheme to bring Tiumen oil to Japan was
clear from at least mid-1971. Discussion centered on the size and the method
of financing the investment in transmission and harbor facilties (the USSR was
asking for a long-term concessional credit, the Japanese preferred shorter-term,
quasi-tied supplier loans), the volume of oil to be obtained by the Japanese on
buy-back, its price and quality, and the adequacy of Soviet reserves for the projected deliveries. It was not until June 1972 that the Japanese were permitted
to send a team to survey the Tiumen oil fields, and the following September
they also dispatched a similar team (with Gulf Oil participation) to Sakhalin to
investigate resources on the island's continental shelf.

Negotiations have proceeded in fits and starts since then, complicated by
government hesitations, the problematic role of American partnership, and the
difficulty of extracting information from the Soviet hosts. The Tiumen oil deal,
beset in addition by Soviet announcement in late 1973 that it could guarantee
no more than 25 million tons a year, now seems to have been put on the shelf,
at least for a while. In a press interview at the end of May 1974, the Soviet
Minister of the Oil Industry, Valentin Shashin (New York *Times,* May 27,
1974) indicated that the oil was needed in the USSR and that the Japanese
would have to wait for seven or eight years, while a duplicate trans-Siberian
railroad was constructed north of the existing one. Shashin may have been
trying to raise the Soviet price on the Japanese deal, hoping to get the railroad
as well as the pipeline financed abroad. But the railroad is obviously of prime
strategic importance, and the Japanese government will want to consider Chinese sensitivities with extreme care. (It may be recalled that the Soviet interest
in Japanese-Soviet energy projects picked up sharply after President Nixon's

visit to Peking in 1971. The latest incident reemphasizes the lesson that there is a politics of Soviet energy trade as well as an economics and that neither aspect can be ignored in dealing with the USSR.)

Other joint projects with the Japanese seem to be intact. In April 1974 partial agreements were reached on the terms of more than $1 billion in loans for three Siberian projects (timber, coking coal, and natural gas, in order of size) and on the scope of the project for exploitation of Yakutsk natural gas (Press bulletin, Moscow Narodny Bank, London, April 26 and May 1, 1974). It is noteworthy that a final go-ahead depends on equal U.S. participation* in the $200 million loan, a figure 33-66 percent higher than the estimates of the previous summer. Negotiations on all the Japanese-Soviet projects—including the Tiumen-Nakhodka pipeline—are under a September 1974 deadline imposed by Moscow in March, on the grounds that thereafter it would be too late to include them in the new (1975-1980) Five-Year Plan (Press Bulletin, April 3, 1974).

As far back as August 1970, on the occasion of an American visit to buy oil field equipment, Shashin had hinted at the possibility of selling sizable amounts of Siberian oil to the United States. American interest tended to focus on gas, however; and in late 1971, the Soviets began talking up the possibilities of a Soviet-American gas deal that would guarantee an approximately $1 billion annual gas supply to the United States over a long period of time. Discussions were pushed forward by the then Secretary of Commerce, Maurice Stans, in his visit to Moscow in December 1971; and a team of American experts was sent over in January 1972. A deal was supposed to be on the verge of completion at the end of 1972 and again in the summer of 1973.

It was clear that the gas was there. Proved reserves in 1971 were estimated at a level 80 times current production, or about 16.5 trillion cubic meters. Potential reserves, including 14.5 trillion of "solid gas" in the Soviet Arctic, were said to reach as much as 87 trillion cubic meters. Gas fields are classified as "giant" if they contain at least a trillion cubic feet (29 billion cubic meters). The USSR has over 30 fields with 3 trillion cubic feet, some half-dozen with 20 trillion or more and the "super-giant" Urengoi, from which North Star gas was to flow, may contain about 140 trillion cubic feet, or 4 trillion cubic meters (Frazier and Netschert 1972).

The subjects at issue between the USSR and the North Star consortium—Tenneco, Texas, Eastern Transmission, and Brown and Root—as in the Japanese oil case, were investment, size of flow, and price. By November 1972 the consortium felt sufficiently confident of both Soviet and American approval

---

*The prospective American partners are El Paso Natural Gas, Occidental Petroleum, and Bechtel.

to announce that it was within 60 days of singing an agreement (New York *Times,* November 4, 1972). Investment in Soviet facilities—field development, pipelines, liquefaction plant in Murmansk—was to total $3.7 billion, of which the USSR would provide $700 million; the Export-Import Bank would lend $1.5 billion directly at 6 percent and guarantee another $1.5 billion 15-year, 7 percent credit supplied by the private sector. In addition, the consortium would build 20 LPG tankers in the United States at a cost of $2.6 billion (New York *Times,* January 9, 1974).

A conspicuous omission from the consortium announcement was an explicit discussion of prices and costs. Initially, newspaper accounts used a figure of $1.25 per thousand cubic feet (tcf) "consumer price" (*Journal of Commerce,* November 6, 1972). Later information indicated that the wholesale price on the east coast would be about $1.50 per tcf, roughly triple the counterpart for domestic gas. At the same time, it was reported that the Soviets, in their eagerness to conclude the agreement, were willing to sell "below cost" at $0.60 per tcf, liquefied at Murmansk (New York *Times,* January 9, 1973). Some observers thought the figure of $1.50 a bare minimum.

The 60 days came and went, and no contract or even "protocol" was concluded. Preliminary agreements of intention were signed in June 1973 in Moscow. Nevertheless, North Star remained in limbo. The explanation is readily obtained: from a national viewpoint, North Star was a political, not an economic, project; and in the developing energy crisis of 1972-73, the questionable economics of the project became more apparent while the alleged political advantages were overcast by fears of excessive dependence on Soviet goodwill.

The economic utility of North Star rested on estimates of extensive shortfalls by 1980 in domestic U.S. natural gas supplies. Indeed, this was already true, but it was obviously related to the tight rein on extraction prices that federal regulations maintained. With a wellhead price of $0.20/tcf, little incentive was provided for exploration and development. At a wellhead price of $0.50 or $0.60/tcf, considerably greater supplies should be forthcoming. (*Petroleum Intelligence Weekly* of April 15, 1974, reported: "U.S. oil reserves may have doubled in the price revolution." The issue of May 6 reported sharp increases in exploration and production activity for both oil and gas.) Was it really necessary to invest such large sums in the USSR, taking into account the cost of U.S. government subsidies—concessional Export-Import Bank loans and guarantees of commercial loans, as well as the subsidies required in building tankers in the United States—when the supply of gas domestically was far from perfectly price price-inelastic?

In a story on North Star that precipitated the consortium's public announcement, the Washington *Post* on November 3, 1972, declared that "the Nixon Administration views the gas deal as one of the biggest coups of its rapprochement with the Soviet Union, both economically and politically," as a project "designed to help bring the U.S. and the Soviet Union closer together." This may not have been an accurate reflection of administration views at that time other than in the Commerce Department. Appearing on national television on January 11, Secretary of the Interior Rogers Morton was openly skeptical; and the White House was reputed to be only lukewarm (New York *Times,* January 9, 1973). A Washington *Post* editorial of December 5, 1972, recognized that "if, as a matter of national policy, this country is now prepared to go as high as $1 or more for its supplemental sources of natural gas, there are many possibilities on this continent," and concluded that "the case for the Soviet deal cannot rest on economics alone." The potential political benefit the *Post* envisioned was that "the gas flows would connect the world's three strongest economies [United States, USSR, and Japan] in a net of interdependence," but its final verdict was that the government's decision would require a balancing of the opposing considerations.

One of those considerations was fear of the consequence of dependence on the USSR. The news that the 1973 Soviet commitment to supply crude oil to the West German National Company, Veba, was underfulfilled by 7 or 16 percent (depending on the source) and that France received 4.5 million tons instead of the 6 million requested may have added to such concerns. Moreover, the Soviets were asking $13-14 a barrel from France, with no privileged discounts on prices of petroleum products. The price demanded of the Germans was even higher, $18 a barrel, whereupon Veba canceled its contract after 16 years of doing business with the USSR (*Economist,* March 16, 1974; *Petroleum Intelligence Weekly,* March 18, 1974).

As negotiations on North Star dragged out, the Soviet side became visibly impatient. In March 1974, D.M. Gvishiani, Kosygin's son-in-law and deputy head of the State Committee on Science and Technology, professed Soviet indifference: the project was "not so vividly interesting for us." In contrast with the consortium's claim that the Soviets were eager enough to be willing to sell the gas below cost, Gvishiani insisted that the USSR had "no immense need" to sell the gas and would do so only if the U.S. side came through with the required $6 billion investment (New York *Times,* March 27, 1974).

But North Star is now caught up in the reevaluation of alternative prospects, the anti-import bias of Project Independence, and a view of detente that is considerably less rosy than that before October. The fate of the project is thus far from clear. There is considerable skepticism about the intrinsic economics of the deal, centering on the expected landed cost of the gas and the relative utility of investing large sums in the USSR rather than in North America. In the new atmosphere of cooling detente, an arrangement where the payoff to the U.S. side is drawn out for two decades beyond the point where the USSR receives, and can start exploiting, American technology has begun to seem unnecessarily one-sided.

What, then, are the prospects for Soviet-American energy deals? How have these prospects been affected by the energy crisis? To provide an answer to these questions, it is necessary to review some generally familiar ground.

The Kremlin's decision to push for rapid trade expansion with the West, particularly imports of advanced technology, is obviously related to the domestic Soviet economic difficulties of the past decade. The economy has fallen off its high growth path of the 1950s because of increasing tightness of labor supply and faltering productivity of resources. The latter is not due to temporary bottlenecks but is a reflection of deep-rooted systemic deficiencies, the inability of the planning system to structure enterprise incentives so as to promote a rapid rate of technological development.

To a considerable extent, Soviet leaders acknowledge this diagnosis, and since 1965 have attempted to reform Soviet economic organization in a number of ways. But these efforts have not succeeded in pulling the USSR back onto the high-growth path, and the government does not seem prepared to institute the more thoroughgoing reform that alone might be capable of doing the job. Thus, in seeking to expand imports of advanced technology—whether as machinery or as know-how (licenses, patents)—the government is hoping to find an alternative means of raising productivity at home.

How is that drive for importation of advanced technology to be financed? Long-term concessional credits from the West would be one possible answer, but they are not obtainable in sufficient volume. Sales of gold would help if the Kremlin could abandon its traditional reluctance to dispose of gold freely, but Soviet gold production and stocks have not been large enough to assume the whole burden. The only other important source of finance for Soviet hard-currency imports has been commodity exports, and the staples have always been raw materials. In particular petroleum has been a major earner of foreign exchange since the late 1950s: in 1971 and 1972, sales of crude oil and refined products to Western Europe (excluding Finland) and Japan were valued at about 500 million foreign trade rubles, equivalent to $600 million or more. With the price increases of 1973, Soviet gross revenues from petroleum exports to hard-currency markets almost doubled, to 950 million rubles, or $1.25 billion, on volume growth of but 7 percent (MVT 1973, 1974).*

In terms of sheer physical presence, the total oil potential in the USSR is undoubtedly very high, although Soviet secrecy on oil reserves obscures the precise relationships (see Becker 1973, pp. 176-85). However, the Ural-Volga fields, the mainstay of production in the 1960s, have begun to dry up; and the

---

*Prices in trade with "socialist" countries were relatively stable, except in the case of Yugoslavia, where a 15 percent increase in tonnage exports yielded a 94 percent jump in revenues for the USSR.

western Siberian fields, the hope of the 1970s, present formidable technical, economic, and human problems of development. Rapidly growing Soviet domestic consumption, in this condition of tight dynamic supply, competes with exports not only to hard-currency markets but also to "soft" outlets in Communist countries. Some 57 percent by weight of Soviet crude and petroleum product exports in 1973 were directed to the "socialist" countries, overwhelmingly to the members of CEMA, in fulfillment of a commitment to supply 243 million tons of crude alone over the period of the Ninth Five-Year Plan (1971-75). In nominal terms, measured by prices received in rubles, the USSR appeared until recently to earn more from its shipments to CEMA than from exports to the West (Campbell 1973, p. 52). But, in a real sense, the benefits of the exchange were reversed. A Hungarian writer has described the disadvantage of the exchange with Eastern Europe in the following terms: "The Soviet Union's export of raw materials and fuels to the [CEMA] countries requires 3-3.5 times more equipment than would be required to manufacture the machines it receives in exchange. The value of the raw materials and fuels exported by the Soviet Union to the member countries is three times greater than what it imports from them" (Doboszy 1974). Given the backwardness of much of its manufacturing sector relative to Western standards, the USSR seemed prepared of offer oil at a lower nominal price in Western markets because the transferable proceeds brought in a more valuable basket of imports than did the oil trade with Eastern Europe.

Thus, it was not surprising that the USSR resented its role of energy supplier to its CEMA allies and had been pressing them to satisfy a larger share of their needs in the world market, presumably in the Middle East and Africa. However, the East Europeans could not be cut off in the immediate future, and in the meantime Soviet domestic needs were continually increasing. To these factors it is necessary to add one more—the high opportunity costs of oil exports, whether to hard- or soft-currency markets, reflected in the costliness of mining European-region coal fields and the difficulties of developing the remote coal and gas supplies of Siberia.

The meteoric rise in petroleum prices during 1973 has raised some significant questions about the Soviet oil trade. Obviously, exports to hard-currency customers should now be much more attractive to Soviet planners. How will this affect the prospects for joint Soviet-Western development of Siberian oil and gas deposits? The price explosion might render such projects sufficiently more interesting to make it worth the Kremlin's while to offer more attractive terms to investors or be more forthcoming on political matters at issue with the West. Alternatively, since the rate of return on investment in Siberia from Soviet funds will be increased substantially, the priority ranking of such investment will be raised accordingly. Perhaps the change would be great enough that if foreign investors' terms, political or economic, seemed stiff, Moscow would be willing to put much more of its own money into the enterprise. This may be at least part of the meaning of Shashin's apparent dismissal in May 1974 of the Japanese Tiumen-Nakhodka oil project.

To provide an appreciation of which is the more likely course would require a more thoroughgoing inquiry into the Soviet thinking on the economics (and politics) of Siberian development than either space or the data permit. But a prime issue is surely the degree to which imported capital, equipment, and know-how are necessary for the exploration of Soviet oil and gas deposits. Development of Siberia has been hindered by the difficulties of operating in an inhospitable environment. The purely engineering (as distinguished from the manpower) problem may be viewed as one of both mastering new technology and widening a bottleneck. The first involves learning to produce and operate specialized equipment suitable for the permafrost environment. The second requires closing a gap in the production of required equipment and supplies—field equipment, pipelines, pumping stations. Is the solution based on domestic resources alone only a matter of time? But the technological backwardness of the Soviet oil and gas industry, particularly in drilling, is not accidental. It is long-standing and intimately related to the class of problems centering on the incentives for innovation that has so often been discussed by Western observers. The USSR, therefore, does not export, but imports petroleum exploration and production equipment from the West. It does not seem likely that the need for imported machinery, pipe, and materials will be quickly overcome. Moreover, the scale of the investments required to tap these vast but inaccessible deposits, apart from the deficiencies of Soviet technology and operation, may make it difficult to dispense with Western participation in the Siberian ventures.

The conjecture seems reinforced by consideration of the problem of East European imports. The supplying 80 percent of Eastern Europe's petroleum needs is fulfilled at the cost of forgoing additional Soviet imports of Western technology through expanded petroleum exports. Recent price trends would make it even more desirable, from the Soviet point of view, to cut the East Europeans loose; but this may be politically infeasible as currency deficits shoot up in fraternal socialist countries. A partial solution may be sought in persuading East Europeans to contribute more substantially to the development of Siberia in exchange for a stable supply from the USSR; but this still puts a premium on a rapid expansion of Soviet reserves, at rates that may not be practicable without Western aid. Doboszy suggests that unless development is speeded up sharply, the CEMA countries will incur an oil deficit by 1980 of 150-170 million tons. Unless Soviet planners foresee a substantial decline in the price of Middle East oil, rapid development of the Siberian fields will still appear to be a high-priority need of the next decade.

CHANGING ROLES IN THE MIDDLE EAST

The June (1967) Arab-Israeli war was initially judged a Soviet disaster and then came to be seen as the prelude to a brilliant victory. It required the shock of the July 1972 expulsion of Soviet forces from Egypt to lead many to question the solidity of the Soviet position in the Middle East. So, too, the October (1973) war was viewed as an American defeat and a recouping of Soviet fortunes, but by mid-1974 formal relations had been reestablished between the United States and the major Arab protagonists of October, Egypt and Syria; Kissinger had practiced his "shuttle diplomacy," and President Nixon had made a triumphal tour of Mideastern capitals. In the wings, the Soviets were consumed by irritation and jealousy.

Nevertheless, it is probably a delusion to think that the last revolution of the kaleidoscope is the final one. The Soviet position has not totally collapsed, and the American has yet to be firmly constructed. Cairo and Damascus have too much at stake in the Soviet alliance to discard it—in political support alone, not to speak of the extraordinary volume of arms supplied over the past two decades. For the short run, one must acknowledge that nothing has been settled in the Arab-Israeli conflict; and all the intractable problems remain—rights of the Palestinians, Jerusalem, recognition of Israel's legitimacy, and the borders of "security." Increasing Soviet sponsorship of the Palestinian Liberation Organization may severely complicate the effort to reach a settlement. The forthcoming peace negotiations will put the Arab-American idyll to a severe test.

Supposing that a settlement of sorts is reached, it is not unlikely that the Kremlin will be able to shape its role accordingly. In an attenuated state, the Arab-Israeli conflict may provide a more difficult arena for Soviet maneuvering than in the halcyon days of Nasser and the war of attrition on the Suez Canal. Perhaps Moscow will find frequent occasion to think itself betrayed by erstwhile clients or allies. The combination of American influence bolstered by Arab oil money does not seem like a Soviet map for the "path of noncapitalist development." Sadat's de-Nasserization and desocialization have already aroused outcries in the Soviet press. Perhaps even the Syrians may someday give grounds for such complaints. Yet the Soviet connection is far too valuable for Egypt, as well as Syria, to be yielded lightly; and Moscow may have the consolation of helping to revive the politics of balancing off the powers with which it began its new Middle Eastern course in the mid-1950s.

The foregoing relates to the arena of the Arab-Israeli conflict. In focusing on the energy crisis and its longer-range effects, it may be more interesting to move a thousand miles eastward, to the Persian Gulf. Soviet interests in the Persian Gulf may be subsumed under three headings (see Becker 1973):

1. Proximity to the USSR. To both tsars and commissars, the Persian Gulf has long been an area of great interest, apart from the value of the oil. The fact of contiguity alone would suggest that Moscow would want to insure friendly regimes in the member states. Political backwardness, radical nationalism, and governmental instability increase both risks and opportunities for the USSR.

2. Oil. As noted below, Soviet interests are multidimensional: some concern the Soviet oil trade and others reflect the strategic role of Middle East oil for the West, and therefore the leverage provided for the Soviet Union's continuous effort to remove Western presence and influence.

3. The region's "in-betweenness." Peter Calvocoressi's (1972) term summarizes the principal value of the area (before oil) to the British Empire—the locational link between the Mediterranean and the Indian Ocean. To some extent the region serves the same function for the USSR, which has important interests in the west and a major security concern in the east. A growing blue-water fleet and the Great Power consciousness that brings the military force into being support this role. Reopening of the Suez Canal will bring the Black Sea much closer to the Arabian Sea and will undoubtedly stimulate an increase in Soviet naval traffic on the periphery of the Persian Gulf region. However, what keeps the Soviet navy out of the Persian Gulf is not the present length of its transit routes from Crimean or Siberian waters but the fear of assuming a high profile in an inhospitable environment.

Up to now the Soviets have cast a very small shadow in the Gulf, apart from their minor role in the region's oil trade. Reasons on both the "pull" and "push" sides can be cited. Conservative, traditional societies have shown a considerable measure of stability even under the impact of oil-based development. With the important though still localized exception of the rebellion in Dhofar, dissident movements do not seem to have taken solid root in the Gulf states; radical-nationalist activity is conspicuous by its absence.

For its part, Moscow has been cautious about pushing its way in. The moment it leaves the safety of anti-Zionism and anti-oil imperialism, the Soviet Union risks plunging into the maelstrom of regional rivalries. Awareness of this problem—of the skill required to support Iran and Iraq simultaneously, to be gracious to King Faisal, because he unbent to send a congratulatory telegram on November 7 and yet support the cause of "national liberation" in South Arabia—makes the Kremlin wary of taking clear positions on regional issues other than Palestine and oil. Such circumspection was particularly clear in Moscow's reactions to several recent crises: the intermittent flare-ups between Iraq and Iran over the Shatt-al-Arab and over land border incursions, the Iranian take-over of three Gulf islands in November 1971, and the second round of the Kuwait-Iraq conflict in March 1973.

Nevertheless, there are strains in the region's political situation that may someday upset the current apparent balance and provide new opportunities for

Soviet involvement. Among them are the potential for dissidence in oppressed immigrant minorities, the possibilities for nationalistic agitation present in the continuing dependence of the Gulf sheikhdoms on British civil servants and army officers, and the dislocations that could be caused by eruption of one or another of the region's many smoldering conflicts. In the latter category, the friction between Baghdad and Teheran is of particular concern to Moscow, especially in view of the continuing conflict between Iraq and its Kurdish minority. Soviet support of Iraq is a constraint on Iranian action but also spurs the Shah to engage in an arms race, while the Iraqi Baath regime would like to move the Kremlin from its cautious stance. Moscow has already taken a clear stand in support of the Dhofar dissidents, the Popular Front for the Liberation of Oman and the Arab Gulf (although the Kremlin has so far ignored the last two words in the movement's title and has not made any commitment to revolution in the Gulf states), and has even ventured to rebuke Iran for its military involvement on the side of Oman's sultan against the dissidents (for example, in a Radio Moscow broadcast in Persian to Iran, 16:30 GMT, February 12, 1974. See also *Pravda*, September 19, 1973 and Moscow Radio's Arabic broadcasts on January 8 (17:00 GMT), February 10 (19:00 GMT), and February 12 (17:00 GMT). For translations, see the *Daily Reports* of the Foreign Broadcast Information Service). It is possible to conceive of conditions under which Moscow would oppose the Shah's ambitions in the Gulf more vigorously, leaning its weight more openly to Iraq's side. While not a highly probable development in the near future, the contingency would promise heightened U.S. involvement, with consequences that would suggest parallels to the crises of the eastern Mediterranean.

It may be that the most significant force for change at the present time is the explosion in petroleum prices and producer government revenues, as well as the concomitant changes in producer-consumer relations. In 1973, the six Gulf members of OPEC more than quadrupled the government take per barrel of crude. With such extraordinary increases in revenues, the region's conservative states may be hard put to control the pace of social and political change in their territories. At the same time, the terms on which oil is produced and sold in the Middle East are undergoing radical changes.

To trace the possible effects on the USSR, and therefore on U.S.-Soviet relations, one should begin by noting that the "pure" petroleum component of Soviet involvement in Gulf affairs has a number of dimensions:

1. The USSR now imports a relatively small volume of crude oil and natural gas from the Middle East and North Africa. The 1973 figures were 13 million tons of crude and 11 billion cubic meters of gas—3 and 5 percent, respectively, of Soviet output (*Izvestiia*, January 16, 1974)—and these imports substantially exceeded the levels of 1970 and 1971 (MVT 1973, 1974). For reasons outlined earlier, Soviet imports from the Middle East were expected to grow rapidly, as were the purchases in the region by the East Europeans. But CEMA must now

reckon with the abrupt escalation of world market prices for crude, which must affect the Soviet view of the opportunity costs of hydrocarbon development in the USSR and, therefore, of the projected balance between supplying East Europe's needs and earning hard currency. The basic considerations suggest an influence in the direction of more rapid development of Siberian resources, if possible.

2. Oil is most of what makes the Middle East a strategically important region. Its oil is vital for Europe and Japan, and might well have become so for the United States if not for the embargo. Middle East oil revenues were important for American and some European balances of payments. The concessionary arrangements between international (largely "Ango-Saxon") oil companies and the host countries were Soviet propaganda's favorite horrible example of imperialist exploitation. This was the main lever with which the USSR sought to pry the West loose from the Gulf and make room for the penetration of Soviet influence (for instance, a Radio Moscow commentary broadcast in Arabic on January 4, 1974 (16:00 GMT) bore the title "The Liquidation of Oil Imperialism Is the Need of Our Time"). However, the concessionary era is almost over and full "participation" or total nationalization is on the horizon. How will the USSR perceive its opportunities and risks in the new era of cartelized national oil companies?

Crude oil may be produced, priced, and sold by Middle East national oil companies; but it must also be refined, transported, and marketed. These "downstream" activities are still in the hands of international companies. So long as they are, the producer countries will chafe at the gap in their control of the oil flow and Soviet propaganda will have a convenient focus for anti-Western agitation. Whether Moscow will be able to offer concrete help to the producers in eliminating the gap is another question. Technological backwardness has hindered Soviet drilling operations in Egypt and may raise similar problems for Soviet aid in setting up downstream operations for the Gulf. When the industrial consumers are rushing headlong to do the same job in exchange for a secure crude supply, it is not at all clear that the Soviet Union enjoys a competitive advantage.

This also suggests some of the difficulties that will beset CEMA attempts to secure considerably larger volumes of oil and gas than are now imported at prices the bloc can "afford" to pay. Presumably, CEMA will continue to suffer from a shortage of hard currency, despite the Soviet windfall derived from OPEC's successes, so that straight purchases in the market will not be desirable. Then the bloc will undoubtedly seek to utilize its political leverage with the national companies of the producers to achieve more favorable terms of trade under arrangements to exchange capital and technical assistance for the required crude. That effort may have to wait for a considerable decline in prices before it has real chance of success. The alternative of trading arms for oil looks less promising in the present situation than it did before, for there is a surfeit of hard currency in the region, making local governments capable of satisfying their needs from Western sources. Moscow might have an understandable interest in tapping the vast hard-currency pool in the Gulf; but the competition is tough and the Kremlin's freedom of action is constrained by its regional commitments, relatively limited though they may still be.

Lest this be judged a completely optimistic view of possible developments, it might be useful to make explicit one implication of the discussion: the Soviet interest in the stability of Persian Gulf regimes should not be unduly high. Whether this will mean a significant possibility of U.S.-Soviet confrontations in the Gulf over the next decade will depend partly on Moscow's perception of the costs of involvement in terms of the threat to its more central objectives in other regions of the world.

CONCLUSION: U.S. POLICY TASKS AND GOALS

Whatever the twists and turns that U.S.-Soviet relations may take, there is hardly likely to be a more pressing foreign-policy problem for either side than avoiding armed conflict between them. Since the Cuban missile crisis, the danger of nuclear confrontation has not been especially high; but inasmuch as nuclear war (in any form) must be regarded as a disaster, the probability of its outbreak must be brought considerably closer to zero than we have yet managed to do. It is not clear that the major Soviet-American arms limitation agreements of recent years have contributed significantly to this goal. More likely, it is still the "balance of terror" in its simplest form that has borne the major responsibility for keeping the superpowers some distance from the brink. (For a discussion of the evolving rules of superpower military engagement in the Middle East, see Becker 1974.) Undoubtedly the "atmosphere" has changed substantially for the better. Reduction of fear, hostility, and suspicion may help prevent uncontrollable escalation of a minor crisis into a major showdown. Nevertheless, the most significant challenge to both sides in the decade ahead is to realize detente-*razriadka* in its most elementary sense: to slacken the crossbow's string, to unload the weapon's charge, and thereby construct a more secure foundation of superpower relations than a balance of terror. We have hardly begun to advance on this road.

To restate a truism that is often overlooked, the danger of war arises not merely from the existence of armed forces, however large they may be, but also from the clash of opposing interests and perceptions. In the last seven years, the Middle East has provided the setting for at least three international crises—1967, 1970, and 1973 (on the last two, see Becker 1974). There is not likely to be a dearth of issues for conflict between the superpowers in the coming decade—over the Middle East, Europe, southern and eastern Asia, or corners of the world that now seem remote from involvement in Great Power politics. With respect to the developing countries, the next decade is likely to bring significantly exacerbated conflict with the developed West, as the "hemisphere of paupers," to use Boumedienne's (1973) phrase, will seek to change the rules of the game of the international division of wealth. One much-discussed effect of the energy crisis is the eagerness of raw-material producers to try to use oligopolistic organization in order to affect their terms of trade. Already copper and bauxite producers are attempting to emulate OPEC, to cut themselves a larger slice of the pie. It does not seem likely that OPEC's huge success can be duplicated by other raw material producers (Varon and Takeuchi 1974), but the effort is likely to be made in a number of cases. In any event, the probability of political agitation and unrest seems high, and this is the major point to both Moscow's and Washington's views.

The Soviet Union has some difficulty in getting itself accepted as an "honorary pauper." For this reason, at least in large part, it abhors such a principle of international classification and much prefers to enlist the disadvantaged under the banner of socialism against imperialism and neocolonialism. Nevertheless, Moscow will do its best to fan the flames of the developing countries' resentment and keep the fire directed at the West. How far it will succeed in this effort remains to be seen, but the past decade has shown that "the major transforming forces of the world are less subject to the control of the two superpowers than each had taken for granted in an earlier period" (Shulman 1973, p. 40). In the coming battle of the developing countries to close the gap with the industrialized world, the USSR may be hard put to keep from being identified with the exploiters.

In formulating policy to deal with the clash of opposing U.S. and Soviet interests, the U.S. government will thus be concerned not just to neutralize or remove sources of conflict that could embroil it with the USSR, but also to hinder the latter from the execution of its objectives of narrowing the perimeter of U.S. influence, eroding the international base of support for U.S. policy, and expelling U.S. presence from the areas in which it is still felt.

Shortly after the Nixon administration took office, Dean Acheson (1969) expressed his jaundiced view of the new slogan for U.S. relations with the USSR: "We are not about to move from an era of confrontation to a phase of negotiations. We have been negotiating with the Soviet Union all along. We shall be involved in confrontation into an indeterminate future. The two go hand in hand in the Soviet view." Acheson may have been partly determined to defend pre-Nixon foreign policy. He was perhaps insufficiently conscious of the winds of change in the USSR. But the acid in his comment also serves to remind that the two societies have not yet found a basis for long-term understanding and cooperation.

It is unstylish now to take seriously the ideological themes of Soviet foreign policy. The motivating force of Soviet action is traced to nationalism and bureaucratic politics. Nevertheless, in its dealings with the USSR, the United States is confronted with the task of comprehending a world view and a pattern of elite reactions that is not just different from ours but is consciously ideological and includes the assertion of an unbridgeable chasm between the two societies. Much has changed in Soviet thought and action, but permanent incompatibility of the two patterns of human organization remains an ubiquitous theme of Soviet self-examination.

"Containment" as a foreign policy has often been pronounced dead; but its underlying rationale remains a persistent, if unacknowledged, foundation for U.S. relations with the USSR. It will probably remain an American objective to try to "contain" Soviet thrusts against American interests around the world, in the hope that in time it will be possible to "normalize" the role of Soviet policy and power in international affairs. Marshall Shulman (1973, pp. 49-50), who equates "containment" with "anti-communism" and views it as a negative policy, seeks "the development of an international system which can accommodate change without violence and in which security does not depend upon control of territory. What follows from this is that the guiding purpose of our policy toward the Soviet Union should be to draw it, over time, into constructive participation in this kind of international system." A Soviet reader would insist that this is "containment" in all but name.

10

THE EMBARGO AND
U.S. FOREIGN
POLICY

Joseph S. Szyliowicz

In retrospect, the "crisis" caused by the embargo did not last long. As this book went to press, one high administration official referred to it as a "spasm," and newspapers began to publish stories concerning the glut of oil in the United States and Europe and the possibility that prices would fall. The situation apparently had changed so dramatically in a few months that many observers began to worry that the lessons of the crisis were rapidly fading to dim memories, as the American public reverted to former consumption patterns. U.S. decision-makers, however, could not afford such a luxury, for the embargo had dramatized an increasingly obvious fact—that the international structure of energy supply and demand was undergoing profound transformation and that the United States would soon face difficult decisions related to the supply and cost of energy. While the impact of the embargo was readily apparent on the domestic front, where the announcement of Project Independence symbolized the new concern for energy, the nature of its impact on foreign affairs is more controversial and deserves careful examination.

Such an analysis is of more than academic interest. In our recent travels to the Middle East and Western Europe, we were struck with the disparate views on this topic held by European and Arab scholars, diplomats, and government officials, on the one hand, and by American diplomats, on the other. In the view of the Arabs and Europeans, U.S. policy, especially in the Middle East, has undergone a profound and fundamental change. According to U.S. officials, however, U.S. policy has remained essentially what it was prior to October 1973, though events created new conditions that made it possible for the United States to move actively to implement that policy. Moreover, they

I would like to express my appreciation to Bard E. O'Neill for his comments and suggestions made during the final preparation of this chapter.

argue, the oil embargo complicated U.S. efforts to achieve its objectives in the Middle East.

Such varying perceptions possess profound significance. If Arab statesmen believe that the embargo led directly to changes in favor of their objectives, then the possibility that similar action might be taken in the future is enhanced. It is therefore most important to address the question of just what impact the embargo actually had on U.S. foreign policy, and we shall now place the findings of our contributors and our own research within the context of the analytical framework that we presented in our introduction.

The tendency of the Nixon foreign-policy apparatus to publicly define the philosophy, goals, and objectives of American policy in Presidential "State of the World" messages (Foreign Policy Reports to the Congress) facilitated this undertaking. We are, of course, aware of the criticisms levelled at these reports and, through them, at the foreign policy of the Nixon Administration. Critics have argued that the tactics conflicted with the objectives, that short-term objectives were emphasized to the detriment of the long-term, that the messages possessed little substance and much rhetoric, and that such critical areas as Eastern Europe and the developing countries were neglected. Moreover, as one experienced Washington administrator noted, ". . . between the generalities of a vague policy document and its implementation by hundreds of people— *most of whom will never have read the policy documents*—lie many places for miscalculation and derailment" (Holbrooke, 1970-71; Hoffmann 1973; Hassner 1971; Brzezinski 1973). In spite of such limitations, however, these messages provide valuable insights into the orientation of U.S. policy, and we shall rely upon them for its official formulation.

THE EMBARGO AND ITS CONSEQUENCES

The catalyst for the embargo was, of course, the Middle East war that erupted on October 6, 1973. This event caught U.S. and Israeli policy-makers by surprise, as did the stunning successes of the Syrian and Egyptian armies. Syria almost recaptured all the strategic Golan Heights, while Egypt overran the much-publicized Bar-Lev Line and proceeded to consolidate its position on the east bank of the Suez Canal. Israel suffered heavy losses of men and material in the initial fighting; and within a few days the Israeli ambassador sought substantial amounts of aircraft, tanks, and other essential military supplies to replace the unexpected and alarming losses. Following some debate within the administration, the United States shipped the requested equipment to Israel, provoking, as Peretz points out in Chapter 5, the Arab decision to use the "oil weapon." The official declaration stated:

... the Arab oil ministers meeting on 17 October in the city of Kuwait have decided to begin immediately the reduction of production in every Arab oil-producing country by no less than 5 percent of the production for the month of September. The same procedure will be applied every month and production will be reduced by the same percentage of the previous month's production until the Israeli forces are completely evacuated from all the Arab territories occupied in the June 1967 war, and the legitimate rights of the Palestinian people are restored (OAPEC Ministerial Council Statement, 1973).

Subsequently, individual Arab states moved to implement this policy in their own way. On October 18, Saudi Arabia decided to cut production by 10 percent; on the following day, Libya increased its prices by 28 percent, Abu Dhabi embargoed the United States, and Iraq proclaimed a 70 percent increase in the price of its oil. The escalation was clearly under way in terms of both politics and economics; and before long, the posted price of oil had climbed to over $11 a barrel, and the United States and Holland, together with Portugal and South Africa, were embargoed.

These developments highlight the political differences among the Arab states, as well as their differing economic situations. They also illuminate the dual nature of the "energy crisis"—the decrease or cessation of supply, and the sharp increase in price. The production cutback commanded the most immediate attention, as the embargo of October dramatically highlighted the vulnerability of the industrialized nations of the West. As the weeks passed, however, the price dimension came increasingly into prominence, as economists warned of the consequences of a new oil price structure for national economies and the international monetary system.

Although in subsequent months numerous reports, rumors and analyses disputed the extent and effect of the embargo, the significant datum is what American policy-makers *perceived* to be happening, for their appraisals formed the basis for the decisions taken. They also illuminate the threefold nature of the "energy crisis"—the cutbacks in shipments to Europe and Japan, the embargo upon the United States and Holland (as well as Portugal and South Africa), and the sharp increase in price. The production cutbacks and the embargo of October dramatically highlighted the vulnerability of the industrialized nations of the West and commanded the most immediate attention but, as the weeks passed and the flow of oil was resumed, the price dimension came increasingly into prominence as economists warned of the consequences of the transfer of wealth to the oil-producing states. They pointed to the impact of higher oil prices for national economies and the international monetary system, and statesmen in the industrialized countries soon found themselves confronted with problems of such severity that talk of bankruptcy and depression became quite common. Domestically, the government was galvanized into action; and internationally, the issue assumed a high priority, as shown by the actions not only of U.S. policy-makers but also of those of Western Europe and Japan.

Western Europe

Goals and Objectives

During the Nixon tenure in office, the Atlantic Alliance was profoundly affected by major transformations and events in the international arena. For one thing, Western Europe's emergence as a major economic entity through the EEC made it a serious competitor of the United States. The United States and the USSR moved to a position of approximate nuclear parity and continued to examine ways of strengthening detente. In the new environment, increasing numbers of Europeans no longer worried greatly about security (Frankel 1971; Wohlstetter 1974; Whitney 1973). Realizing that these developments placed increasing strains on the Atlantic Alliance, the U.S. proposed a thorough examination of American-European relations and declared that 1973 would be the "Year of Europe."

Its goal was the establishment of a broadly based consultative partnership in which military, political, and economic problems could be handled. To achieve this goal, a wide range of objectives were identified. In the political realm, the administration stressed the following:

1. Building a common diplomatic framework and establishing a set of principles that would facilitate the reconciliation of national objectives with the demands of a unified Western policy

2. Redefining the basic partnership

3. Examining the concrete problems that impinge on specific American interests and agreeing on a comprehensive way to solve them

4. Increasing diplomatic consultations with European leaders (*FPR* 1973 pp. 77, 80-81; *Current Foreign Policy* 1973a).

These objectives were, of course, closely related to military issues, especially questions raised by the ongoing SALT and MBFR talks with the Soviet Union, and the adverse effects of continued U.S. military deployments in Europe on the American balance of payments. Within this context, the United States focused on the following objectives: devising and implementing a "realistic" defense strategy that would take into consideration the new strategic balance between East and West and would be conducive to a more equal sharing of burdens; obtaining allied agreement on the need to modernize NATO forces;

maintaining the U.S. military deployment in Europe, lest deterrence be under-mined; agreeing on ways to reduce both Eastern and Western forces in Europe (MBFR) without injuring security (*Current Foreign Policy* 1973a; *FPR* 1973, pp. 77, 82-83).

As far as economic relationships were concerned, the United States was troubled not only by the impact of continued military deployment on its bal-ance of payments, but also by the fact that the EEC's stress on regional auton-omy and a relatively closed European trading system was antithetical to the American emphasis on an open international system and had resulted in an in-ability to deal with problems of monetary reform. In response, the United States outlined several objectives, including the identification of concrete eco-nomic issues to be resolved, the creation of a consultative framework for addressing these problems, the restoration of the integrity of a more open trad-ing system, reforming the international monetary system, and the halting of the drift toward protectionism by reducing tariffs and eliminating the prefer-ential trading arrangements between the EEC and the less developed countries.

Energy questions, however, were not a matter of urgency either within Europe or in U.S. policy toward Europe until the events of October 1973. The United States had warned in 1971 that in case of an embargo it would not, after 1975, be able to supply oil, as it had in 1956 and 1967; but the warning had little impact, and attempts by the Europeans to develop a cooperative en-ergy policy were not productive owing to French intransigence (Laqueur 1974a, p. 242). Perhaps partly for this reason, there was little response to U.S. offers of cooperation in energy, and U.S. officials did not place much emphasis on this topic. In a major address devoted to U.S.-Europe relations, for example, Kissinger made only passing reference to the problem, as did President Nixon in his May 1973 message on energy (*Current Foreign Policy* 1973a; Grose, 1973). The Foreign Policy Report failed even to mention the problem in the section dealing with Europe (*FPR* 1973: 77-81).

Methods

Kissinger's awareness of the need to revitalize American-European rela-tions dictated the choice of techniques, but in many cases these were ineptly applied. Though the United States stressed persuasion, offering of rewards, granting of rewards, and to a much lesser extent the implicit threat of punish-ment, it often acted unilaterally, usually with little regard for European sensi-bilities.

The United States did try, however, to improve relations. Persuasion was continually exerted on all levels, including many state visits between American and European leaders. It also offered political rewards by indicating its con-tinuing support of European unity and of European demands for a free flow of ideas and information between blocs. On the economic issues, the United States suggested that it was willing to reduce tariffs and eliminate other barriers in order to foster a more open trading system, and to cooperate in dealing with energy problems. When it came to security issues, Undersecretary of State Kenneth Rush made it clear in testimony before the Senate Foreign Relations Committee that the administration was committed to maintaining current troop levels in Europe and to participating in the modernization of NATO forces (*Current Foreign Policy* 1973b). At the same time, however, there was a subtle de facto threat of punishment in hints that unless the European states took steps to improve their forces and help offset the American balance-of-payments problems associated with U.S. deployments, the administration would come under increased Congressional pressure to reduce those forces (*Current Foreign Policy* 1973a; Finney 1973).

These efforts had little result, and relations remained tense. The Europeans, however, deserve much of the blame for the strained atmosphere. Often divided among themselves, they did little to improve the situation; and the active opposition of some European states, especially France, which feared the possibility that the United States would be able to dominate European affairs if such comprehensive schemes as a consultative partnership and a new Atlantic Alliance were implemented, further complicated efforts to revitalize relations. Thus, in the weeks prior to the embargo, the goal of consultation was far from being achieved (see Brzezinski 1974, p. 46).

Post-Embargo Developments

While the goals and objectives of U.S. foreign policy remained essentially the same after the embargo, the following months were among the most turbulent in the history of the 25-year alliance. The European states, heavily dependent on petroleum imports from the Middle East, were caught unprepared, for the EEC's efforts to develop a common energy policy that would in time decrease its dependency and in the short term minimize the dangers of energy dependency were still at a preliminary level when the Arabs acted. The reaction was one of near panic, for a subsequent EEC report predicted a depression if adequate energy supplies were not available (Farnsworth 1973a).

The Arab action and the European reactions soon generated political conflict within Europe and with the United States. The first difficulty arose when the United States was denied access to European bases when it sought to resupply Israel during the October war. Other actions that irritated Washington included the scramble for bilateral energy agreements, the political concessions to the Arab states over Security Council resolution 242, and the moves by Europe to develop its own policy toward the Middle East and to coordinate with Japan but not with the United States. Moreover, only the Netherlands had been embargoed; but the other countries, ignoring Dutch pleas for community solidarity, refused to divert any of their oil. The United States pledged to help the Dutch in an emergency (Farnsworth 1973b; Gwertzman 1973b; Saikowski 1973).

Seeking to restore harmony to the alliance, Kissinger outlined the U.S. approach to the crisis in a major speech delivered in London on December 12. The plan called for the creation of an "energy action group" composed of "senior and prestigious individuals" from producing and consuming nations who would develop a collaborative program on all aspects of energy. Kissinger also seized the opportunity to address the larger question of trans-Atlantic relations. Speaking of the "uneasiness of the United States" over "recent practices of the European Community in the political field," Kissinger commented that presenting the "decisions of a unified Europe to the United States as *faits accompli* not subject to effective discussion is alien to the tradition of U.S.-European relations" and, consonant with U.S. pre-embargo policy, continued:

> We are determined to continue constructive dialogue with Western Europe . . . so let us rededicate ourselves to finishing the task of renewing the Atlantic community . . . let us complete the work before us; let us agree on a set of declarations equal to the occasion so that they may serve as an agenda for our governments and as example and inspiration for our peoples . . . let us then transform these declarations into practical and perceptible progress. . . And let us move quickly to improve the process of consultation in both directions. . . . (Prepared text, New York *Times*, December 13, 1973)

While the European reaction was generally favorable, the French, in particular, were disturbed by two points in the Kissinger initiative: the possibility that the plan would undermine their own efforts to establish a special relationship with Arab states, and the fear that the United States implicitly aimed at maintaining its influence through continuing European dependence on it. Hence, when the issue was raised at an EEC meeting in mid-December, the final communique called for a concerted effort to deal with energy problems within the community, but to do so while simultaneously isolating the Dutch to avoid antagonizing the Arabs. Dutch anger and frustration were somewhat mitigated by the actions of companies that quietly diverted non-Arab oil to Rotterdam (Goshko and Randal 1973; Farnsworth 1973d; Morgan 1973a; Kemezis 1973b).

The Washington Energy Conference

Despite lack of concrete response to his proposal, Kissinger indicated that the United States would persist in its efforts to create a cooperative arrangement; and President Nixon personally invited the foreign ministers of major European nations to a meeting scheduled for February in Washington (U.S. Department of State 1974a; Apple 1974). Almost immediately French Foreign Minister Michel Jobert warned that, while France would attend, it would oppose any "syndicate of rich nations."

As the date for the conference approached, the climate was further soured by several developments: a French decision to strengthen the competitive capacity of its economy by floating the franc; a proposal by the Western European countries to cooperate in a two-way declaration of guiding principles with Japan, without the participation of the United States—considered an open rebuff of Kissinger's suggested three-way declaration; publicized European doubts of American willingness to share its oil; the continued French and British pursuit of bilateral oil agreements; and a counterproposal by France that a UN conference be held (Rowen 1974; Oka 1974b, 1974c; Oberdorfer 1974; Shuster 1974b; Marder 1974d).

As if to dramatize its stance, France negotiated an oil deal with Iraq on the eve of the Conference (Lewis 1974b). At the same time, Foreign Minister Jobert obtained an agreement from his European colleagues that the Washington conference should not be a decision-making meeting, should not lead to the creation of new institutions, and should not interfere in any way with the freedom of action of the EEC members.

The Washington Energy Conference opened on a very shaky footing on February 11, 1974. Besides the suspicious posture of the European countries, particularly France, the Arab oil producers issued statements ranging from distrust to outrage. Seemingly unperturbed, Kissinger, in his opening speech, called for an ambitious and wide-ranging effort of cooperation among consumers in the areas of conservation, research and development, emergency sharing, finances, development of alternative energy sources, assistance to less-developed nations, and consumer-producer relations. The United States was willing, according to Kissinger, to share its technology and fuels, and to invest heavily in efforts to address the various problems (U.S. Department of State 1974b). French Foreign Minister Jobert immediately reiterated France's position that the conference was a forum for exchanging views, not a commission for formulating new policy or establishing transnational programs, and called on the delegates to avoid an attempt to impose a "new world energy order."

In the next few days, the basic philosophic differences crystallized over U.S. efforts to ensure that the work of the conference would be continued.

And, despite intense French opposition, including a formal dissent in the official communique, West Germany, Great Britain, the Netherlands, and Belgium, with the United States and seven other nations agreed on a comprehensive action program, financial and monetary measures to preclude competitive depreciation of currencies, plans for a conference with producers, and the establishment of an Energy Coordinating Group (ECG) composed of senior officials and ad hoc working groups (Text of the communique of the Washington Energy Conference; Berger 1974; Delarue 1974).

The Aftermath

Whatever satisfaction Washington enjoyed in the early afterglow of the conference soon dissipated as the Europeans, in a new energy-related action, offered the Arab states a program of broad cooperation without consulting Washington. While he denied threatening anyone, State Department spokesman George Vest warned that the United States reserved "the right to take similar action if it should be appropriate" (Marder 1974f). The downward swing of trans-Atlantic relations continued as Nixon warned that failure to cooperate with the United States in political and economic matters would lead to Congressional pressure for a substantial cut in U.S. forces in Europe. "The day of the one-way street," he asserted, "is gone" (Marder 1974e; Morgan 1974a; Shuster 1974c). This explicit threat may have been prompted by other factors as well as energy, but the surprise announcement that Europe would cooperate with the Arabs cannot be discounted.

It was in this atmosphere that the bilateral agreement between Saudi Arabia and the United States was consummated. Although the State Department Director of Fuel and Energy, George M. Benski, stated that the Saudi deal did not constitute a "barter" for oil, the Europeans vehemently rejected that official line. They pointed out that Kissinger had been negotiating with the Saudis at the same time that he was berating them for making bilateral arrangements and that they were only informed of the deal, not consulted (Koven and Ottaway 1974).

Tensions abated in the following weeks as both sides moved to improve relations. The administration deployed a strong lobbying effort to persuade the Senate to reject Senator Mike Mansfield's proposal for a reduction of 125,000 in the U.S. troops stationed abroad and supported the establishment of an "oil facility" within the International Monetary Fund for the purpose of helping European and other nations with severe balance-of-payments problems. The OECD nations pledged to avoid protectionist trade moves for one year, and Europeans agreed to reduce import duties on up to $1 billion in American exports each year, a move that Nixon called "a major step toward improved Atlantic relationships" (New York *Times,* May 31, 1974; Claiborne 1974). The

EEC council also began to consider a major program aimed at reducing European dependence on imported oil (Commission of the European Communities 1974).

Though Kissinger expressed U.S. reservations about a June 10 EEC decision to pursue its dialogue with the Arabs, the atmosphere was decidedly less acrimonious than in March. Kissinger had in mind at this point an informal "gentlemen's agreement"—that Europe would consult the United States without being bound by the results. The formula was accepted at the NATO foreign ministers' meeting in Ottawa in June and endorsed in a formal declaration signed by the heads of state in Brussels in July (*Declaration on Atlantic Relations* 1974, art. 11; Whitney 1974; Hayworth 1974; Shuster 1974d).

Signs of improved relations were also evident in energy matters; and by October 1974 the ECG had made remarkable progress as reflected by the detailed draft agreement concluded in Brussels on September 20 which called for the establishment of a new International Energy Agency linked to OECD. France, however, remained on the fringes, although upon assuming power the new President, Valery Giscard d'Estaing, let it be known that his government was hopeful of finding a formula to coordinate its policies with the ECG (Kleiman 1974; Farnsworth 1974b; Lewis 1974c; Kemezis 1974a).

The Impact of the Embargo

Clearly, the energy crisis profoundly affected American-European relations. It greatly exacerbated existing problems in several areas, causing sharp exchanges and bitter feelings; but, paradoxically, the end result was positive. Despite the difficulties of the "time of troubles," U.S. foreign policy goals and objectives remained constant and discernible progress toward achieving them was made. In fact, the future could be viewed with confidence—a situation very different indeed from the picture of collapse painted by Walter Laqueur (1974b) and others a few months earlier.

As noted earlier, the goal of U.S. policy was to establish a consultative mechanism based on a common political perspective. By midsummer 1974, arrangements had been worked out that brought that goal much closer than before the embargo. The agreement to consult had been accepted; what remained to be worked out—a no less difficult task—were the principles and mechanism to institutionalize consultations.

The degree of movement toward the goal is evident in a consideration of the extent to which U.S. objectives were achieved. Two of these were largely fulfilled—there had been, and would continue to be, increased consultations with European statesmen; and many of the concrete problems affecting U.S. interests were being examined in an attempt to find acceptable solutions. Less, though tangible, progress had been achieved on redefining the relationship between the two parties and in establishing a diplomatic mechanism and set of principles to ease conflicts between national objectives and Atlantic unity.

The most critical change was the new and higher priority that Washington accorded to the energy question in general and its relations with Europe in particular. The embargo brought the issue of consultations to the fore; and Kissinger, believing that a "horizontal approach" was required to deal with the energy problem, seized the opportunity to address the issue. He did not achieve his original objective; he was forced, because of European opposition, to abandon his emphasis on a comprehensive Atlantic charter that combined political, economic, and military issues in favor of separate declarations by NATO and the EEC. And, at the time of writing, only the former had been agreed upon. Nevertheless, substantial progress was made in revitalizing a spirit of community among the allies. To what extent the new atmosphere was a result of the embargo and its consequences, is, however, less clear. One could argue that the United States had to modify its policies in any event, and that the changes in government in Germany, and particularly in Britain and France, brought to power leaders more favorably disposed toward cooperation with the United States than their predecessors.

Japan

Goals and Objectives

As in the case of Europe, U.S. relations with Japan in the pre-embargo period had been affected by major exogenous changes, most notably the emergence of Japan as an economic superpower and the American detente with Moscow and Peking. Also similar to the U.S.-Europe relationship was the goal of the administration in relation to Tokyo: establishing a consultative partnership to deal with political, security, and economic issues.

The need for such a goal was even greater in the case of Japan than Western Europe, for Japan was not accorded a high priority by U.S. foreign-policy-makers. This was clearly manifested by the "shocks" administered to Japan by the Nixon administration's failure to consult Tokyo prior to the President's trip to China and its decision to act unilaterally in dealing with the trade problem between the two countries. These events had a profound impact on Japan, which had always had a very special sense of vulnerability stemming, at least in part, from wariness about perceived anti-Japanese feeling in many countries, including the United States.

Given the negative impact of these developments, Washington saw a need to intensify consultations with Japan and defined its major objectives as maintaining a consensus on policies and increasing its diplomatic discussions with Japan on global issues.

While nothing much was said about security matters in the 1974 Presidential foreign policy report to Congress, Secretary of State Rogers noted that the administration endorsed the objective of reinforcing Japanese confidence in the American security arrangements; in particular, the United States indicated its desire to reduce friction by consolidating and rationalizing its base structure in Japan.

The United States was also reported to be pressuring Japan to play a larger role in defense of the Japanese islands, to modernize its armed forces—preferably through purchase of U.S. arms—and to assist in the regional defense effort by providing such items as trucks and radios to South Korea. For various reasons Tokyo was not favorably disposed to the last two requests (Halloran 1973a; U.S. Department of State 1973).

When it came to economics, the United States was troubled by the trade imbalance with Japan, so the administration's interconnected objectives were to reduce the trade deficit, increase mutual access to trade, and create mechanisms to monitor and adjust trade (*FPR* 1973, pp. 94-105). At a general level, the United States sought the contribution of Japan to the development of principles that would guide the cooperation of industrial democracies in the effort to reform the international monetary system. More specifically, however, the United States, with the cooperation of the European states, brought intense pressure on Japan to resolve the economic imbalance. In response, Tokyo took steps to revalue the yen, reduce import quotas, open domestic industries to foreign investment, and liberalize capital flows and tourist expenditures (Beecher 1972; *Foreign Policy Outlines* 1973).

Methods

In pursuing these objectives, the administration emphasized threats and nonviolent punishments rather than persuasion and offering and granting rewards. This was because Washington, despite its rhetoric, apparently felt that only such harsh tactics would bring about desired results. In regard to Japan's foreign policy, for example, the United States used threats to dissuade Tokyo from seeking to develop more friendly relations with China; only after Nixon's visit was concluded did the United States endorse a Japanese-Chinese rapprochement. It did indicate, however, that as in the case of Europe, it was willing to grant rewards in the form of lowered trade barriers as a part of reciprocal agreements.

Post-Embargo Developments

As was the case with Western Europe, the oil embargo created additional complications and strains in relations. First, it dramatized Japan's extreme dependence on imported oil from the Middle East. Under such circumstances, energy was inevitably a prime determinant of Japanese foreign policy; and it was hardly surprising that the Arab cut in oil production caused near panic and feverish diplomatic activity. Although Tokyo successfully resisted the request of Sheikh Yamani that it sever diplomatic relations with Israel, it nevertheless agreed to endorse the Arab version of Security Council resolution 242 and publicly stated that its policy toward Israel would be reexamined in the light of future developments.

Although it feared that Japan's political concessions would hamper Kissinger's diplomatic efforts, the United States limited its response to expressions of regret, a reaction that was officially described as "mild." This moderate U.S. reaction was due to several factors: Japan's vulnerability in terms of energy had been acknowledged the previous summer at high level negotiations in Washington; the United States could not guarantee adequate supplies of appropriately priced oil; and Tokyo avoided any extreme action, such as terminating diplomatic or economic relations with Israel (Oberdorfer 1973; Morgan 1973b).

Where Japanese economic policies were involved, however, Washington was more concerned, because Japan adopted a "vertical approach" and concluded barter agreements with Iran, Iraq, and Algeria soon after endorsing the Arab position. Yet even here, the differences on policy were ameliorated by Japan's support of U.S. policy regarding the Washington Energy Conference.

As a result, we believe Arad's conclusion in Chapter 8—that the United States "lost a great deal of influence" after October 1973—is somewhat overstated. While relations since the embargo have been marked by disagreements, the basic content of U.S. foreign policy toward Japan has not changed; and there is little if any evidence to suggest that American influence has been appreciably eroded (see, for example, Oka 1974a).

The Soviet Union

Goals and Objectives

The centrality of the Soviet Union in the search for a Middle East settlement and for a stable international order was, of course, obvious. Believing that the Soviet acceptance of strategic balance made fruitful discussions possible, the Nixon administration defined the U.S. foreign policy goal in its relations with the Soviet Union as the creation of mutual interests in maintaining and developing an international structure based on self-restraint in the pursuit of national interest (*FPR* 1973, p. 27).

Following the May 1972 summit meeting in Moscow between President Nixon and First Secretary Brezhnev, at which agreements were reached on

SALT (albeit partial), naval cooperation to reduce the chances of dangerous incidents, the exchange of information and personnel in the areas of health and technology, and on the need to increase trade and improve economic relations, the United States outlined several objectives: continuing to build on its accomplishments (presumably the conclusion of satisfactory SALT and MBFR agreements); the establishment of mutual respect for the security needs and willingness to balance legitimate interests of the United States and the USSR; European participation in negotiations on Europe; reducing the possibility of confrontation in disputes, such as the Arab-Israeli conflict, by exerting influence on the parties directly concerned; and furthering technological cooperation and increasing trade with the USSR (*FPR 1973*, pp. 32-35, 38-39, 60-70. For the texts of the Nixon-Brezhnev declaration and the joint communique following the May 1972 summit meeting, see New York *Times*, May 30, 1972. On the SALT accords see ibid., May 27, 1972 and June 14, 1972.).

Methods

As Becker has emphasized in Chapter 9, distrust and suspicion, rooted in profound ideological and nation-state differences, continued to characterize Soviet-American relations, despite the atmosphere of detente, so the threat of punishment remained an important foreign-policy technique. By maintaining second-strike capability on the nuclear level and significant forces in Europe, Washington sought to convince the Soviet Union that it would respond militarily to any Soviet military moves against itself or its allies. At the same time, however, the United States increasingly emphasized persuasion. Continuous diplomatic discussions at several levels, punctuated by period summit meetings, took place during both Nixon administrations.

Reinforcing these efforts was the enormous reward potential that the United States possessed because of its great technological capability. Above all, the Russians were concerned with obtaining modern technology, and Washington did permit various agreements embodying technology to be completed. On a less significant level, at least as far as the Soviet Union was concerned, the United States made concessions involving the long-standing dispute over lend-lease payments and economic relations and endorsed exchanges in the areas of health, science, space, the environment, medicine, and the performing arts. Moreover, in the sensitive area of security, the United States granted a significant, if limited, reward by agreeing to numerical inferiority in terms of missiles (although not warheads) in order to arrive at a preliminary agreement in the SALT talks.

While these methods seemed to have the desired effect of lessening tension and reinforcing a mutual interest in maintaining and developing an international structure based on self-restraint in the pursuit of national objectives, it was trenchantly evident, as Becker has noted in Chapter 9, that many of the thorniest issues—such as SALT II, MBFR, and a Middle East settlement—had yet to be resolved (also see Wohlstetter 1974). Although cognizant of the complexity of these matters, the administration appeared determined to continue its quest within a framework having the threat of punishment as an important backdrop, but that laid greater day-to-day emphasis on persuasion, offering rewards, and granting concessions. Since this was not conceived as a unilateral effort, the United States expected reciprocation on the part of the USSR.

Post-Embargo Developments

Energy, as Becker has pointed out, did not prove to be a central consideration in Soviet-American relations; detente retains that privileged place and, despite the obvious disappointment on both sides over the failure to reach significant agreements in the SALT and CESC negotiations, each country has indicated its continued commitment to furthering detente. On the Russian side, *Izvestiia* said, in April 1974, that a return to the Cold War was "unacceptable" to the Soviet Union and that Moscow would work "unswervingly" for the improvement of Russian-American relations (Kaiser 1974; Browne 1974). The United States also continued to pursue the same objectives as in the pre-embargo period.

Events in October 1973 could easily have affected this policy, for the USSR deliberately took a number of steps that seriously jeopardized the momentum of detente. These included the Soviet failure to consult the United States when it became aware of the imminence of war; its massive airlift of supplies to the Arabs; its implicit threat of intervention and apparent readiness to move troops, which precipitated the U.S. "red alert"; and its exhortations to the Arabs to use the "oil weapon" (Shuster 1974a). Further, its endorsement of the French policy of independence during the oil crisis proved irritating (Lewis 1974a).

The U.S. commitment to detente was so strong, however, that it proved remarkably understanding of Soviet actions. State Department officials pointed out that, while the USSR obviously approved of the Arab embargo—among other things, it earned windfall profits from the increase in oil prices—it did not mastermind the oil cutoff. Moreover, its Kremlinologists seemed convinced that Moscow was wary of the new power wielded by the Middle East states, over which the Soviet Union had little influence, as well as of the idea of increased Western cooperation in the face of the oil crisis. Finally, the State Department suggested that Moscow's dependence on Western technology for its internal development schemes made it unlikely that it would adopt policies discouraging trade and investment by the United States and other industrialized states. Nor was much apprehension evidenced on the larger question of whether the Soviets would attempt to gain a controlling position in the oil states (Seeger 1973; Wren 1974; Gumpel 1974). Aside from the fact that most of these states remained concerned about "Communist designs" on the area, the USSR, it was felt, lacked the technology to replace the oil companies in downstream activities. The U.S. reaction to Soviet efforts to maintain its position in the Middle East by assisting Syria and Iraq, by moving closer to the Palestinian guerrillas, by endorsing revolutionary activity in Oman, and by cautiously exploring the possibility of improving relations with hostile Libya was also quite mild.

The United States deliberately overlooked the USSR's interruption of the momentum toward rapprochement with the West in order to further its objectives in the Middle East. It also sought to ensure that its own activities not endanger detente. Fully aware of the dangers implicit in the success of his diplomatic efforts in the Arab world, Secretary Kissinger extolled the Soviet Union for its "very useful and crucial role" in organizing the Geneva Peace Conference, consulted with Soviet officials in Cyprus, Damascus, Moscow, and Geneva—and, to counteract the visible satisfaction of some of his colleagues in Washington with the strengthened U.S. position, specifically declared that the United States had neither the intent nor the capability to destroy Soviet influence in the Middle East.

Such a stance was consistent with the pre-embargo objective of acknowledging that the Soviet Union possessed significant interests in the area and was designed to make possible the achievement of pre-embargo goals. In sum, if any change in American policy vis-a-vis the USSR occurred in the wake of the energy crisis, it was largely in the area of methods.

The People's Republic of China

Goals and Objectives

If the United States were to move toward the establishment of a stable international order, the hostility and estrangement that had characterized American-Chinese relations for two decades had to be altered. Indeed, given the Kissinger belief that the major powers had to legitimate a new "structure of peace," it was impossible to continue the policy of isolating Peking. Hence, the Nixon administration decided that opening a dialogue with Peking was absolutely essential, and sought to normalize relations with the PRC, confident that a strong, independent China would serve the American interest (*FPR* 1973, p. 7).

Accordingly, the Nixon administration's first articulated goal vis-a-vis China was the establishment of a civilized discourse with the leaders in Peking (*FPR*

1972, p. 4). To achieve this goal, the United Stated identified a number of short-run objectives to be pursued, including the initiation of diplomatic discussions, the establishment of liaison offices in each country, an increase of trade, and the inauguration of a philosophical dialogue with Chinese leaders to define the shape of the American-Chinese relationship and its place in the international order (*FPR* 1973, pp. 16-21). By 1973 all the objectives—and hence the goal—had been accomplished because China, concerned with the Soviet threat, welcomed the new U.S. policy.

While U.S. goals and objectives for the next phase of American-Chinese relations have not yet been publicly formulated, it is probably safe to say that they.are similar to those for the USSR. That is, it appears the new goal of American foreign policy toward China is to create mutual interests in maintaining and developing an international structure based on self-restraint in the pursuit of national interests on both sides. Objectives likely to be pursued are further clarification and review of the philosophical basis of the Peking-Washington relationship; increased economic intercourse; additional cultural exchanges; avoidance of military confrontation; establishing full diplomatic relations; and obtaining Chinese participation in controlling the arms race. As in the case of Soviet-American relations, the United States undoubtedly operates on the assumption that such objectives will be achieved only if political decisions include respect for the security needs of both sides and a willingness to arrive at settlements that balance the legitimate interests of both parties.

Methods

In terms of methods, the United States continued to rely on the threat of punishment (deterrence) to defend itself and its allies from possible Chinese military actions, a fact reflecting Washington's awareness of continued ideological and policy differences with Peking. Nevertheless, the Nixon administration emphasized persuasion and rewards as more suitable techniques. It took the initiative in opening the dialogue with China that resulted in visits to China by the President and Secretary of State, and in securing the establishment of liaison offices in both countries. To strengthen this effort, the United States offered and granted rewards: support for China's membership in the UN, and acknowledgment that Taiwan was part of China.

Post-Embargo Developments

U.S. policy toward China was perhaps the least affected by the energy crisis. This is not surprising, given the peripheral role of Peking in the Middle East and its generally detached stance during the oil embargo. This is not to say that China is not concerned with developments in the region. On the contrary, China views Russian efforts to gain increased influence in the Persian Gulf as part of a long-term strategic threat, and therefore welcomes, or at least does not oppose, American attempts to limit Russian influence there (Szulc 1974a). Washington did evidence some interest in Peking's potential role as a major oil producer; but in light of China's limited oil technology and its reluctance to allow foreign investment, substantial Chinese oil production was considered a remote prospect (Leslie 1974). In short, oil and politics did not mix where relations with Peking were concerned.

The Middle East

Goals and Objectives

Of all the regions in the world, the Middle East is clearly the most important in terms of the supply of oil. The grandly phrased goal of U.S. policy, prior to 1973, was to create a "region of peace"—a number of healthy, independent nations, cooperating among themselves, free of external interference, and welcoming the constructive participation of outside powers (*FPR* 1973, p. 141).

To accomplish this goal, the United States identified a number of short-term objectives: settling the Arab-Israeli dispute through a process of negotiation to provide an interim agreement and staged implementation of a settlement of all issues, with the USSR expected to play a responsible role; strengthening ties with such traditional friends as Iran, Jordan, and Saudi Arabia, and restoring relations with the Arab states that severed them in 1967; maintaining the flow of Persian Gulf oil at reasonable prices and in sufficient quantity to meet the needs of the United States and its allies, which necessitated U.S. concern' for the stability of the region; and aiding in development, improving trade, cooperating with oil-producing areas in the sound investment of their large foreign exchange balances, and dissuading the European Economic Community (EEC) from adopting discriminatory relations with the Middle Eastern states that would result in damage to U.S. trade (*FPR* 1973, pp. 134-42; *Foreign Policy Outlines* 1973).

When one considers these objectives and examines the evolution of U.S. foreign policy toward the Middle East in the 1960s and 1970s, it is apparent that American policy-makers were concerned with two major issue areas: the Arab-Israeli conflict, and the complex of questions connected with oil. Since principal states involved were clustered in different parts of the Middle East— none of the major oil producers, mainly located around the Persian Gulf, bordered on Israel—the United States, as John Campbell pointed out in Chapter 6, pursued two independent policies. In terms of the Arab-Israeli conflict, the objective was to obtain a settlement between Israel and its neighbors based on a balance of power. In the Persian Gulf, the United States sought to maintain friendly relations with the oil-producing states, especially Saudi Arabia and Iran, and avoid destabilizing change that might adversely affect U.S. interests in the region.

Clearly, the attempt to isolate the two issue areas was totally dependent upon the position taken by Saudi Arabia in the Arab-Israeli conflict. The United States and its allies would increasingly depend on Saudi Arabia to satisfy their rapidly expanding energy requirements, and Saudi production was expected to rise from 8 million barrels a day to 15 or 20 million by the 1980s. Under these conditions, King Faisal possessed greater potential for influencing U.S. policy than any other Arab leader. If Faisal were to conclude, for whatever reason, that he should use his power to influence the outcome of the Arab-Israeli conflict, the basis for separating these two fundamental issues would be destroyed.

Methods

To accomplish its objectives in each of these areas, the United States used a combination of techniques. In the Arab-Israeli conflict, it sought to establish a context suitable for the peaceful resolution of the differences between the two sides through limited and cautious attempts to persuade them to cease military confrontations and to begin the process of negotiation—with, it was hoped, the cooperation of the USSR. The most significant initiative toward this end between 1967 and 1973 was Secretary of State William Rogers' plan to bring peace to the area that led to the cease-fire along the Suez Canal in the summer of 1970, ending the war of attrition. In conjunction with such efforts, the United States granted Israel rewards in the form of additional military equipment and promised Cairo the prospect of effective negotiations in the future. At no time, however, did Washington seem willing to apply significant pressures on Israel to return substantial portions of the territories occupied in the 1967 war—the Sinai, Gaza Strip, West Bank, and Golan Heights. Rather, the United States limited itself to acknowledging that its support of Tel Aviv did not necessarily extend to Israel's territorial acquisition, at the same time supplying Israel with the sophisticated weapons believed necessary to maintain the balance of power in the area.

Simultaneously, to strengthen Jordan, which was perceived as a moderate state opposed to radical Arab elements and amenable to peaceful settlement, the United States granted military and economic assistance to Amman. To underscore its support, it engaged in a dramatic show of force on behalf of King Hussein during the September 1970 battles between the Palestinian guerrillas and Jordanian forces, a move that also implied a threat of punishment for Syria, should it continue to back the armed invasion of Jordan by Palestine Liberation Army units based in Syria.

Although the Arab-Israeli conflict remained the major consideration in policy-making circles, increasing attention came to be paid to the Persian Gulf region. As late as the end of 1970, however, two national security study memoranda, dated November 9 and December 22, concluded that the United States had minimal strategic interests in the Persian Gulf (Miller 1974). The new awareness that American dependency on Middle Eastern petroleum would rise substantially in the months ahead forced a reappraisal of this position and increased concern with the security of the region.

While Moscow was known to be supporting the efforts of such revolutionary states as Iraq to subvert the traditional regimes in the area, Soviet interference with oil supplies was considered unlikely. To counter revolutionary efforts and preclude any Soviet moves against states friendly to the United States, Washington, as Alvin Cottrell pointed out in Chapter 7, maintained a small, symbolic naval presence in the Gulf. This presence could be viewed not only as a low-level threat of punishment to deter any adventuristic moves by the Kremlin, but also as a reward and support to friendly states whose existence was menaced by radical Arab groups and governments.

Among the dangers faced in the Persian Gulf were guerrillas, who could be used to sabotage oil installations or to interfere with oil shipments by attacking tankers or by blocking such "choke points" as the narrow navigable channel of the Strait of Hormuz at the mouth of the Gulf. Moreover, the radical-conservative cleavage that characterized Arab politics in the 1960s and early 1970s gave rise to fears that existing governments in the conservative oil-producing states might be replaced by regimes willing to sacrifice oil income on behalf of the confrontation with Israel. Iraqi-sponsored subversion in Iran, Oman, and Pakistan, and the fear that such action, if successful, might spread to Saudi Arabia, Kuwait, and the Gulf sheikhdoms, were particularly troublesome. In Oman, for example, Baghdad joined the People's Democratic Republic of Yemen in supporting rebels in western Dhofar Province. Iran and Britain sought to counter this move by aiding the Sultan of Oman. In Pakistan and southeastern Iran, the Iraqis extended support to dissident tribesmen attempting to carve out an independent Baluchistan (Cottrell 1973, p. 48; *Time,* May 5, 1973; New York *Times,* May 15 and July 4, 1973). Palestinian groups and various organizations, such as the Popular Front for the Liberation of Oman and attempts by Irq to move against Kuwait in 1961 and again in 1973 (the latter involving skirmishes by conventional forces) were also cause for concern.

To counter such activities, the United States relied primarily on supporting friendly states; and it granted military assistance (rewards) to a number of states in the region, particularly Iran, which acquired impressive amounts of sophisticated military equipment. Iran, however, wished to enter into a "special relationship" with the United States involving multifaceted economic arrangements that included Iranian investments in the United States and massive purchases of equipment and technology in return for oil. The United States, however, despite its concern with the status quo and with maintaining good relations, proved reluctant to enter into such a bilateral agreement.

The United States proved even more reluctant to accept a similar offer by Saudi Arabia in 1972. After considerable hesitation and deliberation, it ultimately declined, because such an agreement would run counter to traditional American support for multilateralism and free trade (Koven and Ottaway 1974; Schmidt 1974b; Hoagland 1974c). Several other reasons must also be taken into account, however. First, such arrangements ran counter to the principle of most-favored-nation dealings in energy with Canada and Venezuela; second, an agreement with Saudi Arabia would probably have irritated Iran; and third, supplying the Saudis with sophisticated military equipment—particularly in an election year—would have raised objections that such hardware might find its way into the hands of the front-line Arab states in any new eruption of hostilities with Israel.

The Post-Embargo Scene

The events of October 1973 had a profound impact upon the region and upon America's role there. The post-October setting was very different from the prewar scene, and changes in U.S. policy must be assessed not only in terms of the embargo but also in terms of the changed military relationships within the Middle East. As Campbell points out in Chapter 6, from a political viewpoint, the Arabs won the war: they achieved their objective of breaking the existing stalemate and, in so doing, gained a new sense of confidence. Conversely, the Israeli feeling of superiority and, indeed, the very axioms of their strategy, were shaken if not shattered.

The Arab success was the result, at least to some extent, of their improved military capabilities—an improvement due to their obtaining from the USSR the large quantities of modern, sophisticated equipment necessary to fight a "first-class war." The relationship between quality and quantity was highlighted by the fighting, in which Israeli qualitative superiority was offset, to some degree, by Egyptian and Syrian quantitative superiority (Sax and Levy 1974). Therefore, while Israel retained its military advantage, the margin of that advantage had diminished; and in light of sharp increases in oil revenues, it is quite possible that the Arabs will achieve military parity or perhaps even superiority by combining qualitative improvement with quantitative dominance. In the October war, however, the Israelis were prevented by a U.S.-sponsored cease-fire from gaining a clear-cut military victory over Egypt by isolating the Second Army as well as destroying the already-trapped Third Army (O'Neill 1974; Griffith 1974). Soon after, Kissinger made the first of his many trips to the Middle East.

Though he failed to persuade King Faisal to lift the embargo, Kissinger's trip underscored the American policy of restraint and reliance primarily on persuasion, while taking care to make it clear that the United States was not a "paper tiger." Kissinger specifically declared, "It is clear that if present measures continue unreasonably and indefinitely, then the United States will have to consider what countermeasures it may have to take" (Denver *Post*, November 22, 1973); and Undersecretary of State William Porter, pointing to the Arab need for American investments, technology, and industrial assistance, warned that oil was "a two-edged sword."

These comments were taken seriously, and Sheikh Yamani, reacting almost instantaneously, warned that military moves would force the Arabs to destroy the oil fields and that implementation of other measures would lead to substantial reductions in oil shipments—an action that not only would damage the United States but also would lead to the collapse of the European and Japanese economies. Yamani's statement reflected a basic tenet of the Arab strategy: to bring pressure to bear on the United States by threatening the economic well-being of its allies (Hielscher 1973). As a further indication of Arab determination, King Faisal reiterated his official position that oil shipments to the United States would not be resumed until three conditions were met: complete Israeli withdrawal from all the occupied Arab territories; the guarantee of Palestinian right of self-determination; and affirmation of the "Arabism" of Jerusalem (*Al-Jumhuriyah* [Cairo], November 22, 1973; *Al-Anwar* [Beirut], November 22, 1973). It should be noted that the last two points were vaguely worded, providing the Saudi government with negotiating flexibility.

Concomitantly with his discussions with the oil producers, Kissinger moved to effect an Israeli-Arab disengagement and, prior to departing on this mission pledged that the United States would use its influence to bring about a settlement. He also indicated that the United States felt the oil embargo was no longer appropriate, now that it was taking an active role in negotiations and had supported the implementation of Security Council resolution 242. As a token of U.S. flexibility and commitment, he did not rule out U.S. guarantees or even the permanent stationing of U.S. or Soviet forces in the region. These remarks were clearly designed to reflect the U.S. policy of restraint and to foster an appropriate atmosphere for the forthcoming negotiations (Gwertzman 1973a). Kissinger's positive approach was welcomed by Saudi and Algerian officials, who declared they were encouraged by his statements (*Al-Akhbar* [Cairo], December 3, 1973).

Like the United States, Saudi Arabia adopted a "carrot and stick" policy, as evidenced by its actions a few weeks later when the posted price of oil was increased from $5.11 to $11.65 a barrel. To soften the impact, Yamani announced that Arab producers would increase production by 10 percent in January and would supply "friendly" nations with their full oil needs—a move suggesting that the Arab states did not wish to cause an economic catastrophe in the West that would inevitably harm them as well (Silk 1973a).

Two major initiatives were launched early in 1974. Nixon convened the Washington Energy Conference, and Kissinger traveled to the Middle East to secure a disengagement on the Suez front. Both moves were relatively successful. The Washington conference produced the first steps toward trans-Atlantic cooperation on energy, and Kissinger secured an Egyptian-Israeli accord. Kissinger was warmly hailed by Egyptian President Sadat, and the stage was set for the establishment of close ties with Cairo. Moreover, a major step had been taken toward lifting the embargo, though that would have to wait for the completion of Sadat's extensive discussions with the sheikhs, presidents, and kings of the Arab world.

Aware of this, Kissinger told a Congressional committee on January 31 that far more important than the lifting of the embargo were the issues of adequate production in the future and the stabilization of prices (Gwertzman 1974a). His optimism, echoed in Nixon's address to Congress, in which he gave the impression that the embargo would be lifted momentarily, irritated the moderate Arab leaders, who had not had time to work out the necessary arrangements among themselves or with the more radical states. As a consequence, they issued statements casting doubt on when the embargo would be lifted; these, in turn, irritated Kissinger, who used the term "blackmail" for the first time on February 6 to describe the embargo and warned that its continuation "cannot but affect the attitude with which the U.S. would have to pursue its diplomacy"—that is, slow down his efforts to achieve a settlement (Marder 1974a; Gwertzman 1974b; Ellis 1974).

Nevertheless, in early February, Kissinger began his shuttle between Damascus and other Arab capitals and Jerusalem in an effort to achieve a Syrian-Israeli disengagement at the Golan front; and though agreement was not reached until late spring, the welcome news that the embargo would be lifted came in mid-March. Earlier that month rumors of such a move were widespread, but this time American officials maintained a discreet silence until the official declaration by the Arab states.

The lifting of the embargo and the new agreement with Saudi Arabia was made possible by decisions taken in Riyadh. To understand them it is necessary to consider why King Faisal applied the embargo in the first place. A number of factors can be identified. First, he felt that the United States simply did not understand his feelings concerning the Arab-Israeli conflict; and the decision by the United States to support Israel brought his credibility into question, since he had been warning Washington of his concern. Second, one must consider the political forces within the Arab world. If he had not acted, his regime would have been seriously endangered by the wave of resentment that would have followed. Conversely, his decision to act gave him a new image; with this move Faisal was transformed from a "reactionary ally of U.S. imperialism" into a leading Arab nationalist. Finally, one must note the happy convergence of economic and political advantage that accrued to him.

At no time, however, did King Faisal wish to endanger his relationship with the United States, for he shared Washington's concern with the need to contain Soviet influence, which he perceived as presenting a threat to the survival of his monarchy. Hence, throughout the embargo period he carefully sought to avoid a sharp confrontation with the United States and never allied himself with such radical regimes as Iraq and Libya, which were opposing any settlement with Israel on the basis of Security Council resolution 242. Thus it was not surprising that Riyadh readily agreed with Cairo that U.S. policy had changed significantly, even though none of Faisal's original three demands (which he subsequently modified) were met. Indeed the formal OAPEC statement announcing the lifting of the embargo which the Saudis had been instrumental in drafting was surprisingly mild and general. It stated:

> The ministers re-evaluated the results of the Arab oil measures in light of its main objective, namely to draw the attention of the world to the Arab cause in order to create the suitable climate for the implementation of Security Council Resolution 242. . . . The ministers took cognizance of . . . the signs which began to appear in various American circles calling (in various degrees) for the need of an even-handed policy. . . . American official policy . . . assumed a new dimension vis-a-vis the Arab-Israeli conflict. . . .

The announcement lifting the embargo indicated, however, that U.S. policy had not yet reached a position "compatible with the principle of what is right and just toward the Arab-occupied territories and the legitimate rights of the Palestinian people," so production would not be fully restored to pre-embargo levels and a review of the situation would be made later (New York *Times,* March 19, 1973).

Saudi Arabia did raise its production to prewar levels, however, and even fought for lower prices. In an eventful OPEC meeting it gained a three-month freeze on oil prices, but at the same time warned of the need to resolve the Arab-Israeli conflict expeditiously. Saudi Arabia's new policy was hailed by U.S. Ambassador James Akins, who commented:

> Saudi Arabia is acting very responsibly and even altruistically. They
> feel an obligation on this issue. I am not sure that my own govern-
> ment or any government in Europe would take this position in
> similar circumstances (Hoagland 1974a).

In early April the United States and Saudi Arabia announced an agreement to
strengthen economic, technological, and military cooperation. The agreement
included a U.S. commitment to reequip and train the Saudi National Guard
and the creation of mechanisms "to broaden and open the entire United States-
Saudi Arabian relationship," but the State Department was at pains to deny
that the United States was now engaging in the kind of bilateral deal for which
it had so righteously castigated its allies on previous occasions. Its spokesman
declared:

> We are not engaged in discussions with the Saudis to gain a preferred
> nation position at the expense of other consuming nations with respect
> to the purchase of Saudi Arabian oil. . . . The United States will con-
> tinue to press for multilateral solutions to the world petroleum prob-
> lem (Ottaway 1974).

This view, of course, was not shared by all, and one informed American observer
flatly stated, when the agreement was formally signed on June 9th, that oil was
". . . the catalyst that precipitated the new special relationships between the
Saudis and the Americans" (Silk 1974).

Whether or not the agreement represented an about-face, the United
States sought to achieve a number of objectives that centered on oil, including
increasing U.S. influence in the region, alleviating its balance-of-payments problem aggravated by the new oil prices, strengthening the security of the Persian
Gulf area, assuring U.S. access to oil as well as providing political and financial
incentives for expanded oil production, and easing financial problems by obtaining investment of Saudi funds in international aid efforts and long-term
programs of investment (Hoagland 1974a, 1974b). Another probable aim was
to stymie European and Japanese efforts at bilateralism by demonstrating that
the United States could dominate in any scramble for bilateral arrangements.

The United States also moved to further strengthen the new relations
with Cairo, where President Sadat was cooperating in the effort to achieve a
disengagement in the Golan, and Kissinger asked Congress for $250 million
in aid for Egypt. To encourage the Israelis and Syrians, he asked for $350
million and $100 million, respectively. While the latter sum was part of

a contingency fund, an official acknowledged that "this money could be used to resettle refugees, clear away mine fields, and the like"; and Kissinger later told the House Foreign Affairs Committee that he had promised Damascus he would request aid if an agreement were reached (New York *Times,* April 25, 1974). Since the aid to Egypt was also to be used to rehabilitate border zones, there could be no mistaking the symbolic link between aid and a settlement.

Shortly thereafter, the United States seized another chance to demonstrate its new flexibility by voting in the UN Security Council for a resolution condemning the Israeli reprisal raids against six Lebanese villages, without mentioning the massacre at Qiryat Shemona that had provoked the reprisal. The symbolic significance of this vote should be emphasized: a year earlier, the United States had abstained on a similar resolution.

While this vote, together with the agreement for assistance to Syria, created an atmosphere conducive to a disengagement agreement, Kissinger's persistent efforts were still required to take advantage of the opportunity. His ability to do so further strengthened the U.S. position in the Middle East and paved the way for Nixon's acclaimed trip to the area. The commitments undertaken on that trip further symbolized the new American role.

Diplomatic relations were reestablished with Syria, fulfilling a stated objective; in Cairo, Nixon offered to sell a nuclear reactor to Egypt and agreed to establish working groups in investment, agriculture, technology, health, and cultural exchanges; in Israel, he stated that the rapprochement with the Arabs would not lessen U.S. friendship and support, offered to sell Israel a nuclear reactor, declared his intention to seek $350 million in military assistance in the coming year, and discussed a long-term aid program. On this trip, however, Nixon carefully refrained from the promises to maintain the balance of power that had characterized his previous speeches (Shaw 1974; Kilpatrick 1974).

As Nixon departed the Middle East, it was clear to experts and diplomats that a new chapter in U.S.-Middle Eastern relations had begun. In the words of the Egyptian ambassador to Washington, speaking on Cairo radio ". . . the United States' relations with the Arabs have changed from hostility, alienation and estrangement to understanding, friendship and readiness to help solve the Middle East question on a sound basis. . . . President Nixon's visit to Egypt was an important historical event, for it was a turning point in U.S.-Egyptian relations" (The Egyptian *Gazette,* June 21, 1974).

The Impact of the Embargo

In retrospect, it is clear that significant changes did occur in U.S. policy in the Middle East, though a marked degree of continuity can also be discerned. The goal of "creating a region of peace" remained unchanged. Similarly, the objectives that had been articulated remained constant, with the qualifcations that a new objective, that of restoring the oil flow, became paramount; and that the priority accorded to particular objectives both in the Middle East and in the context of American global policy changed dramatically.

The high priority accorded the Middle East question was matched by the change in methods employed there. The former policy of limited and cautious persuasion on the Arab-Israeli issue was replaced by the intensive and highly active "shuttle diplomacy" of Henry Kissinger. To implement his efforts, Kissinger combined rewards and veiled threats of punishment, and many observers felt that U.S. rewards were now dispensed far more generously to Egypt and Syria than had been the case for many years. Moreover, the United States did not hesitate to press home to the Israelis the point that any settlement necessitated concessions involving risks on their part, risks they should be prepared to take in the interest of peace.

It should be emphasized, however, that the United States deliberately pursued a policy designed to demonstrate that it was not reacting to "blackmail." In particular, it continued to support Israel; and Kissinger, combining threats and rewards in his negotiations with the Arab oil states, did not yield to the original demands formulated by OAPEC and announced by King Faisal.

The results of this diplomatic maneuvering enabled the United States to achieve its new objective—restoring the flow of oil—as well as some of its former objectives. In particular, diplomatic relations with Syria and Egypt were restored and ties with friends in the area, notably Saudi Arabia, were strengthened. Other objectives—working with the oil-producing states to promote economic stability, maintaining the security of the region (particularly the Persian Gulf area, where relations between a number of states, such as Iran and Iraq, were strained) and the resolution of the Arab-Israeli conflict—still remained to be achieved, and difficult problems were anticipated.

By midsummer 1974, therefore, the United States enjoyed greater influence in the Middle East than it had for many years. These achievements were made possible by the new priority accorded to a settlement of the Arab-Israeli conflict. That settlement represented an important objective in the region for many years; but after the failure of the Rogers Plan, the issue had lain dormant because of a general feeling that the existing deadlock could not be broken without significant structural changes in the region. Those changes were wrought by the events of October 1973. For the first time in years this issue occupied the attention of the foreign-policy decision-making system at the highest levels, and its preeminence was intensified by the destruction of the former separation of the Arab-Israeli issue from the oil question raised by the Arab embargo. Here too, however, change did not occur overnight; and one could trace the merging of the two issues, beginning with the 1967 failure of an embargo attempt.

What role, then, did the embargo actually play in bringing about the changes in U.S. policy—changes of style and method more than substance? This is a difficult question to answer, for one must separate two events—the October war and the actions of OAPEC. In our view, there is little doubt that the October war would have sensitized American leaders to the dangers of the status quo and forced a new American effort to resolve the issue, which might have succeeded over the long term. Oil served as a lubricant, however, increasing the pace and intensity of the effort.

Finally, one must note that the question of higher prices remained to be resolved, and that this issue, too, would inevitably have arisen, even without an embargo. After all, the Shah of Iran, one of the leaders in the drive for higher oil prices, did not participate in the embargo and publicly called on the Arabs to change their policy (*Al-Hawadith* [Beirut], November 23, 1973). His position on this issue was far more obdurate than that of Saudi Arabia, which continued to press for lower prices; during a June meeting of OPEC, Saudi Arabia sought a 7 percent reduction in the posted price—a reduction that would have reduced Iran's income, but not its own. After bitter debate between Saudi Arabia and the 11 other members, including Iran, a compromise decision that did not result in higher prices was reached. The compromise, however, was a temporary one; and it remained to be seen whether this split in OPEC was a harbinger of things to come (*Middle East* 1974, p. 41).

In this regard, too, one may conclude that the results of the embargo were most noticeable in the acceleration of existing trends. Without the Arab action, the speed and magnitude of the change would probably not have been as great; and consumer nations would have enjoyed greater opportunity to take steps to deal with the situation—a situation that presents grave challenges to international monetary arrangements.

Finally, one must note the increased attention paid to questions of the security requirements associated with maintaining the flow of oil. The Persian Gulf and the Indian Ocean are critical in this regard, and now the State and Defense Departments support a Navy proposal they had previously downplayed, to establish a base on Diego Garcia (Miller 1974). Whatever the outcome of the debate, there is no doubt that the strategic importance of the Persian Gulf is fully accepted by top-level decision-makers and that its security and stability will receive high priority in the future.

THE FOREIGN-POLICY DECISION-MAKING SYSTEM

Psychological Variables

In Chapter 1, we presented an analytical framework that identified a number of critical variables accounting for the content of foreign policy. Since foreign policy, like any policy, involves choices, it is imperative to identify the major actors in the decision-making process. We have already noted that in the Nixon administration, foreign policy decision-making was concentrated in the hands of two men—the President and his Secretary of State, Henry Kissinger, who, prior to assuming that post in September 1973, was the White House Advisor for National Security Affairs

Nixon came to power convinced of his own mastery of foreign affairs, and soon found that Kissinger's *Realpolitik* approach to policy converged closely with his own philosophy. Moreover, Kissinger possessed the ability to provide systematic and comprehensive conceptualizations that Nixon felt were essential ingredients of an effective foreign policy, as well as the organizational capacity to provide the President with carefully argued and articulated foreign policy alternatives (Smith 1971).

Kissinger's imprint on foreign relations is evident to any knowledgeable reader of the *Foreign Policy Reports,* for one can find a coherent view of the international system that contains numerous reflections of his ideas and concepts before entering government.

To understand U.S. foreign policy, therefore, it is necessary to analyze Kissinger's perceptions concerning the international system, and we shall do so using the concepts presented in Chapter 1. While it has often been difficult for scholars to apply such an approach—since many leaders do not possess a coherent and explicit set of beliefs (doctrine)—we are fortunate that Kissinger, over the course of his career, has done so and has articulated them clearly in his writings.

Before considering the components of Kissinger's doctrine, however, it is necessary to identify the major value that informs it. Above all, he wishes to create an international "structure of peace." This value, traceable all the way back to his earliest scholarly work—one of the major preoccupations in writing his doctoral dissertation was to gain insight into means of achieving peace (Graubard 1973, p. 10)—became the specific, articulated concern of both Nixon administrations.

Kissinger's belief concerning the kind of international order that made
peace possible is also clearly reflected in recent U.S. foreign policy moves. In
his view, peace could not be obtained by seeking it directly but, rather, by
creating a stable international order based on general agreements among the
major powers. In Kissinger's own words, "Stability . . . has commonly resulted
not from a quest for peace, but from a generally accepted legitimacy"
(Kissinger 1957). When the administration speaks, therefore, of creating a structure of peace through the participation of all nations, it is really talking about
an understanding, particularly among the major powers, on the acceptable aims
and methods of foreign policy (Graubard 1973, p. 17).

Kissinger further believed that existing conditions were suitable for such
an understanding because, in his view, neither the USSR nor China could be
classified any longer as a revolutionary state seeking to challenge the existing
structure of the international system (Graubard 1973, pp. 273-74). His beliefs
and attitudes were based on an analogy he drew between conditions in the contemporary world and those existing at the time of the Congress of Vienna in
1815. There, the major European states agreed upon a new international system and to pursue divergent aims within accepted limits. It would be wrong,
however, to suggest that this analogy was rigidly held by Kissinger; one of the
important lessons he derived from his study was the primacy of leadership, for
the perceptions and decisions of major actors determine the functioning of the
international system.

Lest there be any misunderstanding, it should be noted that the Kissinger
approach is by no means utopian; it recognizes the fact that because of their
various political and geographical situations, nations will continue to pursue
divergent policies. The task of statesmen, therefore, is to seek a voluntary
agreement on the permissible aims and methods of policy that will constitute
a framework in which states can adjust their differences through diplomacy—a
situation similar to that after the Congress of Vienna.

Kissinger embarked upon the task of creating such a framework and
personally began a serious dialogue with all major international actors,
especially the USSR and China. The purpose of this dialogue was to identify,
develop, and strengthen areas of interdependence in order to create an environment that all the major powers would have a stake in preserving.

Energy and Middle East policy did not receive as high priority as relations with China and the USSR, and both areas were accorded even less
attention than might have been expected because of Kissinger's beliefs and
attitudes. He remained aloof from Middle East issues because of his background and became personally involved only when the great powers were risk-
ing a confrontation in the area (Kraft 1973). The vacuum was filled, for the
most part, by the Department of State. In the case of energy, Kissinger's
disinterest in economic matters ensured that decision-making on such issues

as trade, aid, and investment, as well as energy, would continue to be handled in the traditional manner by a variety of often-conflicting agencies (Malmgren 1972; Szulc 1973).

Bureaucratic Variables

The situation was exacerbated by the character of the organizational structure that Kissinger created to make foreign policy. Both Nixon and Kissinger were always concerned with secrecy and preferred to rely on small groups. Moreover, Kissinger was well-known for his disparaging views on the existing foreign-policy system. He believed that the only way to act creatively and innovatively in foreign affairs was by utilizing the bureaucracy as a source of information and analysis while concentrating actual preparation of the options to be presented to the President in the hands of a small group.

In Chapter 1 we identified three strategies available, singly or in combination, to a leader seeking to escape bureaucratic inertia: He may reshape the organization, create an alternative structure, or use a crisis to effect change. Kissinger obviously chose the second option and created a National Security Council (NSC) apparatus to his liking, while relegating the State Department to a secondary position in foreign-affairs decision-making. In this manner he not only streamlined the policy process but also ensured that he would be in a position to shape policy.

The National Security Council staff was his major instrument. Composed of about 120 persons, the staff had the responsibility for preparing memoranda on major foreign-policy issues and for writing option papers that served as the basis, after Kissinger had personally approved and summarized them, for President Nixon's decisions. As a result the focus on policy options was greatly sharpened and policy-making was very centralized, with Kissinger the major actor (Leacacos 1971-72).

The NSC organization found itself fully occupied in dealing with the priorities that Kissinger established—detente with the USSR and developing a new relationship with China. Since these involved intensive negotiations requiring a great deal of preparation and activity consuming extensive amounts of time, almost by default many important issues were handled by other agencies that did not possess the power, influence, and open-mindedness of the National Security Council staff.

This was particularly true of Middle Eastern affairs, which was the domain of the State Department, an agency that has been regarded as conservative, cautious, and unimaginative by scholars and practitioners alike. Criticism of the department has been extremely widespread, and its validity can be demonstrated by the fact that "the harshest attacks have come from former high-ranking officials of State and the White House staff, people who were in an unusually good position to observe the problem" (Holbrooke 1970-71, p. 67).

In the case of energy, however, a different set of bureaucratic considerations were operative. Here intra-agency difficulties were compounded by inter-agency rivalries and competition. There was no agency in Washington concerned with energy policy as a whole; rather, numerous agencies—including the Departments of State, Treasury, and Interior, the Office of Management and Budget, the AEC, the FPC, and the Office of Emergency Preparedness—were concerned with various aspects of energy. In the absence of a broad overall strategy, little coordination was evident, so that energy policy was a case of "bureaucratic politics" par excellence. Each organization had its own narrow perceptions of the problem, and its own interests to defend, its own clients to satisfy, and, since decisions involving energy possessed strong political implications, great attention was paid to the demands of various groups and the political consequences of any decision. Hence policy was essentially determined in ad hoc, piecemeal fashion by each organization without any concern for coherence, or was arrived at, on those occasions when representatives of the different agencies met, through "satisficing." Such a situation was inevitable, given the absence of coordination, which could come only from strong executive leadership that accorded a high priority to energy-related issues.

Under these conditions it is not surprising that the structure and content of energy policy were totally inadequate to meet national needs. In short, the basic reason for the "energy crisis" does not lie with the familiar scapegoats—oil companies, environmentalists, or even political decision-makers in the administration—but, rather, in the structure and organization of the decision-making system itself. In this case, one may more appropriately speak of the "nondecision-making" system, for following a detailed investigation, the New York *Times* found ". . . a complex but traceable pattern—not so much conspiracy as of national complacency, and, above all, government inaction going back decades. Not so much bad policy—although hindsight exposes that, too—as not policy at all" (Charlton 1974).

This assessment, however, merely emphasizes the absence of an overall energy policy and, as we have suggested, the situation was even worse because ad hoc, conflicting decisions that often proved counterproductive were the norm. Such conflicts extend to foreign policy as well, because energy was considered primarily as a domestic, and not a foreign policy, issue area. There was little awareness at any level of government or in any agency of government of what Lincoln in Chapter 2 refers to as the "interpenetration" of domestic and international dimensions of energy, and the linkage between domestic policy and its international aspects were seldom considered.

The State Department was concerned with energy questions, primarily insofar as the interests of the major oil companies were involved; one such event event proved to be a watershed—the Teheran negotiations between OPEC and the oil companies in 1971. Undersecretary of State John Irwin represented the United States and, after his return, became one of the few men in Washington who demonstrated any concern with the foreign-policy aspects of energy. The atmosphere in the capital may best be illustrated by noting that Irwin felt compelled to take a major and unusual initiative—he personally arranged a meeting with every high official concerned with energy to emphasize his concern. Not until then is there any indication that the top level of the administration gave serious attention to the international aspects of energy.

To further emphasize its concern with this situation, the State Department issued a document entitled *The U.S. and the Impending Energy Crisis* that contained the following conclusion (1972, p. ii):

> The USG [government] should no longer delay action while studying our energy problems and should start taking action. We have had numerous studies and should continue to study and review our energy problems but at the expense of delay. *Decisions must be taken* in the United States within the next two years. . . . (emphasis added)

This lack of top level attention and decision should perhaps not be surprising, for until the early 1970s, all policy-makers, like the American public as a whole, were convinced that energy was a cheap and inexhaustible resource. President Nixon's Task Force on Oil Imports concluded in 1970 that the United States would need little foreign oil, and that most requirements could be met by Venezuela and Canada until about 1980. It was not until these forecasts were shown to be remarkably inaccurate that official Washington began to worry about the implications of a dependency that they had assumed would never occur. Even then, however, policy emerged at a snail's pace, a pace that was further slowed by the fact that 1972 was a Presidential election year.

After the results were tabulated, some actions were taken. In March 1973, an informal interagency group was established to study the international dimensions of the energy situation, and on April 18, President Nixon delivered a major message on energy to Congress. That message, which had been advocated by General George Lincoln, the head of the Office of Emergency Preparedness since 1971, called for decreased dependence on external sources, to be achieved through conservation, greater exploitation of domestic resources, relaxing environmental standards to permit the increased use of coal, high expenditures on energy research and development; he also announced the abolition of the long-controversial oil-import quota. The message, however, demonstrated little sensitivity to the international implications of energy problems in general, or to the need of greater U.S. self-sufficiency in particular, though Nixon did advocate cooperative arrangements, such as oil sharing in times of crisis, cooperative research programs, and the development of international means to maintain energy flows (Hunter 1973, pp. 66-67).

The President's *Foreign Policy Report* issued a month later evidenced no greater awareness of the complexity and significance of energy matters in foreign policy. The President made but scant reference to energy questions; and when he discussed the new challenges for the future, he mentioned space exploration, pollution, and crime but ignored energy issues. It was noted that the U.S. objective was to assure the continuing flow of energy resources by addressing the problem as a common interest shared with Japan and Western Europe, and the importance of the Middle East in terms of energy supplies was acknowledged in passing; but the time and attention devoted to the issue reveal that it remained a secondary consideration (*FPR* 1973, pp. 35, 39, 105, 140).

Another Presidential message dealing with energy was delivered on June 29. Nixon reiterated his call for increased conservation; proposed a five-year, $10 billion program of research and development on alternative sources of energy; announced the creation of a White House Energy Policy Office; and urged Congress to establish a Department of Energy and Natural Resources and an Energy Research and Development Administration. A slight international flavor was added through a reference to consulations between the State Department and oil producers and consumers. The overall significance of this speech was assessed by a knowledgeable analyst in these words: ". . . the absence of broader foreign policy concerns from the message indicates that serious debate and decision on them have once again been postponed" (Hunter 1973, p. 67).

Whatever policy there was, therefore, had to be carried out in the absence of fundamental decisions and represented, at best, preliminary steps. Essentially, the United States had begun to examine ways of cooperating with its allies on energy questions; but it did so very cautiously, and even reluctantly because its relatively low dependence on imported oil meant that any sharing arrangements would involve less oil for the United States. Nevertheless the United States did move toward closer cooperation and Secretary of State Rogers in September 1973, when he met with high Japanese officials, called for the establishment of an oil-sharing arrangement among the United States, Japan, and Western Europe; pooling of information on negotiations with producers; development of new energy resources; and the creation of joint research and development projects. Subsequently, it was announced that the United States, with Western Europe, Canada, Japan, and Australia, was examining plans for oil-sharing arrangements in case of emergency (*Current Foreign Policy* 1973c).

Hence, prior to 1973, energy considerations were, at best, of secondary importance in our foreign relations. By the summer of 1973, the importance of energy-related questions had become apparent, but there appears to have been little sense of urgency or impending crisis. Energy questions did receive increased attention; but little, if any, serious thinking was yet done about the overall significance of the changes taking place, and the kinds of basic decisions that were required had not been made.

The Functioning of the FPDMS

Policy toward the Middle East was also characterized by incrementalism. The possibility that conservative oil-producing states would use their oil resources to support moves by other Arab states to influence U.S. (and Western) policy on the Arab-Israeli conflict was never entertained seriously in Washington, although in the spring of 1973, a national intelligence estimate warned that a renewal of the conflict could lead to an interruption in the flow of oil, if oil facilities were destroyed (Charlton 1974). The general feeling in the FPDMS was that the Arab states were too disunited to effectively implement an embargo; and that Saudi Arabia would, at most, not increase its production to meet the rising demand of consuming nations. Only James Akins, then White House Advisor on Energy, took seriously the possibility of an embargo (Akins 1973). In fairness, however, it should be noted that many experts, including the economist Morris A. Adelman, also rejected the idea that oil could be used for political ends, arguing that cooperation between oil producers was required and that such cooperation would not be forthcoming (Adelman 1972, 1972-73; see also Adams 1973; Krasner 1972; Burrell 1972). Oil industry spokesmen also shared this view. The executive director of the Petroleum Industry Research Foundation, for example, declared about a month before the embargo that the use of oil for political ends "has not happened yet and is not likely to happen in the immediate future" (Lichtblau 1973, p. 3).

The reason for such faith on the part of government officials, businessmen, and academicians is particularly hard to understand when we consider the fact that in the spring and summer of 1973, numerous warnings were issued by King Faisal and his spokesmen that oil was linked to the Arab-Israeli issue. Also, high officials of two major American oil companies with close ties to the Saudi government were warning of the need to change policy. Nor were such warnings lost in transmission. The oil companies possessed close ties to the Department; and Sheikh Yamani personally told Kissinger, Rogers, and Sisco that Saudi Arabia would use the "oil weapon" unless the United States moved more forcefully to secure Israeli withdrawal from the territories it had occupied in 1967. Why the United States chose not to heed this warning awaits further study, but Saudi sources point out that the State Department argued that Yamani did not represent King Faisal on this issue, and a "dialogue of the deaf"–to use Yamani's own phrase–ensued (Sheehan 1974). If this story is true, no better illustration of what happens to new information which clashes with preconceived notions could be provided.

How psychological factors such as these shape policy can be analyzed, as we suggested in Chapter 1, through a consideration of the stages involved in rational problem-solving. When defining the situation, for example, the degree to which actors possess closed or open images is critical; and it appears that policy-makers had fixed views on such subjects as the relationship between the Arab-Israeli conflict and the flow of oil, free trade, and the changing pattern of U.S. dependency on imported energy. Given such perceptions, the actual situation was never accurately defined; and hence none of the other steps–goal selection, search for alternatives, and choice among possible courses of action– could be undertaken.

A similar lack of perception appears to have characterized the policy decisions regarding the Teheran Conference of 1971, when OPEC challenged the oil companies. Much has been written on this topic; but only limited information is yet available on many important aspects, and one can therefore only present a preliminary analysis. The chain of events began in early 1971, when Colonel Mu'ammar al-Qaddafi, who had come to power in Libya in 1969, successfully played off the independent oil producers against one another and against the "seven sisters"–the majors–obtaining a significant increase in oil revenues and establishing a precedent that inevitably led to "leapfrogging" by other oil producers as each state sought to obtain still higher prices. In late 1970 OPEC emerged as the instrument through which the oil producers consolidated new demands for higher income, and many states spoke of ceasing production if the companies did not accede. Undersecretary of State John Irwin was dispatched to Teheran, and he apparently chose not to oppose the demands by OPEC; one scholar has suggested that he actually encouraged the Shah of Iran, who was leading the fight on behalf of the producers, and facilitated his task (Adelman 1972-73).

Threats of a boycott were required for the United States to become an active participant in the negotiations at Teheran. According to an expert witness, "The demand for increased revenues, while alarming, had been an economic matter which would not traditionally have engaged the American government" (Akins 1973, p. 473). Such a stance reflects the degree to which vital questions involving energy, particularly economic ones, never received adequate attention within the FPDMS. The limited concern that was evidenced with the impact of energy prices on national and international economies continued to characterize U.S. policy until the embargo and the accompanying price hikes. Even a few weeks before the embargo, the important question of "petro-dollars"—how to handle the excess revenues of producing countries without disrupting the international economic order—had still not received systematic attention at the policy level. As James Akins told a reporter at the time, "You'll find there is no thought being given to it. . . ." (Fowlkes 1973, p. 1216).

In any case, the Teheran negotiations proved a watershed in the relations between the oil companies and the producing countries, for the balance of power tilted decisively toward the producers. It is not surprising, therefore, that OPEC was "jubilant" at the results; it is perhaps not quite so easy to understand the satisfaction of the United States and its allies, but Akins (1973, pp. 473-74) has suggested that the Europeans were terrified of a boycott and welcomed the assured continuation of supplies at higher prices that need not be passed on to consumers because of company efficiencies and lower transport costs. Unfortunately for the oil consumers, it did not take OPEC long to demand still higher prices as well as "participation," the acquisition of a share in the operations and assets of the oil companies, thus increasing the producers' power and revenues still further.

Hence many have characterized U.S. policy in such terms as a "major blunder"—to use Arad's phrase—and suggest that OPEC's threats should have met a vigorous reaction, for it could be foreseen that success would make OPEC a force to be reckoned with, that powerful cartels raise prices, and that OPEC's success in the economic realm might have profound political implications in terms of a demonstration effect for OAPEC. Such a decision, however, could be reached only after a very careful and systematic analysis of the costs, benefits, and probabilities of success of differing courses of action—and the United States apparently was oblivious to the significance of the occasion. The reasons that have been advanced as to why OPEC's demand could not—and should not—have been resisted are interesting: the companies did not have the power to resist OPEC; the price increases demanded by OPEC involved only a few cents a barrel; Western Europe and Japan were willing to pay higher prices and did not wish a confrontation; since most of the companies involved were American, attempts by the United States to prevent a price rise would be widely regarded as a form of imperialism; OPEC countries were justified in seeking a price increase, since at that time countries like Iran were getting about five cents from a gallon of petroleum selling in Europe for about a dollar. That the whole affair never received serious attention in Washington is also evidenced by the findings of a Congressional subcommittee that "there was astonishing indifference" in the Departments of State and Justice to the negotiations in Teheran; no one even bothered to read the cables flowing in from the field (Mintz 1974a).

The expectation that only incremental change would occur at the Teheran negotiations may have been strengthened by bureaucratic factors. The State Department was primarily responsible for handling the matter, and that institution is widely considered to be deficient where economics is concerned (Malmgren 1972). And State may well have been even less sophisticated when it came to oil-related issues. As one academician (Adelman 1972, p. 71) has acidly noted:

> This agency is deplorably poorly informed in mineral resource economics, the oil industry, the history of oil crises and the participation therein of the Arabs with which it is obsessed . . .

The precise role of such variables, however, merits further study, for we have already noted several indications of the State Department's concern with the lack of priority accorded to the energy questions.

There is also another dimension involved in analyzing U.S. policy vis-a-vis OPEC. One may ask why the United States, in the face of continuing demands for higher prices, retained an essentially passive policy. After all, it could undermine the OPEC cartel by various actions, including such simple steps as making payments by the oil companies to producing countries taxable. Under such conditions the companies would find their position as "OPEC tax-collects" financially unrewarding, and before long the cartel would crumble (Adelman 1972-73; Krasner 1974). Whether such a strategy would in fact work remains a matter of conjecture but one must note that there is little evidence to suggest that the United States ever made a determined effort to achieve lower price levels until late 1974 when, provoked by a domestic economic situation marked by recession combined with inflation, President Ford and Secretary of State Kissinger called for a "global strategy" to deal with the high costs of energy and hinted that the United States was prepared to use its influence to obtain price reductions. If these speeches were indeed part of a coherent policy designed to achieve that goal—and the steps that were taken to establish a common front among the consuming nations which, at the time of writing, had culminated in the proposed International Energy Agency reinforce such an argument—then many observers would conclude that a major shift had occurred in U.S. policy.

Many reasons could be advanced to explain why the United States chose not to challenge OPEC's policies for so many years. By accepting increased costs for petroleum, it could achieve a number of important objectives: it strengthened the position of its allies in the Middle East—Saudi Arabia and Iran—and the higher costs of energy meant that European and Japanese goods would be more expensive and hence U.S. exports become more competitive, thereby easing the U.S. balance-of-payments problem. Moreover, by acceding to the status quo, the powerful oil lobby was quiescent; any change would invite serious political repercussions. Conversely, increased costs for American consumers were not likely to lead to effective interest articulation.

Similar considerations may also have shaped the response of the oil companies. At first they opposed OPEC's demand and sought help from the U.S. government through the State Department. Why should they have done so? After all, when far higher prices were won by the producing countries, the oil companies were able to pass on the increased costs to consumers and earn windfall profits. Here too psychological and bureaucratic factors may be important; the companies may also have relied on past analogies and precedents; traditionally concerned with low prices, they feared that European governments would force them to absorb the higher costs and that their profits would fall. Subsequently, they too discovered a profitable new status quo.

Demands

Reinforcing the psychological commitment to existing objectives and methods was the role of our first input into the FPDMS: demands. Few demands for change were placed on decision-makers; and to have advocated a policy that merged the two issues in the Middle East or a policy designed to change the status of the oil companies would have risked antagonizing powerful lobbies, with substantial political repercussions. Under these conditions, it it not surprising that major decision-makers, who were preoccupied with other issues, preferred to rely on old formulas that had proved quite successful. The very success of past policies, coupled with the risks involved in the implementation of any new policy, further strengthened the commitment to the status quo. Thus, as we argued in Chapter 1, policy tends to be incremental because of psychological factors; and this certainly was the case in policy on the Middle East and energy.

Nor did the public evidence any concern with the topic. It had come to believe that energy supplies were inexpensive and inexhaustible, and was therefore complacent and indifferent. Even the attentive public, while increasingly concerned with pollution, the environment, and utilization of resources, had not yet focused its attention on energy in an international context. Further, the general public was largely unconcerned with developments in the Middle East. Until the early 1970s, Vietnam dominated the domestic debate on foreign policy and, following the Paris settlement, public attention noticeably shifted toward such domestic issues as the environment, inflation, and Watergate. Although some members of the attentive public were concerned with the Middle East during this period, their numbers diminished as domestic matters became of increasing concern.

Nor was there any great pressure for policy changes on either the Arab-Israeli question or energy matters from interest groups. The Zionist lobby was satisfied with the status quo in the occupied territories and with the U.S. decision, in conjunction with the 1970 cease-fire, to meet the Israeli requests for F-4 fighters and other sophisticated military equipment. The oil lobby, too, seemed relatively satisfied with the status quo, especially in foreign affairs. Since there was no national policy, the oil industry happily filled the facuum and continued to wield great influence over energy policy.

The success of both lobbies was attributable to several factors. First, the indifference of the public allowed them to wield a preponderant influence in their respective issue areas. The only notable exception came in the domestic area, where the oil lobby encountered stiff opposition from environmentalists over such issues as the Alaska pipeline. Second, the separation of the two issues permitted each lobby to achieve its goals without endangering those of the other. Had the two issues merged, these groups would certainly have clashed and might have canceled each other out. By the summer of 1973, there were signs that conflict was likely, for executives of major oil corporations were lobbying for a shift in U.S. policy toward the Arab world. Such action, coupled with the increasing warnings of the Saudis, led to doubts about the desirability of keeping the two issue areas separate. As part of its effort to counteract this situation, the Zionist lobby moved to counteract such arguments before they became widespread and published several articles arguing that an embargo was unlikely (see, for example, Luttwak 1973).

The rapid reaction of the Zionist lobby is an indication of its effectiveness. In fact, both lobbies met the criteria for successful articulation in terms of channels and styles discussed in Chapter 1. Each was well-organized, had substantial human and financial resources at its disposal, and used most of the channels available to reach decision-makers. Both the oil and Zionist lobbies relied heavily on elite representation—that is, on sympathizers in administrative and legislative decision-making structures. Many prominent legislators have been identified with each for many years: Senators Long and Kerr with oil, Jackson and Javits with Israel, for example; and oil industry experts have served effectively in the Interior Department. Both lobbies also made extensive use of the local and national media to present their positions and influence public opinion, and they took advantage of all access points to contact and influence state, local, and national legislators and officials. Both were equally sensitive to the need to employ effective styles of interest articulation. When the Zionists lobbied for F-4s for Israel, and the oil interests on the oil-import quotas and depletion allowance, decision-makers understood exactly what was desired, as well as the linkage between their votes and the continued support of the lobbies' constituencies (Stevens 1962; Phelps 1970).

Zionist efforts were facilitated by the ineffectiveness of the Arab lobby, whose efforts were characterized by poor organization, inadequate use of available channels, and reliance on a style that was latent, diffuse, and affective (Phelps 1970). In recent years, however, the Arab lobby has increased its effectiveness and has begun to influence public opinion, particularly among college youth.

Our second input into the FPDMS—support—consists of capability and legitimacy. As was pointed out in Chapter 1, the structure of the international system, which, because of the balance of military power, was largely bipolar, affects foreign policy. Earlier in this chapter, we also noted that American objectives explicitly took into account the emergence of Western Europe, Japan, and China as major new actors of influence, and that Kissinger's vision of a new international order involved these states. While Kissinger and Nixon correctly perceived the changes involving these actors, however, they failed to take into account the impact on this pattern of the emergence of the oil-producing states and never took appropriate action to deal with it.

The other two dimensions of the international system—values and events—can be dismissed fairly quickly. We have seen little or nothing to suggest that systemic values were a factor of any significance in shaping U.S. policy; and, though there were increasing indications that the situation in the Middle East was becoming more precarious, few observers were prepared for the magnitude of the event that was to change the status quo.

Capability

The widespread involvement of the United States in international affairs and the ambitious goals and objectives it pursued rested, of course, on the enormous capability—particularly economic and military—it was able to mobilize. Economic resources made it possible for Washington to offer and grant rewards and concessions in its negotiations with friends and allies. Its military power made it possible, meanwhile, for the United States not only to maintain its deterrent posture vis-a-vis the USSR and China, but also to exercise significant influence over Japan and Europe and its clients in the Middle East.

Despite its impressive capability, however, the United States became more sensitive to the limits of power, particularly in the wake of the Vietnam war. And, as we have emphasized, Kissinger stressed the need for a consultative partnership with Europe and, to a lesser extent, with Japan in order to identify and deal with problem areas. At the same time, however, there was no denying that Washington continued to exercise considerable influence in Europe, partly by exploiting European dependence on American military force for security.

In its relations with potential adversaries, principally the USSR, the preeminent position of the United States in technology gave it a strong card in negotiations concerning detente and other issues. In the case of China, on the other hand, technology played a less important role, largely because of Peking's emphasis on self-reliance and its caution in opening its doors to Western economic penetration. Still, there was no denying that commercial agreements with the Chinese reinforced the improved political relations between Washington and Peking.

In the Middle East, U.S. economic influence and military capability allowed it to establish significant influence over its clients—Israel, Jordan, Iran, and Saudi Arabia. While Israel's extreme dependency on the United States for military equipment meant that Washington had enormous potential influence, we have seen how it refrained from using its capability in negative ways, such as forcing significant concessions on the question of the occupied territories.

In the Persian Gulf, the military and economic capacity of the United States made possible the substantial sales of military hardware to Iran that were believed necessary to maintain stability in the region, but it chose not to respond to Saudi and Iranian requests for a special relationship despite its obvious capability to do so.

Legitimacy

The substantial capability of the U.S. government in the foreign policy arena would not have been possible in the absence of legitimacy, mostly procedural and instrumental, accorded its political society, laws, institutions, and foreign policies. Although certain aspects of foreign policy were subjected to criticism after the Vietnam settlement, there seemed to be a general endorsement of the purposes and goals of foreign policy as defined by Nixon and Kissinger. Nor did this situation change appreciably with the Watergate scandals. In fact, even though the President and members of his White House staff were shown to be involved in what were widely deemed to be criminal and unconstitutional acts, the adverse impact did not appear to spill over into the foreign-policy realm. For one thing, the President was generally considered competent in this area, a notion strengthened by his successful trips to Moscow and Peking. Second, as the Watergate issue continued to mushroom and take its toll in White House advisors, the star of Henry Kissinger rose ever higher; and as Nixon became increasingly preoccupied with the possibility of impeachment, Kissinger enjoyed greater latitude than ever in determining U.S. foreign policy. During his flight to Moscow during the October war, for example, he received a "power of attorney"—the unusual authorization to commit the United States in the President's name without his approval (Kalb and Kalb 1974). Untainted by the Watergate fiasco and basking in apparent success of his Vietnam, China, and detente diplomacy, Kisssinger found that his name had become a household word and that his efforts and ability were increasingly applauded by the media.

The Embargo and Its Consequences

Clearly, the Arab decision represented a major change in the environment of the FPDMS; it was a major event in the international system, one that caught U.S. policy-makers by surprise. The result was a classic case of policy-makers being forced to respond to an unexpected development over which they had little or no control. As they contemplated appropriate responses, the international structure of power was an ever-present factor. In the area of Great Power relations, the need to maintain and enhance the Atlantic Alliance so as to avoid any shift in favor of the USSR was a reality that constantly influenced them. If nothing else, this consideration ruled out harsh threats or the use of punishment against such obstreperous allies as France. Moreover, while the United States might have taken strong action—withholding food or technology from the boycotting Arab states—it was wary of the effects of such a confrontation on its allies. International-system values did not play a salient role in shaping U.S. policy, except perhaps in the search for options. The use of military force, for example, would be rejected almost immediately, as unacceptable in an era opposed to such actions. Other considerations may well have been more significant in negating this option—the Arab threat to destroy the oil fields and the domestic reaction to such action.

The Post Embargo Scene

Shortly after the imposition of the embargo, it became clear that while most Americans responded positively to conservation measures, prolonged deprivation of adequate energy supplies would not be acceptable; and it did not take politicans long to perceive that the American people considered energy a "gut" issue (Broder 1973; Mintz 1974b). To placate the public, which, in Simon's view, questioned the credibility of the government, a substantial public relations effort was undertaken by the administration to persuade Americans that the crisis was real and was under control. The need for such a campaign was obvious, for while most Americans believed there was an energy problem, only 25 percent felt it was the most important issue. Moreover, they were reverting to pre-embargo consumption patterns while blaming the government for developments (Murray et al., 1974).

The implications of this reaction for foreign policy were both general and specific. Generally, it reinforced the new awareness in government that energy could no longer be accorded secondary attention. In foreign policy, this meant doing something about the embargo and prices. On the more specific matter of policy toward the Middle East, there was little pressure from the public to sacrifice Israel on the altar of energy interest. On the contrary, a Gallup poll showed that sympathy for Israel increased from 47 percent in October to 54 percent in December 1973. Interestingly, this reversed a slow downward trend that had been manifest since June 1967. Sympathy for the Arabs was only 7 percent (Blumenthal 1973).

At the same time, interest groups entered the political arena to influence energy policy. Independent truck drivers engaged not only in a transport strike but also in sporadic acts of violence. The Citizens' Forum, a loosely organized umbrella organization representing 137 smaller groups, becan to demand more participation in energy decision-making (Hoyt 1974). Although such groups did not have a major impact, they helped create a heightened awareness of the importance of energy. Moreover, national leaders were only too aware of the reaction of major labor and business groups to the prospect of an economic recession caused by the energy crisis.

As far as the Zionist and oil lobbies were concerned, each found itself on the defensive. The Zionists' fears, which ultimately proved unfounded, centered on the possibility of an anti-Israeli backlash--that the energy crisis would be blamed on American support for Israel (Blumenthal 1973). As far as events in the Middle East were concerned, its natural concern about the concessions Israel was pressured to make in both the Syrian and Egyptian negotiations were offset by promises of continued military and economic aid to Israel. Moreover, the Israeli leadership appeared reluctant to criticize the administration for fear of antagonizing Nixon and Kissinger. The new U.S. diplomacy in the Middle East did, however, prove unsettling, but there was little the lobby could do; its intense efforts to sway the U.S. vote in the Security Council on the Qiryat Shemona question, for example, had no effect (Berlin 1974). Its lack of effectiveness was not due to the Arab lobby, which, though it intensified its efforts to press its case in all possible arena, was not an important factor in the foreign policy calculus (*Congressional Quartly* 1974).

The petroleum companies, meanwhile, came under great suspicion in both public and Congressional eyes. In December 1973, a Gallup poll indicated that 25 percent of the respondents blamed the oil interests for the crisis. In Congress, a number of committees subjected oil executives to sometimes grueling interrogation. In response, the oil companies strengthened their principal lobbying group, the American Petroleum Institute, and began extensive public campaigning. The efforts of the lobbies, therefore, had little impact on the formulation of U.S. foreign policy.

While the American public was clearly distressed by the energy crisis, there was no noticeable weakening of its support for the administration's foreign policy. Although the Watergate issue inexorably destroyed the legitimacy of the President, Kissinger continued to receive accolades—he was named the "most admired man in the U.S." in a December Gallup poll (Saikowski 1974). The extent of his influence not only with the public, but also in Congress, was such that when he threatened to resign because of insinuations that he was linked to illegal wiretaps, a number of influential Senators rallied to his support and the Senate Foreign Relations Committee publicly cleared him of any wrongdoing. Moreover, when President Nixon was forced to resign and Gerald Ford assumed office, one of his first actions was to indicate that Kissinger would continue as Secretary of State. The instrumental legitimacy Kissinger enjoyed was, of course, a product of his apparent foreign policy successes, including the Washington Energy Conference and his peacemaking efforts in the Middle East.

The Bureaucratic Setting and Psychological Factors

Perhaps the most important changes took place here. Although Kissinger moved to the State Department just prior to the October War, amid promises to infuse that department with a new "sense of participation, intellectual excitement, and mission," it was soon apparent that his modus operandi had changed very little. He continued to conduct policy in a personalized and secretive manner, relying on a small group of trusted advisors. While he promised to keep the geographic bureaus of State informed, those who were below the level of Assistant Secretary were seldom privy to his decisions.

Kissinger's move did not affect, as many feared, his dominance over the making of foreign policy. Indeed, if anything, his influence within the Presidential circle increased after Watergate as a result of the removal of his reputed rivals, H.R. Haldeman and John Ehrlichman. Furthermore, apart from Secretary of Defense Schlesinger, there were few powerful personalities within the administration (Marder 1974c; Saikowski 1974). Kissinger's views, therefore, remain crucial to any understanding of U.S. policy, and, as pointed out in our discussion of the pre-embargo FPDMS, Kissinger was generally disinterested in economic matters, gave energy issues but secondary attention, and preferred to leave Middle Eastern policy to others. After the embargo his attitude changed dramatically on each of these points; and this, we believe, was a key determinant of the changes in U.S. policy.

Like everyone else in government, Kissinger became aware of the critical nature of energy considerations and the need to take action to address the various problems relating to them. This meant that international economic issues would have to be given a high priority. The first sign that Kissinger had applied his considerable intellectual skills to this matter came at the Washington Energy Conference, which he reportedly organized single-handedly. There he suggested that the goal of nations should be "Pareto-optimality"—that is, extending the efficient use of resources by moving those such as oil, technology, management, and capital from areas where they were abundant to areas where they were scarce. The key underlying theme—interdependence—was consistent not only with his pre-embargo views in general but also with the agreements made with Saudi Arabia in the spring of 1974 (Silk 1974c; Morgan 1974b). While the latter represented an exercise in bilateral (vertical approach) practice, the administration remained committed to fostering a mutuality of interests through multilateral and horizontal approaches.

In conjunction with the new priority he accorded to energy and economic issues, Kissinger came to believe that the U.S. position in the Middle East required high-level attention; and he took effective, active control of U.S. policy in that region. This, more than any other factor, accounted for the changes in American policy that occurred.

The strong sense of direction given to the foreign policy apparatus was not matched in the domestic arena. While the creation of the Federal Energy Office facilitated the solution of a number of short-term problems, any attempt to achieve Project Independence required long-term planning and coordination. To that end, President Nixon secured the creation of a new energy structure consisting principally of the Federal Energy Administration (FEA) and the Energy Research and Development Administration (ERDA). Possibilities for confusion and interagency conflict are obvious in such an arrangement; and it should be noted that a host of other organizations remained concerned with different aspects of energy, including the Federal Energy Office, the National Science Foundation, the Department of the Interior, the Office of Management and Budget, and the AEC, among others. The outcome is unclear; but the FEA is scheduled to submit a comprehensive energy report, "Blueprint for Independence," by November 1, 1974. Nor did the drive to coordinate long-range energy policy enjoy strong leadership. When John Sawhill was named to head FEA, prestigious *Science* magazine characterized the new appointment as marking "a resumption of a debilitating pattern of rapid change in the top administration of energy matters" (May 3, 1974).

Congress

Generally speaking, it is safe to say that Congress did not play an important role in the changes in American foreign policy resulting from the embargo. Indeed, if anything, Senators and Congressmen seemed awed by Kissinger's expertise and pleased with the attention he was paying them, and therefore appeared willing to accept his lead in foreign-policy matters.

While Congress had little direct impact on the making of energy-related policy decisions, it did exercise some indirect influence through such extra-constitutional and informal techniques as legislative investigations and individual actions. By speaking out on the various aspects of energy problems, and by holding a number of committee investigations—the Senate Permanent Investigative Subcommittee, the Senate Foreign Relations Committee, and the Subcommittee of the Joint Economic Committee—Congressmen continually reinforced and contributed to the new awareness that made energy a high priority in foreign policy. Moreover, some of its investigations uncovered problems that needed to be dealt with in the future. Representative John Dingall's House Select Committee on Small Business, for example, found that government officials had been relying on statistics supplied by the oil industry, despite a 1962 Presidential Petroleum Study Committee report citing the inadequacy of industry data (Mintz 1974b).

Conclusion

The Arab use of their "oil weapon" in order to achieve political objectives was branded by many observers and statesmen as "blackmail." For those on the receiving end, the Arab action was indeed an attempt "to compel a par-particular action by threats." Yet, as the wielders of the oil weapon and their supporters pointed out, the use of an emotive word like "blackmail" was misleading, for it diverted attention from the fact that the Arabs were simply doing what statesmen had been doing for centuries: employing national resources to secure political aims.

In our discussion of capabilities in Chapter 1, we pointed out that a nation's ability to translate its capabilities into influence depends on whether or not its resources are mobilized and usable, the willingness to use them, the credibility of this threat to others, and the degree of dependency of the target state. Although there was a near consensus prior to the October war that the Arab oil producers would not impose an embargo, the October 17 OAPEC decision established the credibility of the Arab threat. Although the United States was far less dependent than Western Europe and Japan, U.S. policy-makers perceived the threat of a continuing embargo as a grave danger. Accordingly they were forced to give energy matters immediate, high-level attention and to undertake a number of initiatives in the domestic field as well as the Middle East and Europe.

As with most foreign-policy changes, those following the embargo were the product of a number of interrelated factors, some of which were especially important. As noted earlier, the oil embargo was a major international event, which both directly and indirectly, through the manifestation of public opinion, the actions of interest groups, and the activities of Congress, sensitized key foreign-policy actors and institutions in the FPDMS to the urgency of energy issues in the context of American foreign policy, most notably in Europe and the Middle East. Once the President, the Secretary of State, and his small group of advisors became aware that energy had to be accorded an immediate high priority, the views of Kissinger—and the limits of his options—became crucially important. Within the constraints set by the international structure of power, Kissinger addressed the energy issue from his pre-embargo doctrine and stressed a multilateral approach with interdependence as its cornerstone. This was evident in his attempts to handle the oil problem within a broad framework of institutionalization and consultation. In the Middle East, the United States sought to foster interdependence through its bilateral arrangements with Saudi Arabia and Iran, and through its new relations with Syria and Egypt. At the same time it continued to support Israel, though demonstrating more flexibility, particularly in style and methods. While the new objectives and the altered methods of U.S. policy that emerged were strikingly consistent with the overall approach to foreign policy articulated prior to the embargo, it is doubtful that the changes that took place would have occurred as rapidly and as intensely without the embargo. And one must not forget that in foreign policy changes of emphasis are often of great importance.

While the role of Kissinger was without doubt an important factor in the achievements of U.S. policy, whatever success he enjoyed was always contingent upon the actions of other actors. His doctrine proved functional precisely because conditions within the international system permitted its application; and one may wonder whether in the absence of such conditions, Kissinger would have sought to implement it and whether the quest for a "structure of peace" would have been stillborn. Without a positive response from leaders in Moscow and Peking, detente with the USSR and rapprochement with China would have remained impossible. Likewise, his efforts in the Middle East would not have yielded the lifting of the embargo or the tentative hopes that a settlement of the Arab-Israeli conflict may now be possible without appropriate responses from Sadat, Faisal, and other Arab leaders.

This fact poses an interesting theoretical point. Clearly, leadership is a critical variable in the making of foreign policy; but the nature of its impact can substantially be affected by the various clusterings of other factors: the institutional setting, the structure of support and demands, and the actions of other states in the system. While this confirms what is generally known, our case study highlights this point. Although we narrowed our focus to the changes that occurred in the wake of the embargo, we found that the independent variables were functionally interrelated in a dynamic way and that it was impossible to derive clear-cut causal relationships.

Nevertheless, our framework did provide an eminently practical organizing device that enabled us to analyze systematically a bewildering array of rapidly changing events. It also permitted us to isolate variables that we assumed, on the basis of theory, to be significant and to examine the nexus between those and U.S. foreign policy. In particular our study confirms the importance of psychological factors in the making of foreign policy. It also confirms the critical role of the President and his closest advisors in shaping foreign policy. This point is worth emphasizing, for many scholars regard policy as emerging from a bureaucratic setting in which actors tend to become depersonalized. This is not to say, however, that bureaucratic factors are unimportant. On the contrary, we have demonstrated that in the case of policy, given medium to low priority, the outcome is the result of "satisficing" within and among agencies.

Our study has also convinced us of the need to conceptualize foreign policy policy more adequately, in a way that is both rigorous and subject to practical application. We utilized "goals," "objectives," and "methods"; but we often found it difficult to separate objectives from methods, because methods may become intermediate objectives. Moreover, goals may be so grandiloquently phrased that they provide little understanding of what is actually occurring. Offsetting this problem to some degree was the administration's use of such concepts in a very explicit way. Yet even here goals may be misleading because of their generality, and objectives may be defined implicitly.

One consequence of a major event such as the embargo is that new goals may emerge that require the identification of objectives and methods. One such goal is Project Independence, which is in the process of being operationally defined. Although there is widespread agreement that "energy security" must be achieved, realistic assessments suggest that the United States can, at best, reduce its need for oil imports from all countries to approximately 20 percent by the 1980s. Under these circumstances the United States would be able to conduct its foreign policy in a "free and unfettered way" for dependency of this magnitude would not be so great as to preclude domestic and international adjustments in the face of pressures based on either price or supply. The achievement of such a goal clearly requires the identification of possible options including conservation, increased efficiency, and the development of new fuel sources and the assessment of the costs and benefits of adopting any or a combination of specific policies in these areas. In the foreign policy realm numerous options are also available to U.S. policy-makers. These have been identified, discussed, or prescribed by our contributors. Which of these will be adopted remains to be seen but it is clear that we live in an increasingly interdependent world. The challenge for the United States is to ensure that such interdependence be characterized by equity as well as symmetry.

In any case, the significance of the problem can no longer be under-estimated, for it is quite possible that if negotiations over the substantive issues in the Arab-Israeli conflict fail and the call to arms is heard once again in the Middle East, the flow of oil could once more be interrupted or new financial pressures brought to bear upon "unfriendly" countries. And, even if such an event does not occur, the larger questions of how mankind will use its finite resources in a way that is appropriate in an age of global interdependence presents a formidable challenge for the coming decades.

Abrahamsson, B. J., and J. L. Steckler. 1973. *Strategic Aspects of Seaborne Oil.* Beverly Hills: Sage Publications.

Acheson, Dean. 1969. Cited in *The Military Budget and National Economic Priorities.* Hearing before the Subcommittee on Economy in Government of the Joint Economic Committee, 91st Congress, 1st sess., 3. Washington, D.C.: U.S. Government Printing Office.

Adams, James Ring. 1973. "The Great Debate." *Wall Street Journal,* April 10.

Adelman, Morris A. 1962. *The Supply and Price of Natural Gas.* Oxford: Basil Blackwell.

_____. 1964. "Efficiency of Resource Use in Crude Petroleum." *Southern Economics Journal* 31: 101-22.

_____. 1972. *The World Petroleum Market.* Baltimore: Johns Hopkins.

_____. 1972-73. "Is the Oil Shortage Real?" *Foreign Policy* 9 (Winter).

AEC. *See* Atomic Energy Commission.

Akins, J. 1973. "The Oil Crisis: This Time the Wolf Is Here." *Foreign Affairs* 51 (April).

Almond, Gabriel A. 1960. *The American People and Foreign Policy.* New York: Frederick Praeger.

_____ and G. Bingham Powell, Jr. 1966. *Comparative Politics: A Developmental Approach.* Boston: Little, Brown.

American Petroleum Institute. 1972. *Annual Report.*

Andrain, Charles F. 1970. *Political Life and Social Change: An Introduction to Political Science.* Belmont, California: Wadsworth.

Apple, R. W., Jr. 1974. "Nixon Is Planning Appeal on Energy to 20 Countries."
New York *Times,* January 4.

Apter, David E., and Charles F. Andrain, eds. 1972. *Contemporary Analytical
Theory.* Englewood Cliffs, N.J.: Prentice-Hall.

Arbatov, Georgii. 1973. "Sovetski-Amerikanskie otnosheniia na novom etape."
Pravda, July 22.

Atomic Energy Commission (AEC). 1973. *The Nation's Energy Future.* Washington, D.C.: U.S. Government Printing Office.

Becker, Abraham S. 1973. "Oil and the Persian Gulf in Soviet Policy in the
1970s." In *The U.S.S.R. and the Middle East,* edited by M. Cinfino
and S. Shamir, pp. 173-214. Jerusalem: Israel Universities Press.

_____. 1974. "The Superpowers in the Arab-Israeli Conflict, 1970-1973."
New York: American Elsevier.

Beecher, William. 1972. "China Is Said to Have Given Japan Military Assurances." New York *Times,* December 14.

Beirut Domestic Service. 1974. As cited in Foreign Broadcast Information
Service, Middle East and Africa, January 10.

Bendix, Reinhard. 1962. *Max Weber: An Intellectual Portrait.* Garden City,
N.Y.: Doubleday-Anchor.

Berg, C. A. 1974. "Conservation in Industry." *Science* 184 (April 19): 264-70.

Berger, Marilyn. 1974. "Jobert Calls Talks a Pretext." Washington *Post,* February 14.

Berlin, Mike. 1974. "U.S. Council Vote Angers Israelis." Washington *Post,*
April 25.

Binder, David. 1974. "Europeans Reluctant at Parley of New 12-Nation Energy
Group." New York *Times,* February 26.

Blechman, Barry M., and Andrew M. Kuzmack. 1974. "Oil and National Security." *Naval War College Review* (May-June): 8-25.

Blumenthal, Ralph. 1973. "Sympathy for Israel Rose After Oil Ban, Poll Finds." New York *Times,* December 23.

Boumedienne, Houari. 1973. Interview by Jean Lacouture in *Le Nouvel observateur* (Paris), September 17-23, pp. 38-39.

Bovin, A. 1973. "Mir i sotsial'nyi progress." *Izvestiia,* September 11.

Brezhnev, Leonid. 1973. "Rech tovarishcha L. I. Brezhneva." *Pravda,* August 16.

————. 1974. "Rech tovarishcha L. I. Brezhneva." *Pravda,* January 31.

Broder, David S. 1973. "Fuel Crisis Poses Peril to Politicians." New York *Times,* November 25.

Browne, Malcolm W. 1974. "East Bloc Looks to Firm Detente." New York *Times,* April 29.

Brzezinski, Zbigniew. 1973. "U.S. Foreign Policy, the Search for Focus." *Foreign Affairs* (July): 708-27.

————. 1974. "The Deceptive Structure of Peace." *Foreign Policy* 14 (Spring).

Burrell, R. M. 1972. "Producers and Consumers of the World Unite." *The New Middle East* (September).

Bushinsky, Jay. 1974. "Israel Uneasy Over Mideast Policy of U.S." Washington *Post,* February 28.

Butterfield, Fox. 1973. "Kissinger Called Unable to Assure Tokyo on Oil." New York *Times,* November 16.

Cabinet Task Force on Oil Import Control. 1970. *The Oil Import Question.* Washington, D.C.: U.S. Government Printing Office.

Cairo Middle East News Agency. 1974. As cited in Foreign Broadcast Information Service, Middle East and Africa, March 19.

Calvocoressi, Peter. 1972. "Britain and the Middle East." In *Political Dynamics in the Middle East,* edited by P. Y. Hammond and S. S. Alexander, Ch. 12. New York: American Elsevier.

Campbell, Robert W. 1973. "Some Issues in Soviet Energy Policy for the
    Seventies." In *Soviet Economic Prospects for the Seventies,* pp. 45-55.
    A compendium of papers submitted to the Joint Economic Commit-
    tee, Congress of the United States. Washington, D.C.: U.S. Govern-
    ment Printing Office.

Carter, Luther J. 1974. "The Energy Bureaucracy: The Pieces Fall into Place."
    Science 185 (July 5): 44-45.

Charlton, Linda. 1974. "Decades of Inaction Brought Energy Gap." New York
    Times, February 10.

Cicchetti, Charles. 1973. *Arctic Oil: An Economic and Environmental Analysis*
 *   of Alternative Transportation Systems.*Washington, D.C.: Resources
    for the Future.

Claiborne, William. 1974. "Europeans Cut Duties on U.S. Exports." Washington
    Post, June 1.

Cohen, Bernard C. 1965. "The Influences of Non-Governmental Groups on
    Foreign Policy-Making." In *Readings on the Making of Foreign Policy,*
    edited by Andrew M. Scott and Raymond H. Dawson, pp. 96-116. New
    York: Macmillan.

Commission of the European Communities. 1974. "Toward a New Energy Pol-
    icy Strategy for the European Community." Communication and
    Proposals from the Commission to the Council, COM (74) 550 Final
    (29 May). Brussels.

Congressional Quarterly. 1974. "Arab-Americans Struggle to Win U.S. Public."
    Christian Science Monitor, March 22.

Cooper, R. N. 1968. *The Economics of Interdependence: Economic Policy in
    the Atlantic Community.* New York: McGraw-Hill.

Coplin, William D. 1971. *Introduction to International Politics: A Theoretical
    Overview.* Chicago: Markham.

_____ et al. 1974. *American Foreign Policy: An Introduction to Analysis
    and Evaluation.* North Scituate, Mass.: Duxbury.

Cottrell, Alvin J. 1971. "An Exclusive Interview with the Shah." *New Middle
    East* (London), March 8.

Cottrell, Alvin J. 1973. "From Iraq with Love." *Near East Report* 17 (March 21): 48.

Council of Economic Advisors. 1974. *Annual Report to the President,* pp. 111-28. Washington, D.C.: U.S. Government Printing Office.

Crabb, Cecil V., Jr. 1965. *American Foreign Policy in the Nuclear Age.* 2d ed. New York: Harper and Row.

Current Foreign Policy. 1973a. "1973: The Year of Europe." Address given by Henry A. Kissinger before the annual meeting of the Associated Press editors (April 23). Washington, D.C.: Bureau of Public Affairs, Department of State.

_____. 1973b. "United States Troop Levels in Europe." Address by Kenneth Rush to the Senate Foreign Relations Committee. Washington, D.C.: Bureau of Public Affairs, Department of State.

_____. 1973c. "Energy: Cooperative Action to Solve Shortages." By William Casey. Washington, D.C.: Bureau of Public Affairs, Department of State.

Darmstadter, J. 1971. *Energy in the World Economy.* Baltimore: Johns Hopkins Press.

Dawson, Richard E., and Kenneth Prewitt. 1969. *Political Socialization.* Boston: Little, Brown.

Declaration on Atlantic Relations. June 19, 1974. Brussels: NATO Information Service.

Delarue, Maurice. 1974. "France—for a European Europe." *Aussen Politik* (2d quarter): 134-45.

Department of the Interior. 1972. *The United States Energy Through the Year 2000.* Washington, D.C. Mimeographed.

Department of State. 1972. *The U.S. and the Impending Energy Crisis.* Washington, D.C. Mimeographed.

Department of State Bulletin, 1973-74.

Deutsch, Karl W. 1968. *The Analysis of International Relations.* Englewood Cliffs, N.J.: Prentice-Hall.

Dirlam, Joel B. 1958. "Natural Gas: Cost, Conservation, and Pricing." *American Economic Review* 48: 491-501.

Doboszy, Istvan. 1974. Cited in *East-West* no. 104 (March 29).

Downs, Anthony. 1967. *Inside Bureaucracy.* Boston: Little, Brown.

Easton, David. 1965. *A Systems Analysis of Political Life.* New York: John Wiley and Sons.

E.G. 1974. *Ekonomicheskaia gazeta* (April) no. 15.

Ellis, Harry B. 1974. "U.S. Softens Tone of Oil Talks." *Christian Science Monitor,* February 6.

Evans, Rowland, and Robert Novak. 1973. "Has U.S. Underestimated Faisal?" Denver *Post,* November 16.

Farnsworth, C.H. 1973a. "Deep Recession Seen for Europe." New York *Times,* December 1.

_____. 1973b. "New Arab Oil Cut to Europe Voided." New York *Times,* November 19.

_____. 1973c. "Market Defers Action on Plan by U.S. to Meet Energy Crisis." New York *Times,* December 20.

_____. 1973d. "Common Market for Energy Shaping." New York *Times,* December 15.

_____. 1974a. "Oil Cooperation Stressed I.M.F." New York *Times,* January 19.

_____. 1974b. "Energy-Policy Harmony." New York *Times,* July 3.

Finney, John W. 1973. "Should U.S. Reduce Its Western European Troop Commitments to the Atlantic Alliance?" New York *Times,* July 26.

Ford Foundation. 1974. *Exploring Energy Choices: A Preliminary Report.* Washington, D.C.: Brookings Institution.

Foreign Policy Outlines. 1973. Washington, D.C.: Bureau of Public Affairs, Department of State (August).

Fowlkes, Frank V. 1973. "Trade Report: Petro Dollar Surpluses Loom as Problem for Monetary System, U.S. Energy Crisis." *National Journal Reports* (August 18): 1211-17.

FPR. See *Report to the Congress . . . .*

Frank, H.J. 1966. *Crude Oil Prices in the Middle East.* New York: Praeger.

Frank, Richard S. 1974. "Trade Report/U.S.-Business Have Partner Role in Expanding East-West Commerce." *National Journal Reports,* January 12, pp. 39-50.

Frankel, Max. 1971. "U.S. Troops: Security Blanket in a Changing Europe." New York *Times,* December 21.

Frazier, Charles H., and Bruce C. Netschert. 1972. "Soviet Gas for the United States?" *American Gas Association Monthly* 54 (March): 4-6.

Friedrich, Carl J. 1968. *Man and His Government.* New York: McGraw-Hill.

Furlong, R.D.M. 1973. "Iran—A Power to be Reckoned with." *International Defense Review* 6: 719-29.

Garnham, David. 1974. "State Department Rigidity: Testing a Psychological Hypothesis." *International Studies Quarterly* 18 (March): 31-40.

Gelb, Leslie H. 1974a. "Kissinger Reassures Soviet of Continued Mideast Roles." New York *Times,* June 7.

_____. 1974b. "Polls Find U.S. Isolationism on Rise." New York *Times,* June 16.

George, Alexander L., and Juliette L. George. 1964. *Woodrow Wilson and Colonel House: A Personality Study.* New York: Dover.

Goshko, John M. 1973. "Europe's Unity Slips Over Arab Oil Cuts." Washington *Post,* November 30.

_____. 1974. "Arabs Lift Embargo Subject to Review in June." Washington *Post,* February 19.

Goshko, John M., and Jonathan Randal. 1973. "EEC Leaders Make Show of Unity on Oil." Washington *Post*, December 16.

Graubard, Stephen R. 1973. *Kissinger: Portrait of a Mind.* New York: W.W. Norton and Co.

Greenstein, Fred I. 1969. *Personality and Politics.* Chicago: Markham Publishing Co.

Griffith, William E. 1974. "The Fourth Middle East War, the Energy Crisis and U.S. Policy," *Orbis* (Winter): 1161-88.

Grose, Peter. 1973. "Oil: Delay and Disunity." New York *Times*, May 15.

Gumpel, Werner. 1974. "USSR—Energy Policy and Middle East Crisis." *Aussen Politik* (1st quarter): 31-41.

Gwertzman, Bernard. 1973a. "U.S. Calls Arab Embargo No Longer Appropriate." New York *Times*, December 7.

_____. 1973b. "U.S. Ready to Help Dutch in Oil Crisis." New York *Times*, December 1.

_____. 1974a. "Kissinger Expects Some Arabs to Ask Oil Embargo's End." New York *Times*, February 1.

_____. 1974b. "Kissinger Warns Arabs on Oil Ban." New York *Times*, February 7.

_____. 1974c. "Kissinger Offers 7-Point Program on World Energy." New York *Times*, February 12.

_____. 1974d. "C.I.A. Chief Doubts Soviet Navy Plans Indian Ocean Build-up." New York *Times*, August 3.

Halloran, Richard. 1973a. "An Ebb in U.S.-Japanese Relations." New York *Times*, February 19.

_____. 1973b. "Japan at Once Self-Confident and Unsure as Nixon and Tanaka Go into Their Talks." New York *Times*, July 31.

Hartshorn, J.E. 1962. *Oil Companies and Governments.* London: Faber and Faber.

Hassner, Pierre. 1971. "Pragmatic Conservatism in the White House." *Foreign Policy* (Summer): 41-61.

Hawley, Donald. 1970. *The Trucial States.* London: George Allen and Unwin.

Hayworth, David. 1974. "NATO Declares Policy Aimed at Revitalizing Tie." *International Herald Tribune* (Paris), June 20.

Heller, H.R. 1974. *International Monetary Economics.* Englewood Cliffs, N.J.: Prentice-Hall.

Hielscher, Hans. 1973. Interview of Saudi Arabian Minister of Petroleum and Mineral Wealth, Ahmad Zaki al-Yamani. *Der Spiegel* (Hamburg), December 3.

Hirst, D. 1966. *Oil and Public Opinion in the Middle East.* New York: Praeger.

Hoagland, Jim. 1974a. "Saudis Tie Level of Exports to U.S. to Mideast Settlement." Washington *Post,* March 28.

_____. 1974b. "Troop Training." Washington *Post,* April 6.

_____. 1974c. "U.S. Shifting Saudi Policy." Washington *Post,* April 8.

Hoffman, Fred S. 1974. "U.S. Pledges Updating of Israeli Air Force." Washington *Star News,* July 1.

Hoffman, Stanley. 1973. "Choices." *Foreign Policy* (Fall): 3-42.

Holbrooke, Richard. 1970-71. "The Machine That Fails." *Foreign Policy* (Winter): 65-77.

Holsti, K.J. 1972. *International Politics: A Framework for Analysis.* 2d ed. Englewood Cliffs, N.J.: Prentice-Hall.

Hottell, H.C., and J.B. Howard. 1971. *New Energy Technology.* Cambridge, Mass.: Massachusetts Institute of Technology.

Hoyt, Monty. 1974. "Fed-up Consumers Organize Energy-Crisis Counterattack." *Christian Science Monitor,* February 22.

Hunter, Robert E. 1973. *The Energy "Crisis" and U.S. Foreign Policy.* Washington, D.C.: Overseas Development Council.

International Economic Report of The President. 1974. Washington, D.C.: U.S. Government Printing Office.

Issawi, Charles. 1972. *Oil, the Middle East and the World.* New York: Library Press.

_____. 1974. "Consequences of the Oil Squeeze." *International Perspectives* (March-April): 9-13.

Jackson, Henry W. 1974a. Address to the Overseas Press Club, April 22. Reprinted in *Congressional Record* 120, no. 55 (April 23).

_____. 1974b. "The Suez Canal and International Stability." Washington, D.C., Senate floor, March 8.

Jameson, Sam. 1974. "Japan Planning More Direct Oil Purchases." Washington *Post,* February 14.

Janis, Irving L. 1972. *Victims of Groupthink.* Boston: Houghton Mifflin.

Joint Committee on Atomic Energy. 1973. *Understanding the National Energy Dilemma.* Washington, D.C.: Center for Strategic and International Studies, Georgetown University.

Kaiser, Karl. 1974. "Europe and America: A Critical Phase." *Foreign Affairs* (July): 725-41.

Kaiser, Robert G. 1974. "Detente Still Soviet Goal." Washington *Post,* March 24.

Kalb, Marvin, and Bernard Kalb. 1974. "Twenty Days in October." New York *Times* Magazine, June 23.

Kaplan, Abraham. 1964. *The Conduct of Inquiry: Methodology for Behavioral Science.* San Francisco: Chandler Publishing Co.

Kegley, Charles W., Jr. 1973. *A General Empirical Typology of Foreign Policy Behavior.* Beverly Hills: Sage.

Kemezis, Paul. 1973a. "Common Market Said to Resist U.S. on Joint Statement." New York *Times,* November 9.

Kemezis, Paul. 1973b. "Many in Netherlands Think Oil Is Being Diverted to Dutch." New York *Times,* December 31.

―――――. 1974a. "Progress Is Reported on Sharing of Oil." New York *Times,* July 10.

―――――. 1974b. "Paris Balks at Sharing." New York *Times,* July 25.

Kendall, Don. 1973. "Cut in Grain Sales to Arabs Doubted." Washington *Post,* November 20.

Key, V. O., Jr. 1972. *Public Opinion and American Democracy.* New York: Alfred A. Knopf.

Kilpatrick, Carroll. 1974. "Nixon Offers Atom Aid for Peace to Israelis." *International Herald Tribune* (Paris), June 18.

Kissinger, Henry A. 1957. *A World Restored.* Boston: Houghton Mifflin.

―――――. 1969. *American Foreign Policy: Three Essays.* New York: Norton.

Kitch, Edmund. 1968. "Regulation of the Field Market for Natural Gas by the Federal Power Commission." *Journal of Law and Economics* 11: 243-80.

Kleiman, Robert. 1974. "Draft of Pact by Oil-Importing Nations Pools Sovereignty." New York *Times,* September 30.

Kohler, Foy D., Leon Govre, and Moshe L. Harvey. 1974. *The Soviet Union and the October Middle East War: The Implications for Detente.* Miami: University of Miami Center for Advanced International Studies.

Koven, Ronald, and David B. Ottaway. 1974. "U.S. Plays New Oil Game." Washington *Post,* April 28.

Kraft, Joseph. 1973. "Secretary Henry." New York *Times* Magazine, October 28.

Krasner, Stephen D. 1973. "The Great Oil Sheikdown." *Foreign Policy* 13 (Winter): 123-48.

―――――. 1974. "Oil Is the Exception." *Foreign Policy* 14 (Spring): 68-83.

Laqueur, W. 1974a. *Confrontation: The Middle East War and World Politics.* London: Wildwood House.

_____. 1974b. "The Idea of Europe Runs out of Gas." New York *Times* Magazine, January 20.

Leacacos, John P. 1971-72. "Kissinger's Apparat." *Foreign Policy* 5 (Winter): 3-24.

Lenczowski, George. 1974. "Probing the Arab Oil Motivation." *International Perspectives* (March-April): 3-9.

Lerche, Charles O., Jr., and Abdul A. Said. 1970. *Concepts of International Politics.* 2d ed. New York: The Free Press.

Leslie, Jacques. 1974. "China Buying Oil Drilling Rigs." Washington *Post,* April 23.

Levi, Werner. 1969. "The Relative Irrelevance of Moral Norms in International Politics." In *International Politics and Foreign Policy,* edited by James Rosenau. 2d ed., pp. 191-98. New York: The Free Press.

Levy, Walter J. 1973. "An Atlantic-Japanese Energy Policy." *Foreign Policy* (Summer): 159-90.

Lewis, Flora. 1974a. "Gromyko Backs French Stand in Energy Crisis." New York *Times,* February 19.

_____. 1974b. "France Is Joining Oil Talks Warily." New York *Times,* February 7.

_____. 1974c. "Paris Assumes the Top Post in the Common Market." New York *Times,* July 2.

Lichtblom, John H. 1974. "Middle East Oil and the U.S. Energy Crisis." Paper delivered at the seminar, "The Mounting Energy Crisis and the Middle East," at Johns Hopkins University, School for Advanced International Studies, September 19.

Lincoln, George A. 1973a. "Energy Security—New Dimension of U.S. Policy." *Air Force Magazine* 56 (November): 49-55.

_____. 1973b. "Energy Conservation." *Science* 180 (April 13): 155-62.

Lindblom, Charles E. 1959. "The Science of Muddling Through." *Public Administration* 19 (Winter): 79-88.

Lipset, Seymour N. 1960. *Political Man.* Garden City, N.Y.: Doubleday.

Lovejoy, W. F., and P. T. Homan. 1967. *Economic Aspects of Oil Conservation Regulation.* Baltimore: Johns Hopkins University Press.

Luttwak, Edward. 1973. "A New Look at the Energy Crisis." *Near East Report,* April 18.

MacAvoy, Paul. 1962. *Price Formation in Natural Gas Fields.* New Haven: Yale University Press.

MacAvoy, P., and R. Pyndyck. 1973. "Alternative Regulatory Policies for Dealing with the Natural Gas Shortage." *Bell Journal of Economics and Management Science* 55: 454-98.

Maclean, John. 1974. "The Dark Side of Kissinger's Winning Style." Chicago *Tribune,* July 14.

Malmgren, Harald B. 1972. "Managing Foreign Economic Policy." *Foreign Policy* (Spring): 42-68.

Mancke, Richard B. 1974a. *The Failure of U.S. Energy Policy.* New York: Columbia University Press.

————. 1974b. "Petroleum Conspiracy: A Costly Myth." *Public Policy* 22: 1-13.

Marder, Murrey. 1974a. "Kissinger Denounces Oil Embargo." Washington *Post,* February 7.

————. 1974b. "Nixon's News Challenged." Washington *Post,* February 1.

————. 1974c. "Kissinger Races Clock in Quest for Lasting Impact." Washington *Post,* April 7.

————. 1974d. "Kissinger to Attend Oil Talks." Washington *Post,* January 31.

————. 1974e. "The Coming Crisis with Europe." Washington *Post,* March 17.

Marder, Murrey. 1974f. "EEC Arab Offer Stirs U.S. Protest." Washington *Post*, March 6.

_____. 1974g. "U.S. Calls Energy Meeting." Washington *Post*, February 22.

Marder, Murrey, and Ronald Koven. 1974. "U.S., France Clash on Plan on World Oil." Washington *Post*, February 2.

Martin, Lawrence. 1972. "British Policy in the Indian Ocean." In *The Indian Ocean: Its Political, Economic and Military Importance*, edited by Alvin J. Cottrell and R.M. Burrell. New York: Praeger.

Matveev, V. 1973. "Kriticheskie al'ternativy." *Izvestiia*, December 25.

_____. 1974. "Realities and Demands of the Nuclear Age." *International Affairs* (Moscow) no 4: 57-63.

Mayer, Lawrence C. 1972. *Comparative Political Inquiry: A Methodological Survey*. Homewood, Ill.: Dorsey.

McCloskey, Herbert. 1956. "Concerning Strategies for a Science of International Politics." *World Politics* 8 (January): 281-95.

McDonald, Stephen L. 1971. *Petroleum Conservation in the United States*. Baltimore: Johns Hopkins University Press.

McGowan, Patrick J., and H.B. Shapiro. 1973. *The Comparative Study of Foreign Policy, A Survey of Scientific Findings*. Beverly Hills: Sage.

Meehan, Eugene J. 1965. *The Theory and Method of Political Analysis*. Homewood, Ill.: Dorsey.

Merkl, Peter H. 1970. *Modern Comparative Politics*. New York: Holt, Rinehart and Winston.

Middle East. 1974. "OPEC Split Results in Compromise." 1 (July/August).

Middle East Information Series. 1973. "The Energy Problem and the Middle East." 23 (May).

Middle East Institute. 1972. *World Energy Demands and the Middle East, Part I*. 26th Annual Conference, Washington, D.C.

Middle East Record 1967. 1972. Jerusalem: Israel Universities Press.

Mikdashi, Zuhayr. 1972. *The Community of Oil Exporting Countries: A Study in Governmental Cooperation.* Ithaca, N.Y.: Cornell University Press.

The Military Balance 1973-1974. 1973. London: International Institute for Strategic Studies.

Miller, Judith. 1974. "U.S. Navy Still Pressing for Base in the Indian Ocean." Washington *Post,* May 19.

Ministerstvo vneshnei torgovli SSSR. 1973. *Vneshniaia torgovlia SSSR 20 1972 god.* Moscow: IMO.

Mintz, Morton. 1974a. "Industry Capitulation Recounted." Washington *Post,* February 1.

_____. 1974b. "Oil Data Seen Scanty." Washington *Post,* January 17.

Moore, William C. 1974. "Diego Garcia Vital to U.S." *Human Events,* August 3.

Morgan, Don. 1973a. "Non Arab Oil Allocation Helps Dutch, Hurts French, Others." Washington *Post,* December 23.

_____. 1973b. "Oil Pressures on Japan Worrying U.S." Washington *Post,* November 24.

_____. 1974a. "Questions Arise on NATO." Washington *Post,* March 17.

_____. 1974b. "Kissinger Seen Weak on Economic Affairs Understanding." Washington *Post,* April 7.

Murray, James R., et al. 1974. "Evolution of Public Response to the Energy Crisis." *Science* 184 (April 19): 257-63.

MVT. *See* Ministerstvo vneshnei torgovli SSSR.

National Petroleum Council of Department of Interior. 1972. *U.S. Energy Outlook, A Summary Report,* p. 53. Washington, D.C.

New Perspectives on the Persian Gulf. 1973. House of Representatives, 93d Congress, 1st sess., hearings of Subcommittee on the Near East and South Asia. Washington, D.C.: U.S. Government Printing Office.

Nixon, Richard. 1973. "United States Foreign Policy for the 1970s: Shaping a Durable Peace." A report by President Nixon to the Congress. May 3.

_____. 1974. "State of the Union Message." *Presidential Documents* 10, no. 5 (February 4), pp. 123-25. Washington, D.C.: U.S. Government Printing Office.

NPC. See National Petroleum Council.

Oberdorfer, Don. 1973. "Feeling Oil Pinch, Japan Starts to Tilt in Favor of Arabs." Washington *Post,* November 9.

_____. 1974. "Europe Seeks Japan Tie, Excluding U.S." Washington *Post,* January 29.

Odell, P. 1963. *An Economic Geography of Oil.* London: Bell.

OECD. See Organization for Economic Cooperation and Development.

Office of Emergency Preparedness, Executive Office of the President. 1972. *The Potential for Energy Conservation.* Washington, D.C.: U.S. Government Printing Office.

_____. 1973. *The Potential for Energy Conservation: Substitution for Scarce Fuels.* Washington, D.C.: U.S. Government Printing Office.

Oka, Takashi. 1974a. "Japan-U.S. Alliance Survives Oil Upsets." *Christian Science Monitor,* March 25.

_____. 1974b. "Will U.S. Share Oil? Allies Ask." *Christian Science Monitor,* February 4.

_____. 1974c. "European Scramble for Oil Perils U.S. Plan." *Christian Science Monitor,* January 28.

_____. 1974d. "Europe's 9 List Thou Shalt Nots for Oil Parley." *Christian Science Monitor,* February 7.

O'Neill, Bard E. 1974. "The October War: A Political-Military Assessment." *Air University Review* 25 (July-August): 27-35.

O'Neill, Bard E., and Joseph S. Szyliowicz, eds. 1973. *American Foreign Policy in the Middle East.* Proceedings of Colorado Association for International

Education Interuniversity Seminar at the U.S. Air Force Academy, Colorado.

Onis, Juan de. 1974. "Saudis Seek U.S. Help to Cut Oil Prices." New York *Times,* June 19.

Organization for Economic Cooperation and Development. 1973. *Oil: the Present Situation and Future Prospects.* Paris.

Organization of the Petroleum Exporting Countries (OPEC). 1973. *Annual Statistical Bulletin 1972.* Vienna.

Ottaway, David B. 1974a. "U.S., Saudis Act to Develop Multiple Ties." Washington *Post,* April 6.

————. 1974b. *Economic Outlook* no. 14.

"Perspectives." *Strategic Survey 1973.* 1974. London: International Institute for Strategic Studies.

Peterson, Peter G. 1972. "U.S.-Soviet Commercial Relationships in a New Era." Department of Commerce press release, August.

Petroleum Information Foundation. 1973. *Background Information.* Paper no. 16. New York.

Petrovskaia, M.D. 1973. "Bespretsedentnyi povorot v Amerikanskom obshche stvennom Mnenii." *SSHA: Ekonomika, Politika, Ideologiia* no. 10: 32-36.

Phelps, Robert H. 1970. "Mideast Lobbies: Uneven Match." New York *Times,* April 6.

Pollack, Gerald A. 1974. "The Economic Consequences of the Energy Crisis." *Foreign Affairs* 52 (April): 402-71.

Randal, Jonathan. 1974. "France Presses Bilateral Deals." Washington *Post,* February 2.

Report to the Congress by Richard Nixon, President of the United States. 1972. Washington, D.C.: U.S. Government Printing Office.

Report to the Congress by Richard Nixon, President of the United States. 1973. Washington, D.C.: U.S. Government Printing Office.

Rose, Sanford. 1974. "Our Vast Hidden Oil Resources." *Fortune* 89 (April): 104-07.

Rosecrance, Richard N. 1973. *International Relations: Peace or War?* New York: McGraw-Hill.

Rosenfeld, Stephen S. 1974. "Pluralism and Policy." *Foreign Affairs* 52 (January): 263-72.

Rowen, Hobart. 1974. "Europe in Disarray." Washington *Post,* January 27.

Ryzhenko, F. 1973. "Mirnoe sosushchestvovanie i kassovaia bor'ba." *Pravda,* August 22.

Saikowski, Charlotte. 1973. "New Facts Raise Stakes for U.S." *Christian Science Monitor,* December 3.

————. 1974. "Kissinger Shapes Consensus." *Christian Science Monitor,* January 30.

Sax, S. W., and A. Levy. 1974. "Arab-Israeli Conflict Four: A Preliminary Assessment." *Naval War College Review* 26 (January-February): 7-16.

Schmidt, Dana A. 1974a. "Nixon's Trip: What Did it Achieve?" *Christian Science Monitor,* June 10.

————. 1974b. "Saudi Carrot Stick Tactics." *Christian Science Monitor,* April 15.

Schmidt, Helmut. 1974. "The Struggle for the World." *Foreign Affairs* (April): 437-51.

Schurr, Sam H., and Paul T. Homan. 1971. *Middle Eastern Oil and the Western World: Prospects and Problems.* New York: American Elsevier.

Seeger, Murray. 1973. "Soviet-Urged Boycott a Two-Edged Sword." Denver *Post,* December 25.

Sharp, Jonathan. 1974. "China Inscrutable—Vast Untapped Oil Reserves?" *Christian Science Monitor,* January 14.

Shaw, Gaylord. 1974. "Wage Peace, Nixon Urges Israelis." St. Louis *Globe-Democrat,* June 17.

Sheehan, Edward R.F. 1974. "Unradical Sheikhs Who Shake the World." New York *Times* Magazine, March 24.

Sheliag, V. 1974. "Dra mirovozzreniia—dva rzgliada na voinu." *Krasnaia zvezda,* February 7.

Shell Oil Company. 1973. *The National Energy Outlook.* Houston, Texas.

Shulman, Marshall D. 1973. "Toward a Western Philosophy of Coexistence." *Foreign Affaris* 52 (October): 35-58.

Shuster, Alvin. 1974a. "Strategic Analysts Gloomy on Detente." New York *Times,* May 10.

————. 1974b. "Iran Agrees to Sell British Large Extra Supply of Oil." New York *Times,* January 26.

————. 1974c. "Nixon's Criticism of Allies Stirs Bitterness in Europe." New York *Times,* March 17.

————. 1974d. "Allied Chiefs Sign NATO Declaration." New York *Times,* June 27.

Silk, Leonard. 1973a. "Arab Brinkmanship." New York *Times,* December 26.

————. 1973b. "Vast World Power Shifts Expected Through Arab Oil." Denver *Post,* November 15.

————. 1974a. "Kissinger as Economist." New York *Times,* February 13.

————. 1974b. "Oil Fueled U.S.-Arab Tie." New York *Times,* June 10.

Simon, Herbert A. 1957. *Administrative Behavior.* 2d ed. New York: The Free Press.

Singer, J. David. 1969. "The Level of Analysis Problem in International Relations." In *International Politics and Foreign Policy,* James Rosenau, ed., 2d ed., pp. 20-29. New York: The Free Press.

Smith, Hedrick. 1971. "Foreign Policy: Kissinger at the Hub." New York *Times,* January 19.

Sondermann, Fred A. 1961. "The Linkages Between Foreign Policy and International Politics." In *International Politics and Foreign Policy,* edited by James Rosenau, pp. 8-17. New York: The Free Press.

Spritzer, Ralph S. 1971. "Changing Elements in the Natural Gas Picture: Implications for the Federal Regulatory Scheme." In *Regulation of the Natural Gas Processing Industry,* edited by Keith C. Brown, pp. 113-36. Baltimore: Johns Hopkins University Press.

Sprout, Harold, and Margaret Sprout. 1965. *The Ecological Perspective on Human Affairs.* Princeton: Princeton University Press.

Stanley, Timothy W., and Darnell M. Whitt. 1970. *Detente Diplomacy: United States and European Security in the 1970s.* Cambridge, Mass.: Cambridge University Press.

Statement Before the House Near East Subcommittee. 1973. By Joseph S. Sisco. Department of State press release no. 197 (June 6).

Stauffer, T. R. 1974. "Oil Money and World Money: Conflict or Confluence?" *Science* 184 (April 19): 321-24.

Stevens, Richard P. 1962. *American Zionism and U.S. Foreign Policy.* New York: Pageant Press.

Stocking, G. 1970. *Middle East Oil.* Nashville: Vanderbilt University Press.

Strategic Survey 1973. 1974. London: International Institute for Strategic Studies.

Szulc, Tad. 1973. "Foreign Policy: the Economic Problem." New York *Times,* January 20.

_____. 1974a. "The Chinese See Russia's Threat Changing in Asia." *International Herald Tribune* (Paris), July 8.

_____. 1974b. "Is He Indispensable? Answers to the Kissinger Riddle." *New York* Magazine, July 1.

Tahtinen, Dale R. 1974a. *Arms in the Persian Gulf.* Washington, D.C.: American Enterprise Institute for Public Policy Research.

_____. 1974b. *The Arab-Israeli Military Balance Since October 1973.* Washington, D.C.: American Enterprise Institute for Public Policy Research.

Tanzer, M. 1969. *The Political Economy of Oil and Underdeveloped Countries.* Boston: Beacon Press, 1970.

Teltsch, Kathleen. 1974. "U.N. Envoys Weigh U.S. Israel Vote." New York *Times,* April 26.

Teune, Henry, and Adam Przeworsky. 1970. *The Logic of Comparative Social Inquiry.* New York: John Wiley and Sons.

Text of Arab statement in Vienna on end of embargo. 1973. New York *Times,* March 19.

Trofimenko, G. A. 1974. "SSSR, SSHA: Mirnoe soshushchestvovanie kak norma vzaimootnosheniia." *SSHA: Ekonomika, Politika, Ideologiia,* no. 2: 3-17.

Turpin, William N. 1972. "Foreign Relations, Yes, Foreign Policy, No." *Foreign Policy* (Fall): 50-61.

United States Cabinet Task Force on Oil Import Controls. 1970. *The Oil Import Question.* Washington, D.C.: U.S. Government Printing Office.

The United States Oil Shortage and the Arab-Israel Conflict. 1973. House of Representatives, 93d Congress, 1st sess., Study mission report (December 20).

U.S. Department of State. 1973. *The United States and Japan.* No. 8740. Washington, D.C.: U.S. Government Printing Office.

_____. 1974a. Press conference by Secretary of State Henry Kissinger and Federal Energy Administrator William Simon, January 10.

_____. 1974b. Opening remarks of Secretary Kissinger at the Energy Conference of Oil Consuming Nations at Washington, D.C. (February 11). Washington, D.C.: U.S. Government Printing Office.

Varon, Bension, and Kenji Takeuchi. 1974. "Developing Countries and Non-Fuel Minerals." *Foreign Affairs* 52 (April): 497-510.

Whitney, Craig R. 1973. "West Germany and NATO Allies Seeking to Dissuade U.S. from Sudden Cut in Troops." New York *Times,* June 13.

_____. 1974. "Kissinger Cool to European Bid to Arabs." New York *Times,* June 12.

Wohlstetter, Albert. 1974. "Threats and Promises of Peace: Europe and America in the New Era." *Orbis* (Winter): 1107-44.

Wolfers, Arnold. 1961. "The Role of Power and the Role of Indifference." In *International Politics and Foreign Policy,* James N. Rosenau, ed., pp. 146-51. New York: The Free Press.

Wren, Christopher S. 1974. "Russian Oil Profits from West Climb." New York *Times,* June 5.

Wriggins, W. Howard. 1969. *The Ruler's Imperative.* New York: Columbia University Press.

Yaari, S. 1973. "The Basic Economics of Arab Oil Actions." Mimeographed.

DR. JOSEPH S. SZYLIOWICZ is Professor of Middle East Studies, Graduate School of International Studies, University of Denver. He has served as Director of the American Research Institute in Turkey and has published numerous works on development in Turkey and the Middle East including *Political Change in Rural Turkey: Erdemli, Education and Modernization in the Middle East*, and *A Political Analysis of Student Activism, The Turkish Case*. He is also the coeditor and coauthor of *The Contemporary Middle East, Tradition and Innovation*.

DR. BARD E. O'NEILL is Associate Professor of Political Science, U.S. Air Force Academy. His major fields of interest are the Middle East and Africa, insurgency, and American foreign policy. He has published several articles on these subjects and he is also the author of *Revolutionary Warfare in the Middle East* and coeditor and coauthor of *Political Violence and Insurgency*.

UZI B. ARAD is a political scientist on the professional staff of the Hudson Institute. He is currently directing a research project on "Energy and National Defense, 1975-1985" and is coauthoring a book on U.S. energy independence.

DR. BERNHARD ABRAHAMSSON is Associate Professor of International Economics, Graduate School of International Studies, University of Denver. He has been a staff member of the IMF and has served as Director of the Institute of Maritime Transport, Israel. He has published several articles on international trade and is coauthor of *Strategic Aspects of Seaborne Oil*.

DR. ABRAHAM S. BECKER of the Rand Corporation, is a well known expert on Soviet Policy, particularly in reference to the Middle East. He has published numerous articles and monographs on this topic and is the author of *The Superpowers in the Arab-Israeli Conflict, 1970-1973*.

DR. JOHN C. CAMPBELL of the Council on Foreign Relations is a distinguished authority on U.S. Policy in the Middle East. He has published numerous articles on this topic and has authored *Defense of the Middle East: Problems of American Policy, the Middle East in the Muted Cold War*, and coauthored *The West and the Middle East*.

DR. ALVIN J. COTTRELL is Director of Research of the Center for Strategic and International Studies, Georgetown University. He received his Ph.D. from the University of Pennsylvania and has been a member of the faculty of the National War College. He is an expert on strategic problems and has published numerous books and articles on this topic.

GENERAL GEORGE A. LINCOLN (RET.) served as Director of the Office of Emergency Preparedness from 1969 to 1973. During those years he was a member of the National Security Council. A former Rhodes scholar, General Lincoln served for many years as head of the Department of Social Sciences of the Military Academy and is now an Adjunct Professor of Economics and International Studies at the University of Denver. He is the author of numerous articles and books on international relations, security policy and energy.

DR. RICHARD B. MANCKE is Associate Professor of International Economic Relations, Fletcher School of Law and Diplomacy, Tufts University. He was a staff economist of the Cabinet Task Force on Oil Import Control and has published numerous articles on energy policy.

DR. DON C. PERETZ is Director of the South West Asia North African Studies Program, State University of New York at Binghamton. He is a well known authority on the Arab-Israeli conflict and has published numerous books and articles on Middle East Affairs.

RELATED TITLES

Published by

Praeger Special Studies

ENVIRONMENTAL DETERIORATION IN THE SOVIET UNION AND
EASTERN EUROPE

edited by Ivan Volgyes

ENVIRONMENTAL POLITICS

edited by Stuart S. Nagel

MIDDLE EAST OIL AND U.S. FOREIGN POLICY: With Special
Reference to the U.S. Energy Crisis

Shoshana Klebanoff

THE PRICING OF CRUDE OIL: Economic and Strategic Guidelines
for an International Energy Policy

Taki Rifai

THE SOVIET ENERGY BALANCE: Natural Gas, Other Fossil Fuels,
and Alternative Power Sources

Iain F. Elliot